Developing Respec[t]
Connection in Our Relationships
from a Torah Perspective

LOVE
PEACE
and
PURSUE
IT

RABBI ARYEH GOLDMAN

ISBN:
Hardcover: 978-1-0879-4970-3
Paperback: 978-1-0879-7586-3
E-book: 978-1-0880-4746-0

Publishing services provided by JewishSelfPublishing. The author
acts as the publisher and is solely responsible for the content
of this book, which does not necessarily reflect the opinions of
JewishSelfPublishing.

www.jewishselfpublishing.com
info@jewishselfpublishing.com
(800) 613-9430

The author can be contacted at aryehgoldman123@gmail.com.

◆ מכתב ברכה ◆

RSA Rabbinical
Seminary
of America

ישיבת רבנו ישראל מאיר הכהן זצוק"ל
בעל ה"חפץ חיים"
Dedicated by the Ginzberg Family

76-01 147th St., Flushing NY 11367
718.268.4700 / Fax: 718.268.4684
office@rabbinical.org

Rabbi Dovid Leibowitz זצוק"ל
Founding Rosh HaYeshiva 1933-1941

Rabbi A. Henach Leibowitz זצוק"ל
Rosh HaYeshiva 1941-2008

Rabbi Dovid Harris שליט"א
Rosh HaYeshiva

Rabbi Akiva Grunblatt שליט"א
Rosh HaYeshiva

Dr. Ira Kukin ע"ה
Chairman Emeritus

Dr. Allan Jacob
Chairman of the Board

אייר תשפ"ב לפ"ק

שמחנו לראות גליונות מאירים מספר "Love Peace and Pursue It",
פרי עמלו וגיעתו של תלמידנו היקר מחשובי ישיבתנו הק', ה"ה הרב
אריה גולדמאן שליט"א. המחבר שליט"א כיהן כאחד מחברי ההנהלה
בישיבתנו הק' ולמד ולימד והדריך ועידד ועזר הרבה מתלמידינו במשרה
זו. עכשיו המחבר שליט"א מרביץ תורה לרבים בעיר לאס ויגעס.

הנה הרב המחבר שליט"א רחש לבו דבר טוב להוציא לאור עולם ספר
על תורת בין אדם לחבירו שנכתב בשפה המדוברת במדינתנו ובעהשי"ת
תהי' לתועלת גדולה לכל המעיינים בו. וכבר כתב הרמב"ן בפרשת
ואתחנן (דברים ו' י"ח) ד"ועשית הישר והטוב" היא מצוה כללית שבין
אדם לחבירו, דמלבד המצות הפרטיות והמסויימות שבין אדם לחבירו,
נצטווינו שכל היחס לזולת יהיה על פי הישר והטוב. ולזה נחזיק טובה
להרב המחבר שליט"א שסידר וערך בטוב טעם ודעת ספר נחמד שהוא
אוצר בלום על תורת האדם ומדות בין אדם לחבירו והדרכה לבני תורה
מבקשי השי"ת, הנוגע להלכה ולמעשה בכל יום ויום ע"פ "ועשית הישר
והטוב".

ולמרות שמחמת טרדות הישיבה לא הי' לנו פנאי לעיין בו כדבעי מ"מ
אנו מכירים היטב הרב המחבר שליט"א שהוא תלמיד חכם ואינו יוצא
מתחת ידו דבר שאינו מתוקן. ואנו מברכים אותו מעומק לבבנו שימשיך
לזכות את הרבים, וימשיך עוד להפיץ מעיינותיו חוצה להגדיל תורה
ולהאדירה.

הכו"ח לכבוד התורה ולומדי',

דוד הריס

עקיבא אליהו גרונבלאט

◆ מכתב ברכה ◆

Rabbi Shaya Cohen
ROSH HAYESHIVA

It is a very special privilege to write a few words of Bracha, in appreciation of this unique Sefer. Following faithfully the approach of Rav Yisrael Salanter, Rabbi Aryeh Goldman, a distinguished Talmid Chacham and Baal Mussar, has delineated the method, based on Chazal, to make significant changes in our Middos and our actions.

This work goes into great detail about the necessary process and although it is extensive, its detail would seem the best approach to effectuate lasting change.

Rabbi Goldman has tackled the issue of changing ones Middos and actions from a wide variety of perspectives and I am confident that this Mussar approach will do wonders for those who avail themselves of it seriously.

I wish Rabbi Goldman continued success in his spreading of Torah and Mussar and may this powerful Sefer guide and facilitate great changes and improvements of character and deeds in all those who take advantage of all its wisdom.

בברכת התורה,

Rabbi Shaya Cohen

YESHIVA CAMPUS: 1213 BAY 25TH STREET, FAR ROCKAWAY, NY 11691
PHONE: 347-619-9074 ~ EMAIL: YESHIVAZICHRONARYEH@GMAIL.COM

"ITS WAYS ARE WAYS OF PLEASANTNESS and its pathways are peace" (*Mishlei* 3,17). Upon this *pasuk* the *Yalkut Shimoni* in *Parshas Yisro* brings that Hashem said, "The entire Torah is peace, and to whom shall I give it? To a nation that loves peace (the Jewish nation)."

What greater endeavor can there then be than to acquire the love of peace and to pursue it? Clearly the quality of shalom/peace encompasses the entirety of character refinement which our Sages teach us is a critically needed foundation for the acquisition of Torah (Rabbeinu Yonah, *Avos* 3:7), and is the ultimate good to be achieved through the study of the Torah (*Mesilas Yesharim*, chapter 11). This endeavor requires great wisdom as indicated by the Rambam in *Hilchos Dei'os* (chapter 2).

For close to two decades Rabbi Goldman *shlit"a* has successfully imparted this rare wisdom to his students and to all who have been fortunate to seek it from him. I have been privileged to benefit personally from many presentations by Rabbi Goldman *shlit"a*, and I have heard the deep appreciation of other listeners who experienced a profound and positive impact. One who reads with an open heart will be able to see that wisdom in the pages to come. Moreover, through the pleasantness of his personal character Rabbi Goldman has acquired the "Crown of a good name," the highest honor described by our Sages (*Avos* 4:17).

We can certainly expect that the written words of this work that emanate from a heart that loves pleasantness and peace will reach and enter the heart of the reader and be a source of understanding, inspiration, and guidance to achieve the love and pursuit of peace with the help of Hashem.

With great esteem and appreciation for my very dear friend and colleague I extend to Rabbi Goldman *shlit"a* my heartfelt blessing for long, healthy, and successful years of imparting the beauty of the Torah to the beloved Jewish nation.

בכבוד ובאהבה,
יהודה אריה ליב שמידמאן
Yehuda Shmidman

In the introduction to the *Sefer Cheshbon Hanefesh,* the author describes the greatness of the human creation. He explains how the Creator brings down human souls one by one to the lower world to be joined with the animalistic part of man for a limited period of time. Our purpose in this world is to cling to the ways of Hashem and to do good to His creations. Because the animalistic side of man (known as the *nefesh habehamis*) knows only what is sweet in the moment, it is the task of the human mind (known as the *nefesh hasichlis*), derived from the *neshamah,* to maintain our direction in life.

The Torah is the roadmap to keep us oriented in the proper way, not to fall pray to our physical desires and our egos.

In this unique *sefer,* Rabbi Aryeh Goldman sets forth how the Torah enables us to maintain our direction in every aspect of our relationships with other people. It demonstrates the extent to which we are obligated to show kindness to our spouses, our children, our friends, and our associates.

What is remarkable about this *sefer* is its specificity. The classic *mussar seforim* elaborate on the *middos* that a person must cultivate, but they do so only in general terms. This *sefer* elaborates on the Torah approach in a way that makes it immediately applicable. The reader can apply the Torah guidelines directly to his life.

I highly recommend this sefer.

From a proud and loving father,
Rabbi Dr. Abba Goldman

CONTENTS

– PART 1 –

PROPER SPEECH

◆ CHAPTER 1 ◆

HOW TO DEVELOP PROPER SPEECH   10

• CHAPTER 2 •

IDEALS AND VALUES RELATING TO
PROPER SPEECH 58

♦ CHAPTER 3 ♦

PROPER APPLICATION OF THE
TORAH'S IDEALS AND VALUES   73

♦ CHAPTER 4 ♦

THE MOTIVATION TO DEVELOP
PROPER SPEECH   80

– PART 2 –

RESPONSIBILITY IN RELATIONSHIPS

INTRODUCTION 99

◆ CHAPTER 1 ◆

THE SOURCE AND IMPORTANCE OF OUR RESPONSIBILITIES 102

◆ CHAPTER 2 ◆

OUR RESPONSIBILITIES ACCORDING TO THE TORAH 113

• CHAPTER 3 •

THE FOUNDATION OF OUR RESPONSIBILITIES IN OUR RELATIONSHIPS   124

◆ CHAPTER 4 ◆

PROPER ATTITUDES AND PERSPECTIVES ABOUT OUR RESPONSIBILITIES   142

◆ CHAPTER 5 ◆

ACCEPTING RESPONSIBILITY FOR OUR
MISTAKES   165

– PART 3 –

FINDING CLOSENESS IN OUR
RELATIONSHIPS

INTRODUCTION   175

◆ CHAPTER 1 ◆

UNCONDITIONAL LOVE AND
COMPASSION   177

◆ CHAPTER 2 ◆

THE TORAH APPROACH TO DEALING WITH CHALLENGES IN RELATIONSHIPS 185

◆ CHAPTER 3 ◆

SELF-IMPROVEMENT AS THE BASIS FOR IMPROVING OUR RELATIONSHIPS 194

♦ CHAPTER 4 ♦

UNDERSTANDING THE RELATIONSHIP AND THE PEOPLE IN IT 210

♦ CHAPTER 5 ♦

DEVELOPING TOOLS AND STRATEGIES FOR IMPROVING OUR RELATIONSHIPS 229

• CHAPTER 6 •
A TORAH-BASED STRATEGY FOR
REBUILDING OUR RELATIONSHIPS 248

PREFACE

RABBI PINCHAS BEN YA'IR (*AVODAH Zarah* 20b) states that Torah study is what brings us to careful mitzvah observance. Rav Yechezkel Sarna (in his footnotes on the *Mesillas Yesharim*) explains that the Torah guides us to all aspects of personal development — not just mitzvos that connect us to Hashem (*bein adam laMakom*) but also those that relate to interpersonal relations (*bein adam lechaveiro*) and to the improvement of our basic character traits (*middos*).

The Torah contains all the wisdom we need to determine our proper goals in life and to develop our ideals, values, and behaviors so that we can achieve those goals. However, we need teachers and role models who can help us access that wisdom. Our teachers unlock the wisdom of the Torah through their teachings and the way in which they live.

I have been blessed to have had many special *rebbe'im* in Yeshiva Tiferes Yisroel in Brooklyn, WITS in Milwaukee, and Yeshiva Chofetz Chaim in Queens. Their teachings and their conduct have taught me the lessons of the Torah, and for that, I am eternally grateful.

In particular, I deeply appreciate the fact that my *chaveirim* and I were blessed to have had Rav Henoch Lebowitz as our *rebbi* in Yeshiva Chofetz Chaim for many years. One of the most important things he taught us was that the development of *middos* is a significant part of our job as *ovdei Hashem*. He instilled in us many of the Torah's lessons about what the proper *middos* are and how to develop them appropriately. His teachings also helped us develop the skills to glean further insights about character development from the words of *Chazal* independently.

The Gemara in *Ta'anis* (7a) teaches that we learn from three groups of people. Aside from learning from our *rebbe'im*, we can also learn a great deal from our peers and from our students.

Thankfully, I have been blessed with many very special *chavrusas* and friends. Being surrounded by such exceptional people has helped me grow, and I have learned so much from hearing their perspectives.

Rav Avraham Grodzinsky, the *mashgiach* of the Slobodka Yeshivah prior to World War II, tells us in *Toras Avraham* (p. 364) that much of the wisdom in books of *mussar* can only be found "between the lines." I have had wonderful opportunities over the years to learn these *sefarim* with *chavrusas* and with study groups, and those discussions have been instrumental in my ability to uncover some of the wisdom from our great leaders. I thank everyone who has joined me in those sessions.

The *Toras Avraham* (p. 369) also says that in order to fully understand the mitzvos of the Torah, we need to understand how people work, and we need to understand the world around us.

Generally, our understanding of humanity and our perceptions of the world are limited to what we know from our own experiences. However, when we listen (respectfully and empathetically) to the experiences of others, we can learn from them as well.

I have spent time with many friends and students over the years who have shared with me the stories of their lives. They have shared their hopes, dreams, and ambitions as well as their successes. They have also shared their mistakes, fears, shame, and pain. Throughout these conversations, it has always been amazing to me to see that even though, in many ways, we all have different personalities and experiences, at our core, we share the same overall nature and tendencies.

As a result, I have been able to learn much about myself and about humanity in general from the stories and insights that others have shared with me about their lives and about life in general. I am grateful to everyone who has trusted me enough to include me in their lives in such a meaningful manner.

For more than seventeen years, I have had the *zechus* to work for two great organizations: Yeshiva Chofetz Chaim and Las Vegas Kollel. They have provided me with many opportunities for spiritual growth, including the opportunity to learn about character development through the guidance of the Torah. They have also provided me with the opportunity to share those ideas with others. I am grateful to both organizations for everything they have given me.

Hashem has blessed me with a family that has been so good for me: loving, nurturing, and conducive to my spiritual and personal development. I could not have asked for a more special family for myself. For that, I am thankful to Hashem and to my family.

My parents and in-laws have been wonderful teachers and role models. Their knowledge of what it means to live a life with excellent *middos* and proper Torah values as well as their dedication to living such a life have guided and inspired me to try to become the best person I can be.

I offer a special thank you to my brothers, sisters, brothers-in-law, and sisters-in-law.

I would like to thank my wife, Michal, for everything she does for me and for our boys. You are a partner in everything that I do. I would also like to thank my boys, who have brought such happiness to my life. It is my prayer that we should continue to be *zocheh* to many *berachos* from Hashem.

There are several people I would like to thank for their help in creating this book. Much of this book came from my learning with Leigh Silver. He helped me clarify the concepts herein and write them more effectively. He also sponsored the editing and publishing costs for the book. Thank you, Leigh.

I would also like to thank Eliyahu Miller of JewishSelfPublishing, who guided and assisted me in making this book a reality. Thank you, as well, to Mrs. Sarah Rudolph for editing the book. Mrs. Rudolph's insights and suggestions were extremely helpful in clarifying and presenting the content.

Our relationships play a major role in our lives. Our spouses, siblings, parents, and children are certainly central figures in our lives. Extended family, friends, community members, and general acquaintances are also important to us. The friendship, encouragement, and assistance that we receive and that we give to others is essential for our happiness and success in life.

However, relationships are difficult, and it is easy for us to run into conflict. If we deal with those conflicts productively, we can maximize the benefits of our relationships despite the challenges. If we do not, it is easy for conflict to cause our relationships to fall apart.

It is up to us to work hard and do our best to learn how to develop ourselves so we will be more equipped to do our part toward building productive relationships. Then, we need to work hard at putting what we have learned into practice in order to actually become the best that we can be. Together with putting in our best efforts, we can also turn to Hashem and ask Him to help us be happy and productive together.

We should all be blessed with peace, happiness, and success in all our relationships and in all aspects of our lives.

INTRODUCTION

WE ALL UNDERSTAND THAT WE are obligated to love others as we love ourselves and to treat others with respect and compassion. These are some of the most fundamental responsibilities in the Torah. We also know that when we treat others with love, respect, and compassion, it is extremely beneficial for us as well because it enables us to find fulfillment and happiness within our relationships.

We all want to have happy, enjoyable, and fulfilling relationships, and we would be ready to do whatever we can to have them. We also want to be kind and compassionate to others, especially to our family and friends. We know that it is the most appropriate way to act and that it is beneficial for us as well. However, we do not fully live in this way, and we can all benefit from improving ourselves.

The importance of caring about others and treating them accordingly is demonstrated by the Gemara in *Yoma* (9b). The Gemara tells us that the second Beis Hamikdash was destroyed because *sinas chinam* (unjustified hatred) was rampant. The Gemara explains that the Jews at that time learned Torah and observed the mitzvos: They kept Shabbos and ate kosher food, they kept Pesach and Succos, and so on. However, they were not careful enough about the mitzvos that relate to loving others and treating them accordingly. That was enough of a problem to make them unworthy of having the Beis Hamikdash.

Rav Yisrael Meir Kagan (1839–1933), in the introduction to *Chafetz Chaim*, teaches us that every generation since the destruction of the Beis Hamikdash has struggled with the same issues, and that is why Hashem has not yet rebuilt the Beis Hamikdash.

The fact that we have been unworthy of the rebuilding of the Beis Hamikdash for the past two thousand years because we have not treated each other properly is a clear indication that we need to improve our treatment of others.

Treating Others Well

From time to time, we may reflect on how we treat others: Do we generally treat others with the proper compassion, kindness, and respect? Do we need to improve the way we treat others? Most of us would probably admit that we are not perfect, but we probably think that we generally treat others with compassion and respect. There is often a lot of truth in that assessment; however, the reality is that most of us are very far from fulfilling our responsibility to treat others appropriately.

We certainly do not see ourselves as people who mistreat others so badly that we are not worthy of having the Beis Hamikdash. We may think that it must be other people who are the culprits. *They* should realize how inappropriate their hatred is, and *they* should realize the significant impact of their actions!

However, we may think twice when we remember that the Gemara teaches us that the problems of *sinas chinam* apply even to moral people and to people who are dedicated to Torah observance. The Chafetz Chaim reminds us that throughout the generations, despite widespread dedication to living both moral and Torah-observant lives, we have always had the same unjustified hatred within us that caused the original destruction of the Beis Hamikdash. He also teaches us another important lesson: that it is common for people to mistreat others without recognizing that they are doing so.

We need to reflect on the ongoing reality that even moral people and people who keep Torah and mitzvos are often mean to their friends and family. It seems only reasonable for each of us to be open to the possibility that we too can improve in that area. It is likely that we also often do not treat others appropriately. Therefore, we need to make an honest and careful assessment of our own behaviors in order to identify the areas in which we may need to improve.

The Difficulties of Relationships

The fact that many people who are sincerely dedicated to being good people and observing the mitzvos still have a hard time getting along with others shows us how complicated relationships are. This reality highlights the fact that it is difficult to care about and treat others properly. It is important for us to understand why it is so difficult so that we can discover how we can improve ourselves.

The Maharal (*Derech Chaim* on *Pirkei Avos* 1:12) tells us that the fact that we have a hard time getting along with others is due to human nature. When we understand human nature well, we will realize that a natural part of being human is that it is difficult to get along with others. It is certainly difficult to avoid conflict consistently and effectively as well as maintain peace within our long-term relationships.

He highlights the fact that from the very first moments of human existence, there was conflict. The Torah teaches us about jealousy, insecurity, and murder in the story of Kayin and Hevel (*Bereishis* 4:1–16). This is our introduction to what we can expect of human nature and the human experience.

Any study of human history is filled with endless stories about war and violence. We see in our own times that there is conflict all around us. People from opposing countries or from different religious or political backgrounds will often find themselves in conflict. Even within our communities, synagogues, and families, it is extremely common to find ourselves surrounded by consistent and significant feelings of anger, pain, and resentment.

The aspects of human nature that cause us to have conflicts in our relationships can be referred to as our bad *middos* or our unproductive or inappropriate thoughts, feelings, and behaviors.

The *Mesillas Yesharim* (ch. 11) discusses many of the *middos* that most of us struggle with. We have anger, arrogance, and jealousy. We also have egotistical desires for respect, honor, and power. Our struggles in these areas have many negative implications in our lives. These *middos* interfere with our ability to feel a proper degree of respect and compassion, and they generally lead us to be critical, condescending, and antagonistic toward others. It is explained many times in the *Orchos Tzaddikim* that all our bad *middos* significantly hold us back from having happy and productive relationships with others. The more we struggle with these bad *middos*, the more our relationships will suffer. Even when we are motivated to treat others properly, we will not be very successful if we do not improve our *middos*.

All the *ba'alei mussar* discuss how difficult it is to make significant improvements in our *middos*. Many of these *middos* are connected to our emotional needs. It is often difficult to deal with our emotional needs in a proper and productive manner. Addressing our emotional needs productively requires much wisdom, guidance, and hard work.

The Maharal (*Derech Chaim* on *Pirkei Avos* 1:12) says that because our relationships are so challenging, the only way for us to have peaceful and productive relationships is to develop a love for peace and actively pursue it. That is certainly a tough job!

The Reality of Our Bad *Middos*

The *Orchos Tzaddikim* (Introduction) compares the complexity of our physical health to the complexity of the health of our character. The human body is extremely complex, and maintaining its physical health is therefore an extremely complex matter. To become a doctor, one must spend years learning about the human body: how it works, what types of dysfunctions can occur, and how to address them. Doctors train for many years to become experts in these areas. Only then can they properly diagnose a problem and devise a game plan to deal with the problem appropriately. Another aspect of human complexity relates to our *middos*. They are a complicated part of our humanity. They are connected to our thoughts, feelings, and behaviors. They are also connected to the web of the spiritual, emotional, and psychological aspects of who we are. Therefore, if we want to understand how to develop our *middos* appropriately, we need to study human behavior and emotions.

In a similar manner, the Midrash (*Vayikra Rabbah* 21:5) compares the challenges of making the proper decisions in our lives to the challenges that the captain of a ship faces as he tries to navigate his ship through a stormy sea. Life is full of challenges and adventures, and it is as difficult to consistently make good decisions about right and wrong as it is to successfully navigate the challenges and adventures at sea.

The only way for the ship to survive and reach its destination safely is to have a captain who is trained in the ways of the sea and in understanding the necessary strategies for navigating his ship through the dangerous winds and powerful waves.

The project of developing our *middos* and our relationships is also full of challenges and adventures. We are constantly faced with *middos*-related challenges that threaten our ability to remain on course and reach our destination safely. The winds and waves of *middos* development include our emotional, psychological, social, and spiritual needs. The storm also includes all the needs of others around us. Each relationship brings its own set of highs and lows, challenges and opportunities. The only way for us to properly develop our *middos* is to be like the captain of a ship. We need to learn about our emotional, physical, social, and psychological needs, and we need to learn strategies to navigate every experience in life.

The objective of this book is to provide some direction for how to develop greater compassion and respect for others and how to build more appropriate and productive relationships.

We will need to develop our *middos* and our *seichel* according to the guidance of the Torah. We will need to focus on understanding ourselves and others through the Torah, including understanding our purpose, our nature, and our development. A full understanding of these deep concepts is far beyond the scope of this book. However, the book will hopefully provide some clarity about these matters and how they can help us improve our relationships.

– PART 1 –

PROPER SPEECH

INTRODUCTION

IN THE LATE NINETEENTH CENTURY, the Chafetz Chaim reflected on the world around him and noticed a disturbing phenomenon. As he states in the introduction to *Chafetz Chaim* (published in 1873), many people in his generation frequently spoke negatively about others. They used their words to hurt other people's reputations, feelings, finances, and relationships.

He notes that he saw this disturbing behavior even among people who were generally dedicated to behaving according to proper moral values and even among people who were generally dedicated to observing the Torah's laws.

According to the Chafetz Chaim, when people would speak in a hurtful manner, they generally did not seem to recognize that their behavior was inconsistent with their ideals and values. They did not see how it conflicted with the image of a moral and Torah-observant person.

This phenomenon was not unique to the people in the Chafetz Chaim's generation. Rather, the reality that even moral and ethical people frequently speak negatively about others, without even recognizing it, is a common challenge that people have faced throughout the ages.

The Chafetz Chaim's observations should lead us to the following conclusions:

- Even though many of us may not think we speak inappropriately about others in any significant way, we probably do have a problem in this area. Even if we are generally committed to a life of morality and Torah observance, it is still likely that we are speaking about others in a manner that is inconsistent with those goals and ideals.
- The fact that we do not notice the problem in how we talk about others indicates that we do not always understand what it means to speak nicely and appropriately.
- Most people have compelling motivations to speak negatively about

others, which makes it very difficult to have the sufficient dedication and self-control to avoid doing so.

- We have many justifications that allow us to speak inappropriately without recognizing that we are doing something wrong.
- Even when we realize we have room to improve, we generally do not work on improving our speech in the most productive manner. The system that most of us use is not effective enough, as we see that even though we all want to speak appropriately, most of us are not accomplishing that goal very well.

It would be helpful to consider adjusting how we work on speaking properly about others, because the system we generally use to avoid hurting others may not be the most effective.

Most of us use the following approaches:

- We increase our dedication to our morals and Torah observance in general.
- We inspire and motivate ourselves to speak nicely about others.
- We consider the significance of our obligation to speak appropriately about others.
- We think about the fact that we will receive a great reward for speaking appropriately and that we will be held accountable for not speaking appropriately.
- We also think about all the benefits that come to us and to others when we speak in that manner.
- We try to increase our compassion for others and to be more careful not to hurt them.
- We create reminders for ourselves to focus on speaking nicely.
- We try to make a habit of speaking nicely.
- We learn the laws of proper speech and review them to make sure that we remember and focus on them.

This approach does help. When we are dedicated to moral behavior and to keeping the ways of the Torah, it helps to reduce our likelihood of speaking *lashon hara*, especially if we occasionally focus specifically on not speaking *lashon hara*. When we focus on acting with compassion for others and on not saying hurtful things about them, we can start to develop better habits. We should certainly continue to use these strategies to improve how we speak about others!

However, as the Chafetz Chaim says (introduction to *Chafetz Chaim*), many of us with the best intentions and efforts still speak *lashon hara* often. Apparently, if we want to stop speaking critically about others, we cannot just rely on the general development of our motivation and dedication to morality and Torah observance, with an occasional focus on speaking nicely. That does not work well enough!

Why not? Is our dedication to our morals and our Torah observance not good enough motivation to be nice to others and certainly to avoid hurting others by speaking about them behind their backs?

The actual source of the value of "treating others as you would want to be treated" originates in Torah law, as the Torah says (*Vayikra* 19:18), "Love your fellow like yourself" and the Gemara (*Shabbos* 31a) teaches us further that we should not treat others as we would not want to be treated. The Torah even gives us a specific law against speaking *lashon hara* (*Vayikra* 19:16), and the Chafetz Chaim (in the introduction to *Chafetz Chaim*) enumerates many other mitzvos that we transgress when we hurt others with our words. In general, the Torah teaches us that every person deserves to be treated with care, concern, and respect. These values are taught to us clearly in the Torah and in Torah literature. We invest time, money, and energy into keeping other mitzvos in the most ideal manner. It seems we should have the same motivation to fulfill our responsibilities to treat others properly.

When we know we are obligated to follow a Torah law, such as putting on *tefillin*, shaking a *lulav*, eating kosher food, and not having *chametz* on Pesach, we are usually pretty good at it. We go out of our way to invest time, money, and energy to keep the mitzvah appropriately. Why should *lashon hara* be any different? The same question applies to leading a moral life: Most of us are not bullies or thieves, but we do hurt others with our words. Why do we do that?

In order to identify what might be missing from our attempts to improve our speech, it is helpful to understand why it is that we generally use the less productive approach outlined above.

The Assumptions behind Our Typical Approach

Below are some assumptions underlying our use of our typical, less helpful approach to improving our speech, as outlined above.

Assumption 1: It is easy to define the values of proper speech about others. The values that relate to speaking properly seem to be very clear. Many fundamental aspects of morality, such as caring about others, respecting them, not wanting them to be hurt, and certainly not causing them to be hurt, define what proper speech should be. It is a universally accepted value to treat others as we would want to be treated. We would not want to be hurt, so we should not hurt others either.

Assumption 2: When we are dedicated to morality and to Torah observance, we will be motivated to behave in accordance with those values. We will want to be kind and giving, and we will strive to speak *to* others and *about* others in a manner that is not hurtful.

Assumption 3: Once someone is motivated to not hurt others with his words, it should not be too hard to follow through and act accordingly. Proper motivation and good habits should ensure our success.

Once we are sincere about being a good, moral person who follows the laws of the Torah, then we should certainly be able to commit to speaking positively about others and to fulfill this commitment effectively. The goal seems very clear, and it is easy to see its value and importance; therefore, it should be relatively easy to accomplish the goal. All we should need for this process is to develop good habits, with an occasional dose of inspiration and renewed focus.

Rethinking Our Assumptions

The *Orchos Tzaddikim* (Introduction) teaches us an important lesson about leading a Torah-observant and moral life. He says that our idealism, motivation, and commitment certainly influence how successful we will be in achieving our goals. However, many of our projects are complicated, and in order to succeed in them, we need to work on them properly and productively.

At times, we misinterpret what our true responsibilities are. As a result, our idealism, motivation, and commitment are focused in the wrong direction, and we will not accomplish our goals even if we work hard. At times, that simply means missing out on the positive accomplishments that we really should be achieving. In other scenarios, we may even be doing the wrong thing, and we may cause a lot of harm. It can be damaging if we have idealistic goals, but they are not directed toward what the Torah would consider to be truly appropriate. In the spirit of our idealism, we can justify behavior that can be hurtful to ourselves or others.

In other situations, we may have appropriate goals but may not know how to accomplish those goals. As a result, we are not equipped to implement the process productively. Each project has its own unique dynamics and requires its own process. Each project also has its own challenges that need to be overcome in order for us to achieve the intended goals.

These same concepts apply to the success of the project of improving our speech. For the most part, the success of this project depends on our idealism, motivation, and commitment, but we also cannot be successful without having a clear idea of what the Torah considers to be the appropriate way to speak and without the wisdom that is needed to be able to speak in that manner.

This was exactly the phenomenon that the Chafetz Chaim experienced. It was common for even moral and Torah-observant people to speak hurtfully about others. They were extremely diligent about their mitzvah observance in general. They were extremely careful about keeping all the laws of Shabbos, *kashrus*, and the rest of the *Shulchan Aruch*. However, they were not so careful about the laws of *lashon hara*. Apparently, speaking nicely about others does not result naturally from being a good person and not even from being a person who is generally careful about following Torah law.

We need to recognize the reality that we speak too much *lashon hara* and that we need to figure out how to truly improve in this area.

It is important to know that it is actually very difficult to determine the proper ideals as far as what we can say and why. There is a great deal of room for misinterpretation of these laws. It is also difficult to have enough motivation to really be able to follow through in not speaking about others in a negative way. There are many things that can interfere with our goal of speaking properly, and these challenges are not easy to overcome.

Even if we try to have specific reminders to speak positively about others, and even if we have a frequent dose of inspiration, these methods do not really help enough. There are unique factors that relate to *lashon hara* and make avoiding *lashon hara* a unique challenge. We need to clarify what those factors are, and we need to address them appropriately.

A more productive approach for improvement should include:

- clarifying what the proper ideals, values, rules, guidelines, and goals are (the positive actions that we need to accomplish and the negative actions we must avoid) in relation to speaking about other people;
- making an honest self-assessment to determine how we speak about others and to recognize which areas of our speech need improvement;
- developing proper and productive motivations for appropriate speech;
- identifying and understanding the challenges that cause us to speak inappropriately, including the motivations and the justifications for why we do not speak positively; and
- effectively addressing and dealing with all those challenges, including the dismantling of our justifications.

This approach will not work unless we embrace it, but we will not embrace it unless we understand why we need to change what we have been doing and why this approach will be more helpful than what we have been doing thus far. Most of us do not relate to the need for thought and analysis in relation to these matters. We think we already know the proper ideals and values for speaking properly. And we may be insulted by the notion that we do not even know how to properly determine what is proper and what is not.

We underestimate how often we speak inappropriately, especially because we are quick to find justifications for our criticisms of others.

We realize that challenges do present themselves in life, but we think we just need to remind ourselves of our goals and use our motivation to make the right decisions. Trying to figure out how to improve ourselves seems unnecessary because we know that we are good people, we are motivated to speak properly, and all we should need is a little extra focus and inspiration. In our minds, trying to figure out other means of improving ourselves seems like a waste of time.

The first step in working on speaking more positively is the realization that it is extremely important to do so and to realize that we are a long way away from speaking in the Torah-mandated manner about others. Speaking positively requires a complicated and difficult process, and we need to learn the process and work hard to carry it out.

The objective of this section of the book is to help us develop ourselves in a manner in which we have respect and compassion for others in our thoughts and feelings and in the way in which we speak about them, as well.

This book will use the Torah's guidance to:

- explain what the Torah considers the appropriate goals in terms of determining how to think, feel, and speak about others;
- outline the ideal process for developing the appropriate thoughts, feelings, and speech about others; and
- give examples of the challenges that interfere with our attainment of the appropriate thoughts, feelings, and speech about others — and explanations of how to overcome them.

CHAPTER 1

How to Develop Proper Speech

It is important to approach the project of improving our speech holistically. We need to consider all the different factors that influence the process. We need to identify the factors that cause us to speak properly and the challenges that prevent us from speaking positively.

The Chafetz Chaim (*Shemiras Halashon, Sha'ar Hatevunah*, ch. 13) tells us that in order to improve how we speak about others, we need to begin with an understanding of why we are not speaking nicely about them in the first place. The same way a doctor will try to identify the cause of an illness in order to prescribe the proper treatment plan, so too, if we want to know how to cure ourselves of speaking *lashon hara*, we first need to discover what causes us to speak *lashon hara* so we can address those factors productively.

On the one hand, the cause of speaking *lashon hara* is very clear, but on the other hand, it is somewhat perplexing. We know that we generally speak *lashon hara* when we are angry or jealous or when we feel better about ourselves by lowering someone else. However, it is unclear why it is that so many of us speak *lashon hara* so frequently, when we are motivated to act with morality in general and we are generally motivated to follow Torah Law. We generally do not want to hurt others. We need to understand what it is that causes us to hurt others with our words, and we need to identify the challenges that prevent us from speaking properly.

In the *Ohr Hatzafun* (vol. 1, p. 173), we are taught an important lesson about behavior modification that is certainly applicable to improving how we speak about others. It is written there that our ability to act or speak properly depends on many fundamental aspects of who we are, such as our thoughts, feelings, and *middos*, all of which shape our inner being and affect our speech and behavior.

Many of the strategies that are often used to influence behavior focus on the specific behavior itself and do not take into account what is going on in our thoughts, feelings, and *middos*. For certain projects, such an approach may be effective; however, if we want to make lasting and meaningful change in our behavior, we cannot rely on these strategies alone. Rather, we need to understand the underlying causes of the behaviors and underlying challenges that have previously stood in the way of our having achieved our goal. That insight will enable us to make more meaningful and more sustainable changes in the future.

Similarly, when we want to work on improving how we speak about others, we need to understand the causes of proper speech and the underlying challenges that hinder proper speech.

Pirkei Avos (2:9) teaches us a similar concept. Rabban Yochanan ben Zakkai agrees with Rabbi Elazar that the most productive way to improve our *middos* and behavior is to develop a *lev tov* (good heart), to improve ourselves internally. If we focus on developing a *lev tov*, then good *middos* and actions will follow.

The *Rishonim* tell us that the feelings we hold in our hearts (and the thoughts and attitudes in our minds) shape our behaviors and relationships. They explain that having a good heart includes having all the proper feelings, thoughts, and attitudes so we become loving, kind, and compassionate; happy with what we have and not jealous of others; and genuinely happy when others succeed.

Rabbi Eliezer (*Pirkei Avos* 2:9) agrees that working toward proper *middos* and behaviors begins in our hearts and minds. He says that developing an *ayin tovah* (a good eye) leads to the acquisition of all the other proper behaviors and *middos*. The *Rishonim* explain that having a good eye refers to being happy with what we have or to having a generous and benevolent attitude toward others to the extent that we are even happy for other people's successes. When we have these thoughts, feelings, and attitudes, our actions will also be proper and appropriate.

The Chafetz Chaim tells us throughout his *sefer Chafetz Chaim* that it is important to learn the laws of proper speech because they involve many nuances that many people do not know. He also wrote an entire *sefer, Shemiras Halashon,* that teaches us about the underlying attitudes, perspectives, ideals, and values that relate to proper speech. He teaches us that we need to make sure that all our attitudes, perspectives, ideals, and values are in line with those of the Torah in order to make real improvements in how we speak about others.

Although understanding the relevant laws and values as well as dedication to living in accordance with them put us in a good position to make proper decisions, these approaches are not enough because there are so many other factors that also affect how we speak.

For example, we need to refine the value we place on human life; how we define success and accomplishment; and how we think about other people (groups or individuals). The more respect we have for each individual or group, the more sensitive we will be to not hurting them with our words.

Our feelings have a significant effect on how we treat others. For example, when we feel like we have been hurt by someone, it can be difficult to control how we speak about them. Moreover, the laws of proper speech often depend on our judgment calls. Even if we try to have the self-control to follow the laws about what to say, it is difficult to make the proper judgments when we are hurt or upset due to our biases. When we make the wrong judgments, then our application of the relevant laws will not be accurate.

It is helpful to recognize the value of speaking nicely about others in order to understand the importance of the mitzvah and its potential benefits for our spirituality, our closeness to Hashem, and our rewards in This World and the Next World.

It is also important to understand how damaging our words can be so we will be motivated to avoid causing damage through them and, conversely, to understand how helpful our words can be so we can be motivated to speak in more helpful ways.

In order to significantly improve how we speak about others, we need to approach our goal with wisdom. Our words and behaviors are generally motivated and controlled by our thoughts, feelings, perspectives, attitudes, and *middos*. Therefore, any meaningful growth in our behavior or our words can only happen if we develop these areas productively.

It is essential to work on developing the types of perspectives and feelings that will enable us to have a realistic chance of speaking appropriately about others. It is certainly a long process, but it is necessary to work on developing the core *middos* of compassion, kindness, acceptance, tolerance, empathy, and patience. Through these *middos*, we can develop thoughts and feelings of love, acceptance, understanding, and respect for all people, even those who have done things that are wrong and even those who have hurt us personally. It is a difficult job, but we only need to improve step by step. These are just a few examples of the factors that we need to consider in order to improve our speech.

The following is a list of many of the things that affect how we speak about others:

- *middos*, thoughts, and feelings, such as low self-esteem, arrogance, humility, kindness, compassion, empathy, faith and trust in Hashem, anger, resentment, emotional pain, jealousy, happiness, and fulfillment;
- thinking before speaking;
- love of and respect for others;
- our recognition and belief that we have a responsibility to love and respect everyone;
- our ability to develop love and respect for others — because it does not come naturally;
- our realistic expectations of ourselves or others;
- judging others favorably;
- our justifications for hurting others;
- our biases that motivate us to justify our inappropriate attitudes and behaviors toward others;
- our ability to coexist peacefully and to speak nicely despite the challenges involved;

- our unfulfilled needs, which may lead us to speak inappropriately, such as the need for respect, love, acceptance, or belonging;
- our ability to address all the factors that cause our negative speech (it is especially hard to deal with all the factors combined);
- our dedication and ability to improve our relationships productively;
- our environment;
- our ideals and values (thoughts, attitudes, and perspectives) regarding matters such as Hashem's role in our lives, respect, love, human value, and how to define success and accomplishment;
- knowledge of the laws that regulate what, how, and when to speak about others, our understanding of how to keep those laws, and our dedication to following them; and
- our recognition of how important it is to speak appropriately about others.

When we are not speaking nicely, it is due to a combination of our thoughts, perspectives, attitudes, feelings, *middos*, and needs. In order to improve in a meaningful way, it is necessary to understand our whole inner being, including how different elements of our being affect each other. We need to address all these factors individually and as a whole. It is important to focus on developing the proper ideals and values, taking into account all the above elements in order to work on ourselves productively.

This process requires a lot of self-awareness. We need to identify our thoughts, feelings, and *middos* and to understand how they are causing us to speak negatively about others. Then, we can start the process of making the changes that we need to make. To the extent that we improve ourselves in each of these areas, we will also improve how we speak about others.

The remainder of Chapter 1 will explain most of the factors in the above list in more detail, while a few will be discussed in subsequent chapters.

Chapter 2 will explain the proper ideals and values in relation to speaking properly from a Torah perspective. Defining our ideals and values properly will help define our goals and is a major part of the process of improving how we speak about others.

Chapter 3 will explain the importance of knowing the laws clearly and applying them properly.

Chapter 4 will discuss our motivation to speak properly, which is based on developing more of an appreciation for the importance of speaking positively about others.

Refining Our Thoughts, Feelings, and *Middos*

The way in which we speak about others is often a natural result of our thoughts, feelings, and *middos*.

The Chafetz Chaim, in *Sha'ar Hatevunah* (*Shemiras Halashon*) and throughout his *sefarim*, explains that we often speak *lashon hara* due to our inappropriate thoughts and feelings about others and due to our own bad *middos*.

The Midrash (*Vayikra Rabbah* 9:3) teaches us, "*Derech eretz* (having productive *middos*) precedes the Torah." The *Ohr Hatzafun* (vol. 1, p. 173) explains that this statement refers to the fact that our *middos* are the foundation of many of the mitzvos. Many mitzvos can only be accomplished if we have already laid the foundation for their accomplishment beforehand. Many of the mitzvos that require us to act appropriately toward others or to speak positively about others can only be accomplished through working on our *middos* first. We need to respect others, care about them, not feel jealous of them, and not be arrogant toward them in order to treat them properly.

Throughout the *Mesillas Yesharim*, there are references to the idea that our thoughts and feelings are connected to our words and behaviors — thoughts and feelings influence words and behaviors, and vice versa. The more appropriate our speech is, the more appropriate our thoughts and feelings will be, and the more we develop proper thoughts and feelings, the better our words will be.

It is important to have proper thoughts and feelings because they are important in their own right, but it is also necessary to have the proper thoughts and feelings in order to act properly toward others and to speak properly to and about others.

Critical Thoughts and Negative Feelings

Obviously, how we think about others affects how we speak about them. If we think someone is a great and amazing person and we like them a lot, it is unlikely that we will be motivated to speak about them in a critical manner. On the other hand, if we think someone is a bad or foolish person, we are much more likely to be motivated to speak about them in a critical manner, and we will have much more criticism to share about them as well.

Similarly, if we have feelings of dislike, hatred, or animosity toward others, we will feel compelled to speak about them in a negative way.

When we have critical thoughts about others or have negative feelings about them, we are still obligated to avoid speaking about them in a negative manner. However, if we do not develop appropriate and productive perspectives about others, it is not realistic for us to communicate about them in a positive and productive way. Once we determine in our minds that someone is a bad or foolish person, it is likely that we will find ways to share that opinion with others. Even if we really try to avoid criticizing them, we will not be able to do so. Our thoughts and feelings will eventually manifest.

Therefore, if our goal is to speak positively about others, we need to ensure that our thoughts and attitudes are in line with that goal. We also need to work on ourselves to remove some of our pain, dislike, hatred, or animosity, or we will likely not be able to hold ourselves back from speaking about them in a critical way.

Underlying Thoughts, Feelings, and *Middos*

As we explained above, how we speak about someone is primarily related to our thoughts and feelings: If we do not respect or care about them, that will likely be expressed in our speech. However, if we look deeper, we will recognize that there are certain fundamental *middos*, thoughts, feelings, attitudes, and perspectives that are the underlying causes of those negative thoughts and feelings. If we can identify and work on them, we will be more likely to have positive thoughts and feelings about others, which will certainly lead to speaking less critically about them.

For example, Rabbeinu Yonah (*Sha'arei Teshuvah*, ch. 3) tells us that arrogance affects our criticism in a significant way. When we are arrogant, we tend to think of others in negative terms. We think of them as being bad, foolish, incapable, unworthy, and unimportant. It is also common to develop feelings of negativity, anger, or jealousy toward others when we are arrogant. Therefore, it is difficult to work on not being critical of others without working on our humility.

If we contrast someone who generally has the *middos* of anger, jealousy, and hatred with someone who generally has the *middos* of compassion, empathy, and tolerance, those in the first group will certainly be more likely to be critical of others than those in the second group. It is helpful to work on these *middos* in order to help us to become less critical of others, which will lead to speaking more positively about others.

Our belief in Hashem plays a big role in how critical we are. When we recognize that Hashem determines what our nature, environment, and experiences will be in life and that Hashem designs each person's situation in its own unique way, that fundamental perspective will affect our outlook in many ways. For example, we will not attribute other people's successes and failures to them alone. As a result, we will not be as critical of them for their failures. We also will not be as likely to measure one person's talents or successes in relation to the next person's talents and successes. Very often, we are critical of others because we feel they are holding us back or have held us back from our success. When we recognize that our success is actually controlled solely by Hashem, then we are less likely to hold others responsible for our limitations and criticize them.

How much we value human life in general also affects how likely we are to be critical of others. The less we value human life, the less we will be motivated to respect or care about other people. We will not think that they are important or relevant.

If we are arrogant and critical of others or if we are angry and hurt by others, it is not realistic to assume that we are going to be able to avoid speaking *lashon hara*. We obviously need to work on learning what the right perspectives and attitudes should be and on developing our *middos* productively.

Thinking Carefully before We Speak about Others

One of the biggest challenges we face with regard to speaking *lashon hara* is that we often do not really think before we speak about others. As a result, we often hurt others with our words even though we know that it is wrong to do so.

When we know that we have a presentation to make in an upcoming business meeting, we will spend a lot of time preparing for it. We will think about what we are going to say, why we are going to say it, and how we are going to present it. We will think about how the message will be received and how our audience is likely to react when they hear that message. We will often consider the pros and cons of sharing our message in one manner as opposed to sharing it in a different manner.

In contrast, very little thought tends to go into any of the standard conversations that we have throughout our days. Many of our discussions revolve around other people, and within the discussion, we will often share what is on our mind about those people. Since we generally do not spend any time preparing for these discussions, we say hurtful things that we might have avoided had we thought it through properly beforehand.

At times, we might say something that is hurtful without having recognized at the time that it was hurtful or how hurtful it was. We might realize on some level that we are saying something hurtful to others, but we do not fully recognize that we are truly hurting them. Maybe we felt justified without thinking through whether it was really a good justification, or we did not think through the consequences properly. Sometimes, we act impulsively and make an objectively bad decision that seemed reasonable at the time.

There are several reasons for our lack of focus on what we are saying and our likelihood of saying something hurtful without being fully aware of it.

The *Mesillas Yesharim* (ch. 4) teaches us that one of the biggest challenges we face in achieving any spiritual goal is being properly focused. Even when something is important to us, we still have a hard time focusing on what is proper and productive. We often get distracted by other desires and interests, and we do not do what is really important to us. We are particularly likely to focus on the desires, pleasures, and comforts that are right in front of us and to not focus enough on our long-term goals. Even though the long-term goal may be more of a priority in many ways than the short-term pleasure and comfort, it is more natural for us to focus on the pleasure and comfort that is in front of us than it is to think about the benefits of our long-term goals.

The fact that our words often hurt others only in an indirect and intangible manner also makes it difficult to recognize the need to stop and consider what we are going to say before we say it.

We generally have a strong hesitation to physically harm someone even when we are tempted to do so because we would be very aware that we are hurting the person. Before making a decision to hurt them, we would carefully analyze the situation in order to handle it in a proper and measured manner. It is easier to fall into the trap of hurting others with our words because that type of damage is less tangible, and it is therefore easier to lose focus. The more we are aware and focused on the fact that our words can hurt others, the less likely we will be to say anything that is critical and hurtful.

Loving and Respecting Others

We do not usually speak critically about the people we love and respect. However, there are many people we do not love or respect, and even in our relationships with those we do love and respect, there are times when we do not feel that love and respect. During those times, we are more likely to speak about them in a negative manner. One of the most important ways of improving how we speak about others is to increase our love and respect for them.

There are a number of reasons why our lack of love and respect for others leads us to speak about them in a negative way even though we all know that it is inappropriate to hurt others with our words.

- When we do not like someone or we do not respect them, and certainly when we feel hurt by them or are angry at them, we will often speak about them in a negative manner simply because we want to speak negatively about them. The fact that we know we should not hurt them will cause us to want to hold back to some extent, but realistically, we will often not have enough self-control to consistently refrain from speaking badly about them.

- Generally, one of our motivations for speaking nicely about others comes from our sense that people deserve to be treated with love and respect. However, when we think that someone is a bad person or that they do not care about us, we may not think that they deserve to be treated with respect.

- Additionally, even if we recognize that we need to speak positively, when we do not like someone, we are motivated to find a way to justify speaking badly of them and hurting them. We will tell ourselves we're doing the right thing, even though our behavior is really just caused by our desire.

- Criticism is sometimes communicated in subtle ways. Our words often contain subtle messages that influence whether the overall meaning is critical or not. When we do not like or respect someone, even when we are not willing to criticize them overtly, we are often able to justify criticizing them in a subtle manner.

- When helping someone out requires us to speak about someone else's limitations and challenges, we are allowed to do so. However, many rules and guidelines must be followed in order to be allowed to speak about them. When we do not like the person we are talking about, we are not likely to try our best to speak about them in the most permissible and sensitive manner.

- One of the biggest challenges that relates to all these matters is that even when we want to make the right decisions, we have many biases that affect our judgment. When we have been hurt by someone and we are upset at them, we certainly have a strong bias to want to hurt them as well. Therefore, all our decisions that relate to any discussions about that person, whether they relate to what to say or how to say it, will be affected by our biases. Our biases affect our decisions subconsciously; therefore, it is difficult to anticipate and therefore avoid their effects.

When there are people we do not like and do not respect, we need to do our best to make sure we do not hurt them by speaking *lashon hara* about them. We need to have self-control to hold ourselves back from criticizing them even when we want to do so. It is important to realize that even though someone has hurt us, we do not have the right to hurt them in return. We must be aware of the risk of over-justifying and telling ourselves it is right to speak about others in a situation in which it is not really justified. We must also learn how to speak about other people's shortcomings appropriately in the situations in which we are permitted to and are even advised to speak about them as well as to avoid bias due to our flawed relationship with the person.

However, the most productive way to avoid speaking *lashon hara* in these situations is to improve our relationship with the other person. If the relationship improves, it will be much less of a challenge to avoid speaking *lashon hara* about them.

Similarly, in order to improve our general behavior of speaking *lashon hara*, we need to work on becoming the type of person who is more likely to have productive relationships and more positive thoughts and feelings about others in general.

Recognizing Our Responsibility to Love and Respect Everyone

We all say the words that everyone should be treated with care, concern, and respect. That seems to be what we are expected to think and to say, and we may think that we really believe it. However, when we analyze our thoughts more closely, we will see that we tend to think that many people do not actually deserve to be respected and cared for. Once we do not *think* they deserve to be treated with care and respect, then we often *treat* them and speak about them accordingly.

It is important to analyze these matters objectively and to ask ourselves whether or not everyone really does deserve respect and care. We obviously know that there are some people we should respect and care about, but does that principle really apply to everyone?

We should analyze the matters of care and respect individually because there are certain differences in how we look at them. Every person has their own system for measuring who deserves care or respect; however, there are generally a few basic factors that we all must consider.

Care

When we measure how much we should care about someone, we will often consider how close they are to us (either as family or as a friend) or how much they have done for us.

The question is not whether we should feel more care and concern for those who are close to us or those who have helped us. It is part of human nature to care more about those who are closest to us, such as our family and friends. The Torah teaches us the same concept — that we should prioritize helping the people who are closest to us before we help others. Similarly, it is both natural and appropriate to care more about those people who have helped us out than about others who have not. The importance of showing gratitude to those who have helped us is a well-known Torah concept.

The question is really whether we need to care about the people who are not so close to us and have never helped us. On the one hand, it is easy to say, "Of course, we care! We care about everyone!" On the other hand, when we are honest with ourselves, we may not really believe it so much. It is hard to really care about others in a meaningful way!

We may also think that we should not be responsible for caring about people who are not "good people." We might think that people who are not moral, ethical, or Torah observant do not deserve to be cared for. Certainly, when it comes to people who have not been pleasant to others, we may think, "Why should I care about him, if he does not care about others?" Especially when we or someone we care about has been hurt, we often think, "Why should I care about him? If he has hurt me or someone I care about, he does not deserve my care and concern!"

Are these perspectives accurate? What are our responsibilities to those who have done things wrong, in general or specifically to us or our loved ones? We ask ourselves these questions, whether consciously or not, all the time. Should I care about that person? If so, how much? What has he done for me? Is he a good person? Is he a friend?

These are very reasonable considerations, but they often hold us back from caring about other people. If we want to work on caring more about others, we need to resolve these questions appropriately.

Respect

The same is true of respect. We often think it is okay to speak negatively about the people in our lives because they do not deserve our respect or the dignity of our sensitivity to their needs. Therefore, it is important to ensure that we have an accurate understanding of who deserves respect.

One of our considerations about whether someone deserves respect or not relates to whether the person is a great person or not. If we think that someone is only average, and certainly if he is a bad person, it may not seem like they should deserve much respect.

We may also ask ourselves what our responsibilities are to the "average person." We may think that we are only obligated to respect someone who is special in a meaningful way. Do we need to respect everyone?

We tend to measure how much we should respect someone based primarily on what we consider their value to be. We all recognize that every person has objective value as a human (even a new baby has value), but each person's value is also affected by his accomplishments. How we measure a person's success affects our respect for them.

Unfortunately, most people measure success in a manner that causes them to conclude that most people do not deserve very much respect. All people have shortcomings, and it is easy for us to see their shortcomings and to conclude that they do not deserve to be respected.

How much we respect another person is related to how we determine human value in general: how we understand who we are and our purpose in This World as well as how we define and measure human success and failure. It also relates to how we determine each specific person's individual value and success within that general framework. In order to respect others properly, we need to have the proper "value system" for people in general, and we need to apply it to each person appropriately.

Unfortunately, very few people spend time thinking about how to respect others properly. We think we already have a clear value system and understand how to apply it to each individual person. However, the reality is that we often do not really understand the basis for an assessment of human value. We do not have an accurate understanding of our purpose in This World, and we have a distorted impression of how to accurately measure human success. Therefore, our conclusions about whom we should respect and how much we should respect them are often not appropriate or productive. What makes the situation worse is that we generally do not even realize our measuring system is wrong, so we do not realize that we need to fix anything.

If our value system is wrong, there will be many people whom we will not be able to respect even if we are extremely motivated to respect others. If there is a person who does not deserve respect according to our understanding (perhaps due to his social, financial, or intellectual status or due to his values or moral choices), then there is no way to fully respect him. How can we have respect for someone we do not really think deserves respect? At times, we will be able to treat the person in a respectful manner, but the fact that we do not respect them will cause us to also mistreat them, and we certainly will not be able to have respect for them in our minds and hearts.

Therefore, if our goal is to respect every person, we need to learn how to change our value system to match the Torah's system, according to which every human has incredible innate value.

The Value of Every Person

There are a few quotes that highlight the true value of every person. For instance, the Torah says that Adam was created in the image of Hashem (*Bereishis* 1:27). The Mishnah in *Pirkei Avos* (3:14) teaches us that every man is created in the image of Hashem. The Mishnah in *Sanhedrin* (4:5) teaches us that every person is obligated to say, "The world was created for me." The *pasuk* in *Vayikra* (19:18) says, "Love your fellow like yourself."

The true Torah perspective is that every person is created in the image of Hashem. Everyone has an eternal soul, and Hashem created the entire world for the purpose of our individual missions in This World.

There is plenty to love and respect about each person when we truly understand who they are and what their essence is. We are all familiar with our responsibility to love others, and that applies to everyone!

It is true that it is difficult to respect and care about people who are not close to us, and it is especially difficult to care about those who seem to be "bad people," particularly those who have hurt us. However, it is our responsibility to do our best to care about them and to respect them.

The more we appreciate the greatness of the human soul, the easier it is to be motivated to care about others and respect them.

We tend to sense that it is appropriate to feel unconditional love, care, concern, and acceptance for all people. We should treat everyone equally and respectfully, and everyone should be equally valuable to us. We often expect ourselves and others to love and respect everyone with a full heart.

This sounds nice, but it does not fully reflect how our minds really work, and it is not reflected in many of our actions. Sometimes, we do act accordingly, such as when we see someone who is suffering. When we see an individual in front of us who is experiencing physical or emotional pain, we often try to offer comfort and encouragement and try to help them in any way we can. When there is a national crisis, we often hear about people from around the country who mobilize to help strangers physically or financially. At times, people put their lives in danger in order to help others. Yet, we also still hurt each other with our words, and there is a great deal of conflict in This World. All these examples seem to indicate that we do not really care about each other so much.

Even within many close relationships, sometimes, it seems that we care about each other a lot, yet at other times, we demonstrate negative feelings toward and are critical of each other. We do not always offer help when we can, and we sometimes even hurt each other.

Both sides are true. The same person can be extremely nice to one person and extremely mean to another. Even within the same relationship, a person can sometimes be extremely loving and kind, while at other times, he can be extremely unhelpful and hurtful to the same person.

Conflicting Behaviors in the Same Person

The fact that we have seemingly contradictory thoughts, feelings, and behaviors is basic human nature. Every human has strong feelings of compassion, empathy, care, and concern about others because each of us has a *neshamah* that, by nature, wants and needs to act with kindness, compassion, and love. Our *neshamos* can motivate us to act with true and sincere kindness.

If the *neshamah* existed as an independent being, it would naturally have boundless love and compassion for others, and nothing could interfere with that.

However, as humans, we were also created with another part of our nature, which is very egocentric. We are selfish and concerned only about ourselves. Our egocentric nature causes us to focus on our desires — we want pleasure, comfort, respect, and honor. There are many *middos* that come along with this nature, such as jealousy, anger, and the tendency to be mean and hurtful to others — especially when these *middos* help us get what we want. Our desire to feel good about ourselves can lead to arrogance, which can cause us to be critical, mean, and hurtful to others. At the same time, our desire to feel good about ourselves can also lead to a lack of self-esteem, which can lead us to be critical of others and even hurt them in order to build ourselves up.

Both aspects of humanity, the *neshamah* and self-centeredness, are part of every person. Both shape our existence — our thoughts, feelings, and actions.

Our *neshamos* cause us to be compassionate, caring, and considerate to others as well as to do whatever we can to help them, in whatever way possible. Our egocentricity causes us to be selfish, to only focus on ourselves, to care only about ourselves, and to even hurt others when doing so benefits us. Both these elements operate within us and make us who we are.

Even within a relationship that is important to us, even if we have a history of love, care, and concern for the other person, it is still difficult for us to only focus on their best interests because our own interests usually take precedence. Even though we want to do what is right — as a good person and as a Torah-observant Jew — when there is a conflict between what is good for us and what is good for the other person, we will often prioritize our own needs over theirs. We will even do things that hurt them for the sake of our own needs because we are essentially selfish beings.

The selfish or self-centered side of humanity is likely the main source of our speaking inappropriately about others. Our self-centered side creates a need for us to build ourselves up, and that side often manifests when we use our words to put others down when we speak to or about them.

The fact that there are so many people we do not care about or respect makes it very likely that we speak a lot of *lashon hara*. We often find ourselves criticizing others because from our own perspective, there are many things about them that we could criticize, and since we do not particularly like them, it does not bother us to hurt their feelings and their reputation.

The Chovos Halevavos (*Sha'ar Avodas Ha'Elokim*, ch. 1) teaches us that our egocentric self begins to develop long before our *seichel* matures and develops. From when we are born, we already begin to think about our own needs, interests, and desires. We focus our thoughts and energy on taking care of ourselves. We do not have the ability to control our thoughts and behaviors because we are too young to understand this need.

He also explains that the desire for honor, pleasure, and comfort has a more natural course of development than our *seichel* does because we are more naturally inclined to follow that path than the path of thinking about helping others.

This principle teaches us an important lesson: Even though we are good people and care about others and want to help them, especially those we are close to, we need to realize that it is very difficult to care about and be nice to others. Reaching the level where we truly care for others requires a lot of focus, a good game plan, and hard work. With a combination of these elements, we can grow slowly and gradually.

This perspective can help us in a few ways. It can wake us up to the idea that we should not be overconfident that we will treat others in the most ideal manner, whether for the sake of general morality or Torah observance or because we have a good relationship with a certain person. Realistically, the fact that we are selfish and self-centered will interfere with our ability to be as loving, caring, and compassionate as we expect ourselves to be. This awareness will help motivate us to work on improving ourselves.

This perspective can also guide us in understanding how to work on ourselves to become more sensitive about how we speak to or about others. We cannot just work on being a generally moral person or a generally Torah-observant Jew because we will still have our natural tendencies that revolve around our egos and our own needs. We will remain selfish and self-centered, and we will still care more about our own happiness than about that of others. Instead, we must also work on a more fundamental level, to change our inner selves. We need to figure out how to become less selfish and less self-centered. These are not easy matters to accomplish, but at least we know what we need to do.

It is difficult to admit to ourselves that we do not actually care about or respect most people because it is not socially acceptable to think in those terms. However, that is the reality of most people's feelings.

It is also difficult to recognize that this is how we think and feel because there is still that part of us that does care about all people, that does want to be nice to everyone. We want to think of ourselves as good people, so we overlook the fact that the other part of us (and, often, the more dominant part) does not really respect or care about others.

It is important to recognize that our lack of care or respect for others does not mean we are bad people but rather that it is very difficult to truly love and care about others. We were created as selfish beings who naturally focus on ourselves and our own interests and desires, and our selfish nature is reinforced by many of the messages we receive from our environment as we grow up. We are exposed to many people who are selfish, and that has a significant effect on our perspectives and behaviors. We are often exposed to people who are very critical of others, which teaches us to see the world that way.

When we understand that it is both important and difficult to love and respect others, we will be motivated to work hard to develop the appropriate thoughts, feelings, and behaviors. We will also be motivated to learn about what needs to be done to develop these thoughts, feelings, and behaviors rather than assume we already have developed them naturally or expect them to come through willpower alone.

Another reason why it is challenging to learn to respect others is that every person has limitations, which offer many opportunities to criticize them. If we do not learn to understand other people's limitations from a perspective that does not involve judging them as bad or foolish, then that is how we will think about them. Therefore, one of the aspects of how to work on respecting others relates to perfectionism.

Developing Realistic Standards for Ourselves and Others

Most of us do not think of ourselves as perfectionists. We think of ourselves as good people, but we understand that we have limitations, we make mistakes, and we are not perfect.

However, the term "perfectionism" does not only refer to an expectation to be perfect. It can also refer to someone who has unrealistic standards for themselves or others. Perfectionism often comes with a sense of self-criticism or criticism of others when those standards and expectations are not met.

Realistic expectations are based on a proper understanding of human nature, including our needs, our *middos*, and our challenges. They also include an understanding of how difficult it is to overcome challenges.

We all want to do what is right and to avoid doing what is wrong. However, it is often hard to know what is right and wrong; it is hard to be fully motivated to do what is right and to avoid doing what is wrong; and it is hard to overcome the challenges that stand in the way and that cause us to want to do what is wrong.

We all want to run after pleasure and comfort, and that pursuit can interfere with our ideals and values. We want to fulfill our financial, emotional, social, and psychological needs and desires. We often have a hard time taking care of these needs and desires productively, which causes us to be anxious and upset, and it motivates us to try to fulfill those needs as best as we can, even in unproductive ways.

We often underestimate how difficult it is to overcome our challenges, and we expect that we should be able to live up to our ideals and values. We may give ourselves a certain amount of leeway, but we generally expect too much of ourselves and others. That approach leads us to be too critical. We think, "Why can't you just…?" We use this expression for any of the ideals and values that we see others are not living up to or tasks that we think they should be able to accomplish easily.

The basis of perfectionism is a lack of understanding of humanity and of our needs and limitations as humans. We expect that understanding "right and wrong" should be easy and that once we understand what is right and wrong, we should be able to accomplish those goals if we just care about them. Therefore, when we see others not living up to what we would have expected, we are often critical of them. We attribute negative motives to them and judge their "failures." We start to think of them as people who have bad morals and values, or we might think that they must be lazy or angry. Why else would they act this way, if not because they are such bad people?

The Effect of Perfectionism on Respect and Love

Interpreting other people's behavior in this fashion and assuming that they are "bad people" leads to developing a lack of respect for them. Similarly, if we create unrealistic expectations of others, then when they fail to live up to those expectations, we will conclude that they do not love us or care about us.

We need to recognize that there are many good people whose own needs and limitations hold them back from mitzvos that they want to be involved in. If they end up making the wrong decision, that does not make them a bad person. It does not even mean that they do not care about the mitzvos. All it means is that the challenge was difficult, and they did not overcome it this time.

This recognition can help us to respect the person despite their limitations. We will understand that they are really good people, with good morals and values, but they are human, and they also face challenges and failures.

This recognition can also help us understand that even someone who cares about us and loves us may, at times, be insensitive. Their insensitivity may hurt, but we will realize that they still care about us and that the overall relationship can still be meaningful and positive.

The danger of the perfectionist way of thinking is that it is very black and white — all or nothing. Either you are a good person or a bad person, either you love me or you do not. If you are good, you will always be good, and if you do not (almost) always do the right thing, you must be a bad person. If you care about me, you will always be sensitive and care for my needs. If there are times that you are not sensitive to my needs, then you must not care about me.

Realistically, none of us can stand up to such scrutiny. We are human, and we will not always be able to behave appropriately, and none of us can always act with care and sensitivity to others.

Judging Others Properly

We are constantly judging whether other people are worthy of our respect and love. We also judge how they seem to feel toward us: Do they respect us? Do they love us? These judgments shape our relationships.

We have access to a lot of information about other people. We witness their behaviors, we hear what they say, and we hear what others have to say about them. How we process that information is significant. If we process information about others critically, then we will end up with a negative impression of them. However, if we process the information about others in a positive way, then we will end up with a much more positive opinion of them.

When we take in information and judge those around us, we measure their success, achievements, and natural gifts. When we consider whether people are "good people," we assess their deeds in numerous areas. Are they kind? Compassionate? Honest? Calm? Helpful? Modest? The list goes on and on. If we are considering whether someone is smart, we measure their knowledge about many different areas — a person may know math and science, but are they street smart? Are they business savvy? Are they socially smooth? Or are they good with their hands?

Most of us are capable, talented, smart, and competent. However, we are judged in so many areas that we are certainly going to be average at best in some areas and probably below average in many others. That opens us up for criticism.

Within any relationship (husband-wife, parent-child, employer-employee, coworker, friend, neighbor relationships, etc.), our limitations will certainly show, and they will affect the relationship. This demonstration of our limitations puts the other person in the relationship in a position to criticize us. Our limitations, including anger, forgetfulness, laziness, and any other negative *middos* we have, will affect the other person in a negative way. That will cause them to want to criticize us. Even the basic differences in personality that we all have can be viewed by the other person as being problematic, opening up more room for more criticism.

All the different aspects of our personality will come out on a regular basis because that they contribute to who we are. Someone who is critical of one of our *middos* will consistently be exposed to that trait and will therefore be consistently critical of us.

Avoiding Criticism of Others

There are two major elements in not being critical of others.

The first is recognizing that very often, the information we have about the other person in a relationship is inaccurate or incomplete. Although we receive a lot of information about others, it is most often secondhand, and we are usually missing a big part of the story. When we recognize this reality, it is much easier to not be critical of that person because we realize we do not even know what really happened.

The other element is how we interpret information even if we have good reason to believe it is accurate. We need to learn how to think about things differently and gain perspectives that enable us to not be critical of others.

We often make judgments about what other people could have or should have done differently, but the Mishnah (*Pirkei Avos* 2:4) tells us, "Do not judge your friend until you reach his place." When we make judgments about another person, we are often assuming something about them, such as how easy or difficult their circumstances are. Our assumptions are usually inaccurate — in order to really assess the level of difficulty of a person's challenges, we would need to have their individualized nature, experiences, and life circumstances. Any individual's challenges are uniquely experienced by them — and them alone. Nobody else can know what that person's individual situation was like.

However, it is very common to look at another person's situation and think that we know what his challenges are. We think we can assess how easy or difficult it would be to overcome those challenges, and we judge the person based on that assessment.

The Mishnah above teaches us that we are often judging the other person as though *they* were in *our* situation, and in that context, we assess what they could have and should have done. However, even if the same thing happened to us, we may have done the same thing — and even if we would not have done the same thing, that may be because we are different people, and what is relatively easy for us may be extremely difficult for them.

The Mishnah also teaches us that a lot of our criticism comes from misjudging other people's situations and not realizing that things are often much more complicated than they seem from a distance. When we do not know all the factors that are relevant to another person's situation, we often end up with a critical perspective about the person. On the surface, we see that the person has done something that does not seem appropriate or productive. If we think the story is limited to what we see in front of us, then we may conclude that he is bad or foolish.

Based on the lessons from the Mishnah, there are a few strategies we can use in order to be less critical. First, we can focus on the fact that we do not really know the situation and instead think about the fact that if we did know the rest of the situation, we would be a lot less critical. If we recognize that if we knew more about the story, we would likely understand the behavior, that can help us recognize that we do not have a reason to believe the person is bad or foolish.

Second, we can try to investigate the situation and come to a real understanding of the other person's reality and why they made the decisions they made. Getting the facts straight can help make us less critical.

Another aspect of being less critical relates to how we deal with the facts that are in front of us. We can look at the same facts in very different ways. We can see someone who has some form of limitation and think that means that they must be a terrible person. Or we can think to ourselves that even if they have a limitation, they can still be a good person overall. They may be doing a great job based on their situation. There are many situations in which the same facts can be viewed from different angles, and that choice can affect how critical we will be of the other person.

Not Seeing Our Limitations

It also helps to remember that we all have limitations and shortcomings. "There is no man who is so righteous that he does not sin" (*Koheles* 7:20). Everyone makes bad choices, and we all act in ways that are not proper. However, even though this principle applies to all of us, as Rabbi Yisrael Salanter once said, "A person does not see his own limitations." Many of us have a hard time seeing our own shortcomings. We are quick to see other people's sins, but our own sins slip under our own radar. This situation often causes us to feel that we are better and smarter than others. We become arrogant and are therefore critical of other people's mistakes.

There are two reasons why we see others' limitations more easily than we see our own. First, we are motivated to overlook our own limitations, and we are more motivated to see other people's limitations. We want to think highly of ourselves. We want to think of ourselves as smart, capable, and moral. That desire causes us to look for ways to convince ourselves that we have all these qualities. It also feels good when we "rate well" compared to others; therefore, aside from convincing ourselves that we are smart, capable, and moral, we like to think of other people as not having these qualities.

The other reason why we see other people's limitations more than our own is that it is generally easier to see the big picture in our own lives than it is in other people's lives. We can generally understand why we have the limitations that we have. Even if our actions are not always fully justified, we know why they are understandable and even partially justified. On the other hand, when we see other people's limitations without knowing the full context of their situation, we often do not know any of the reasons behind their behavior, and we may end up assuming that their behavior is mostly incomprehensible and unjustifiable.

It is important for us to learn how to address both these challenges: avoiding the temptation to look down on others in order to put ourselves above them as well as understanding where they are coming from and that their limitations do not look so evil when we see them in context.

Seeing our own limitations helps us in two different ways. It helps us recognize that we are not better than others, and it also gives us a more appropriate understanding of how to relate to mistakes and limitations. We learn that mistakes and limitations are parts of life and that the existence of mistakes does not make someone a bad or foolish person. However, it is certainly a challenge to reach that point.

How False Judgements Lead to Slander

The Chafetz Chaim repeats many times in his *sefarim* that it is a problem to hurt someone with our words, even if what we are saying is true. However, it is certainly worse if we hurt someone with our words when the criticism is not even accurate. Most of us are much more hesitant to make up and spread a hurtful story than we are to share a story that we know is true even though it is hurtful. When a story is true, we feel somewhat justified in sharing it either because we think we are just sharing facts and people have a right to know what is happening around them or because we think that since it is true that a certain person did something wrong, they deserve to be held responsible for their behavior.

We come up with various justifications when the information is true. However, the Chafetz Chaim teaches us (*Chafetz Chaim*, ch. 6–7) that most information we receive is not reliable. Even when we see something for ourselves, we often do not have the whole story. Certainly, when we hear things from others, we almost never have the full story.

Therefore, when we share a story based on information that we received from others, we should realize that if we share that story, it is likely that we are spreading false rumors about someone! It is likely that what we are sharing is slander. We may not be trying to make up stories, but we are likely believing false information and spreading it to others.

It is helpful to think about this idea before we talk about someone in a negative way. Not only are we hurting someone with our words, but it is also likely that we are spreading rumors about someone that are not even true! Unfortunately, the reality is that it is that we have already slandered many people in our lives. This recognition can motivate us to be more careful to avoid doing so again in the future.

Sincere Intentions

We may think speaking in a negative way about others is not a problem unless we intend to hurt the other person. If we are not trying to hurt the other person, then we excuse ourselves, even if we end up hurting them.

Judging others inappropriately is an example of this situation — the improper judgment itself is often not done on purpose. Once we have judged that someone is not a good person, there are times that it seems appropriate to speak about them, to let people know that they are not a good person. It may even be true that if the information were true, then it would be appropriate to share it — but since the information is likely not true, the result is that we are sharing information about a person that is hurtful and is not even true.

The reality is that we are obviously obligated to be careful not to hurt others. The fact that we were not intending to hurt them is only a valid excuse if we could not have known better. Doing something wrong due to negligence is not as bad as doing something wrong on purpose. However, we are obligated to do our best to avoid doing the wrong thing, and if we are negligent in our responsibilities, we will be held accountable for our negligence. If we really could have known better, but we are not careful, the negligence is our fault, and we are held responsible for it.

The same way that we would not want to hurt someone physically if we can avoid it, we should also not hurt other people's feelings or their reputation if we can avoid it. We can sometimes cause other people a lot of harm with our words. There are times that it is necessary and justified to speak about other people, but it is important to be as careful as we can to speak as appropriately as possible about others.

Analyzing Our Justifications for Speaking Negatively

The Chafetz Chaim says (introduction to *Chafetz Chaim*) that one of the reasons why we frequently speak *lashon hara*, even though we are generally motivated to keep the Torah and we are generally motivated to keep the mitzvos, is that we have many justifications for our negative speech. The justifications help us feel like we are good people, and we are keeping the Torah, even if we speak a lot of *lashon hara*.

Justifying Sharing the Truth

The Chafetz Chaim frequently discusses the fact that even though slander is universally known to be inappropriate, many people think that it is acceptable to share information about others as long as it is true. The fact that the information is true seems to justify our right even to criticize or hurt others.

We feel justified sharing information we believe to be true for a number of reasons. We may misinterpret the whole concept of not speaking *lashon hara* and think the problem is only in making something up to hurt someone. We may think that the truth should be accessible to all.

However, in reality, *lashon hara* includes any form of unnecessary criticism of someone else or causing anyone any unnecessary pain.

To avoid these justifications, we need to really believe that everyone deserves to be respected and cared for. As we mentioned above, we often do not think that everyone deserves the courtesy of us caring about them or respecting them enough to be careful about how we speak about them.

Sometimes, we feel justified in speaking about someone who has done bad things. We may think that they do not deserve to be treated with sensitivity, especially if they have hurt other people.

We are even more convinced that it should be justified to speak in a negative way about others when they have done something to hurt us personally. We may think that we should not be obligated to care about their feelings or their reputation when they have hurt us. Rather, we feel justified in speaking in a negative manner about them, and we may even feel entitled to do so.

However, every human being truly deserves to be treated with care and concern. Just because someone has done something wrong, that does not mean they have lost that right and that others should speak about them negatively. Even if someone has done something to hurt us, we are still obligated to speak nicely about them.

Another type of justification is when we believe sharing the negative information may be necessary in a certain situation in order to help someone or to protect them.

The truth is that it is generally prohibited to speak about others in a negative way even if the information is true. As long as the information is critical of others or if sharing it can be hurtful to others, it is forbidden. There are times when it is appropriate to share the information if it is truly necessary for helping ourselves or others. However, even in those situations, this is only permitted within certain guidelines. Everyone deserves our respect and our care even if they have hurt us in the past.

Revenge

The Mesillas Yesharim (ch. 11) says that when we are hurt by someone, our natural reaction is to want to hurt them back. He explains that when our feelings are hurt, we search for a means of alleviating the pain, and we turn to revenge as a way of removing some of that pain. He adds that every human being has a hard time not bearing a grudge and not wanting to take revenge.

When we have been hurt in a significant way by someone else, it is likely that we would feel justified in taking revenge. It is very difficult to not have the desire for revenge, and it is difficult to have the self-control to avoid acting upon that desire.

Even though it is very understandable to want to take revenge, that does not make it proper or permitted. We are not entitled to hurt another person just because they hurt us.

We do need to find a healthy and productive way of dealing with our feelings. We cannot expect them to magically disappear on their own. Realistically, if we do not figure out how to deal with our pain, we will harbor bad feelings. We will remain in pain, and we may end up trying to cause the other person pain as well.

The process of dealing with such pain is difficult, and it usually requires seeking advice or at least an empathetic ear. In that process, we have to share the information about the fact that someone hurt us. (As we will discuss below, it is permissible to speak about others in certain limited circumstances.) However, when we share that information, the Torah requires us to do so within the guidelines that the Chafetz Chaim discusses in his *sefarim*. These guidelines not only provide the appropriate way of discussing someone else's shortcomings without hurting them unnecessarily, but they also outline the most beneficial way for us to deal with our emotions in a productive and healing manner.

Hasty Judgment

One reason why we are liable to want to hurt those who have hurt us is that people in general are very quick to determine that others should be punished for their actions. There is obviously a lot of validity in the principle of being accountable for our actions, and there is a system of reward and punishment in the Torah and in any productive society. However, we are often too quick to decide what the guidelines should be for other people's accountability. Our desire for moral superiority over others often plays a big role in our determining that we are entitled to punish others for their actions. We need to learn the proper system from the Torah.

This is certainly true for those in a position of authority. In such a role, we may think that we are entitled to judge others and carry out the punishments. There is an element of truth to that thought process: Anyone in a leadership position is responsible for setting up systems and creating a structure to help people succeed as individuals and as a group. That can include carrying out punishments or other means of holding people accountable for their actions.

A parent or teacher's main roles are to educate and inspire. They also need to create a structure and an atmosphere that is conducive for learning and for growth as a productive human being. When it is necessary to hold a child accountable for their behavior, it is important to do so. However, even in such a situation, the accountability must be enforced with compassion and wisdom. How the accountability is understood by the parent or teacher is very important, as is how it is communicated to the child. Some people in positions of authority might feel a sense of entitlement to punish bad behavior and not to care about the child's feelings. There is not much of a basis for such an approach from a Torah perspective. Rather, we hold the child accountable for his own benefit because we love him and care about him. The difference between the two perspectives affects how we interact with the child in a significant way.

Generally, punishment for wrongdoing is Hashem's job, and we are not capable of judging another person's degree of good or bad.

When we take away our mindset of feeling justified and entitled to judge and punish others, then we are more likely to be careful about not hurting others even when they have behaved inappropriately.

Permitted Speech about Others

There are times that it is necessary and appropriate — even a mitzvah — to share with others the fact that another person is doing something wrong.

When there is an appropriate *to'eles* — when we need to help or to protect someone (anyone, especially ourselves), and the only way to do it is by speaking about the negative aspect of someone else — then we are allowed and even obligated to do so.

The fact that there are situations in which we are allowed to speak about the negative aspects of others makes it easy to think we can say anything at all about them. However, even when there is a benefit in speaking about someone, that does not justify saying whatever we want, to whomever we want, and however we want.

When we know there is something that needs to be addressed and it relates to other people's limitations, it is very important for us to find the proper path to deal with the situation. If we can find the proper approach, then we will not do anything wrong. If we do not use the right approach, we will probably end up doing many *aveiros*!

The proper approach is discussed throughout *Chafetz Chaim*, and it will be addressed to some extent in Chapter 3 of the present book.

Preventing Our Biases from Causing Us to Justify Criticizing Others

We need to make many judgment calls to determine whether or not we are allowed to say something about someone else. We need to assess the necessity of sharing information, whether we have an accurate account of the story, and whether sharing the information will be helpful. There are also questions about whom to tell, when to tell them, and most importantly, how to tell them.

These questions can be difficult to answer even when we do not have any bias, but when we are upset at the person or if we have something to gain by putting the other person down, it becomes even more difficult to figure out the true answers to these questions.

Our biases affect our judgments in terms of our general ideals and values as well as how we apply those ideals and values to specific situations.

The *Orchos Tzaddikim* (*Sha'ar Hasheker*) teaches us that we often determine what is right and wrong based on what we want to be right and wrong. We want to fulfill our desires, needs, and interests, and we do not want to be held back by our conscience telling us that we are doing something wrong. Therefore, we develop our sense of right and wrong in a manner that will justify the behavior we are interested in.

He explains that our personalities, our needs, and our interests all affect our judgment, and we tend to develop our ideals and values based on what fits best with all those subjective aspects of ourselves.

In some cases, our bias is only relevant to a very specific situation, so we are only motivated to justify that particular situation. However, we can also be biased in justifying the way we speak about people or treat people in a more general manner. For example, if a person has a tendency to be arrogant or critical, they will likely be biased in thinking that it is generally not a problem to be critical of others verbally or otherwise. They will be motivated to find ways to justify the fact that they are hurting others throughout the day and will likely find many reasons: justifications related to the person they are talking about, when they are speaking, the person they are speaking to, or how they are speaking about the person being discussed.

Even though these are all important considerations, most of the time, the *lashon hara* should not be said anyway. When we have a bias in sharing the information, we are more likely to end up saying it without even realizing that we are doing anything wrong. When our bias is the type that relates to our general behavior, we may end up justifying our behavior in a very general manner. As a result, our whole value system about these matters will be shaped by our desires!

Often, the process of our desires shaping our perspectives takes place subconsciously, such that we do not even realize it happens. When we think about what the proper ideals and values are, we tend to think of ourselves as being objective; therefore, we tend to trust our judgment about what is right and wrong. This requires a great deal of honesty, self-awareness, and dedication to try to discover the truth and build an objective perspective about right and wrong — in a specific situation or in general.

We need to develop a proper understanding of right and wrong in order to gain a proper understanding of how we should speak to others.

Learning to Coexist Peacefully

Another reason why it is difficult to avoid speaking improperly is that we live in a social world, and all day, every day, we are constantly interacting with other people. As a result, we are constantly affected by other people's limitations and shortcomings, which makes it very difficult to act properly toward them.

We are often hurt by the people around us, whether physically, emotionally, psychologically, spiritually, socially, or financially. There are times when we have already been affected and feel compelled to do something about it — we may need to vent or seek help or advice from others. In other cases, we might be concerned that we will be affected, even though it has not happened yet. Here, too, we will likely need to speak to others about the concern to gain advice or assistance or just to share our feelings. In both of these situations, we may also want to speak to the aggressor themselves about the situation.

Similarly, we are often made aware of situations in which the people around us have been hurt by others or are in a position in which they may be hurt by others. We often feel compelled to speak about the situation in these cases, as well: We may need to speak to our friend directly, or we may need to speak to other people about our friend in order to address the problem.

In some circumstances, the need to deal with other people's limitations is ongoing. For example, those in a leadership position (such as a parent, teacher, rabbi, or employer) or those who live or work together (such as family members, coworkers, classmates, neighbors, or friends) will experience many situations that require speaking about others. Our lives are integrated with those of others, and often, situations need to improve either for one person's benefit, another person's benefit, or for their mutual benefit.

Speaking Up Properly

In many situations, it is appropriate and necessary to have these conversations. It is important for people to be protected from being hurt, and it is appropriate to deal with our feelings when they have been hurt. It is also important to be able to work together as family, friends, and neighbors, and it is necessary to have leaders who are assertive and helpful.

However, it is difficult to have those conversations in the proper manner and with the proper guidelines. When we discuss other people's shortcomings, it is common to be critical and hurtful in the wrong type of way.

One of the main problems in these situations is that even when there is a proper reason to speak to someone when we are the one getting hurt or to get involved and try to help when someone else is getting hurt, it does not necessarily mean that our motivation for getting involved is altruistic. It could be that our motivation to share the negative information is coming from a desire to criticize the person. Perhaps it helps us feel better about ourselves because we feel like we are better than the other person, or it serves as a form of revenge, or we may stand to gain in some manner. When our motivation is not truly to help the other person but for our own personal gain, this will often affect the way we help and the question of whether our involvement is allowed. We may be more critical than is necessary, or we may give advice that is in our best interests rather than the other person's.

In these situations, we are likely driven to speak about the other person by a combination of different motivations. We are motivated by a genuine interest to fix the problem, and at the same time, we are motivated by some sort of personal benefit, as well. Our goal of fixing the problem alone is appropriate and can lead to productive results. However, our positive, productive motivations often blind us to our other motivations. Therefore, if our only motivation to criticize someone were to put the other person down in order to build ourselves up or to take revenge, it would be easy to identify the problem. However, the fact that we also have altruistic motives often causes us to lack awareness of the problem, and we are not careful to avoid hurting others with our inappropriate words. When we have selfish motivations mixed in, our involvement is rendered inappropriate, and this usually leads to unfortunate and unproductive results.

In order to deal with another person's shortcomings appropriately, there are a number of things that have to be done well.

First, the situation has to be assessed properly, which includes clarifying the truth of the information. We need to make sure that we have all the necessary information in order to get a good picture of the situation, and we need to make sure that we are not misinterpreting that information.

Second, we also have to determine whether it is really necessary to discuss the person's shortcomings. Even if our goal is to help, it may not be helpful for us to discuss the other person's shortcomings in this situation. There are many factors that affect each specific situation, and we need to assess each situation properly. Even if we know that discussing the situation will be helpful, there may be other ways of accomplishing the same goal without needing to discuss anything negative about the person.

Even if we know that theoretically, it may be helpful to speak to a person about their limitations or to speak about the person's limitations to others, we need to know how to help the person. It is often extremely complicated to help someone deal with their limitations productively. Often, when we get involved, and we are not really equipped to help, we end up causing more damage than benefit.

In a situation in which it is appropriate for us to speak about someone else's shortcomings, we need to check our own motivations for speaking up, and even when we have the proper motivations, we need to make sure that we help properly.

Addressing Our Unfulfilled Needs

There are times when we criticize others inappropriately merely due to a lack of focus, but there is often something deeper motivating us. Often, we criticize others with our words because we are trying to fill a personal need of our own. Therefore, even if we are motivated to not hurt others with our words, we will still put the other person down.

Whenever we find ourselves speaking critically about others, we should ask ourselves, "What am I trying to accomplish by putting him down? Is there something that I am trying to gain by criticizing this person?"

Self-Esteem

When we are struggling with our self-esteem or when we are jealous of someone, we are likely to want to put them down in order to hurt their feelings or their reputation.

We are all extremely motivated to feel good about ourselves. We are constantly under attack from all kinds of social pressures. We are surrounded by endless messages that tell us we are not good enough.

When we do not feel good about ourselves, we search for ways to try to feel better. Very often, we try to put others down in order to build ourselves up either in our own eyes or in the eyes of others. The worse we feel about ourselves, the more motivated we will be to put others down. We will do whatever we can to ruin other people's reputations in order to feel better. The stronger our need to be respected by those around us, the more motivated we will be to put others down. When we are more respected than others, this makes us feel somewhat better about ourselves.

We need to work on developing a healthy and appropriate sense of self-esteem. We need to feel good about ourselves by finding enough value within ourselves so that we do not have to put others down in order to feel good about ourselves.

We also need to recognize that we are not really helping ourselves when we put others down. Believing we are better than others feels good, but it is not internally rewarding. When we are living a life of meaning, however, we will feel truly fulfilled.

Conflict

When we have a conflict with someone, whether we were hurt emotionally, physically, financially, or in some other manner, we will be motivated to hurt them. We will use our words to hurt their feelings or, sometimes, their reputation. The situation might even turn into a competition about who can hurt the other person's reputation in a more significant manner.

Once we are in a conflict, there are many justifications for speaking negatively about the other person involved. We think, "He hurt me, so I do not have a responsibility to care about his feelings," "He is a bad person, so

I do not have a responsibility to care about his feelings," "I need to share my thoughts and feelings with others in order to deal with my own feelings," or "I need advice and guidance from others to know how to deal with my situation properly."

For the most part, even though these thoughts and attitudes are understandable, they are still inappropriate. It is true that we need to deal with our conflicts proactively — we cannot just ignore them and hope for them to go away. However, we need to figure out how to do that appropriately.

It is productive and appropriate to speak about problems we have with others, but it must be done with the right people, with the right attitudes, and in the right manner.

It is difficult to mend a conflict, and it is also difficult to not speak negatively about someone we are fighting with. Therefore, we need to do our best to mend our conflicts and to be careful about our speech in the meantime.

Addressing conflicts productively requires much wisdom and training. Most of us have had role models who have learned very unhealthy, unproductive, and inappropriate ways of dealing with conflicts. As a result, when we have conflicts, we are often critical, angry, and vengeful toward the other person involved. One of the negative results of such an approach to conflict is that we will often speak in a negative manner about the other person.

A better approach to the situation may include some of the following thoughts and attitudes: "Even though someone did something to hurt me, that does not mean they are bad," "It does not mean that they do not care about me at all," and "It certainly does not mean they deserve to be hurt or disrespected in turn." Rather, we should recognize that the other person was probably not trying to hurt us maliciously. It is likely that in the context of their nature, their needs, and their situation in life, they acted in a reasonable manner. They may have made a mistake and may have done something wrong, and they should be held accountable for their actions. We also need to take the necessary actions to protect ourselves from being hurt in the future. However, we should do our best to avoid acting in a manner in which we are trying to hurt the other person. The goal of protecting ourselves is appropriate and productive, but the mindset of hurting the other person is inappropriate and unproductive.

Jealousy

Jealousy can be very painful. Sometimes, when we see that someone else has something we do not have, it can make us feel bad. We may have negative thoughts about ourselves, such as, "Why can't I have that? Why does he get it and not me?" We may wonder, "Is the reason why he has it and I do not that he is better than I am?"

Thoughts such as these can cause us to need to defend ourselves from the attacks to our ego and our happiness. We feel a need to convince ourselves that the fact that someone else has something we want does not make him better than we are. In order to protect ourselves, we will often tell ourselves that the other person is a bad person in some way.

Our jealousy will tempt us to talk about the other person with our friends because we are upset at him for being "better" or because we do not want others to think of him as being better than we are.

Jealousy is a difficult *middah* to work on because it requires much wisdom and training to do so. We need to work on ourselves to improve our thought patterns and our attitudes that are causing our jealousy, and we need to try not to be critical of others in the meantime.

Addressing All the Factors That Cause Our Negative Speech

We began this book by asking, "Why is it so difficult to speak nicely about others? If we really care about morality and Torah observance, shouldn't we realize that we must care about others, respect them, and not hurt them with our words? We know that it is not proper to hurt others — why do not we stick to our principles? Haven't we tried to motivate ourselves to speak properly and to develop the proper habits of not hurting others with our words?"

However, if we think about all the different factors that make it difficult for us to speak positively, we can understand why it is so challenging even when we are motivated. If we think about how all the different factors combine, we can certainly understand that it is much harder to deal with each of the independent factors. To improve how we speak about others, we need an approach that addresses those challenges productively.

When we combine the factors, we come up with the following picture.

It is difficult to appreciate the importance of not speaking *lashon hara*. We often think of the concept of speaking positively about others as a nice thing to do as opposed to perhaps one of our greatest responsibilities. The fact that most people, even most of our role models, are not so careful about these laws makes it even more difficult to appreciate the value of speaking properly about others. We also often underestimate the pain and suffering that comes from our words.

It is difficult to have genuine respect for the average person because the average person is average, and we generally only consider a person to be deserving of respect if they are unique or special.

It is also hard to care about the average person. We do not have meaningful relationships with most people, and we have many relationships with others that are very challenging. In either situation, it is hard to truly care. Our lives are busy and stressful, and we are often physically, emotionally, and psychologically drained and overwhelmed. With so much to handle, we find it hard to deal with other people's needs or problems, and certainly not their shortcomings.

Most of us are trying to feel good about ourselves. We struggle to find purpose, meaning, and significance in our lives. We often struggle to keep up with our finances, our jobs, and our general responsibilities in life. We often feel that we are not religious enough or that we are not good enough as parents, spouses, or employees. These are only a few of the matters in our lives that cause us to struggle with feeling good about ourselves.

One of the things we do in order to feel good about ourselves is to try to build ourselves up in comparison to those around us. It feels good to think about ourselves as being better than others, so we are often critical of others. We are also motivated to convince people around us that we are special. In order to do that, we might boast about our own achievements, and very often, we also put others down so that we can feel better about our own social standing.

When we have a difficult relationship, and we are upset with the other person, we are often motivated to speak to others about our situation. It is very difficult to express our thoughts and feelings in these circumstances without being inappropriately critical. It is also difficult to hold back from expressing our critical thoughts when we are not supposed to mention them at all.

As humans, we are generally pretty egocentric and are mostly focused on our own needs. Recognizing this helps us understand why we do not naturally care about speaking positively about others. The fact that we are generally egocentric and sensitive to being hurt or insulted and yet live in a world where others are often critical of us or insensitive to us explains why we are often motivated to get back at them and hurt them with our words.

We also live in a world where people have many limitations, and we have to deal with them because we are always interacting with them. We may need to work with them, or help them, or engage with them in other ways. When we see others' limitations, we often have a hard time knowing how to respect them. They might even hurt us because of their limitations, or we may simply not like them!

These things are not easy to change. It is not so simple to just learn to love others, fix our relationships, and respect others properly. The fact that we do not have so much respect for others makes it difficult to even know what the proper ideals are. *Should* we show respect for people who do not seem to deserve respect or kindness? Certainly, when someone has been insensitive to us, it is difficult to know how much love and respect we should show them. Even if we want to avoid speaking about others in a critical manner, we often feel we need to speak about them. We do not think highly of them, we do not like them, and they are getting in our way! This often creates a very big challenge for us. We may want to be good people and follow the ways of the Torah, but it is still difficult to make the proper decisions. Therefore, we need an effective system to figure out how to speak nicely despite these challenges.

What makes the challenge of proper speech even more difficult is the fact that there can be so many justifications involved in these decisions. We may feel like we need to protect ourselves or others, or we may think that the other person does not deserve to be treated well. In some cases, we may think we are standing up for a proper moral value and feel compelled to hurt the person, who seems to be inappropriately standing in our way.

The combination of all these factors can lead to our speaking in a negative manner about others despite our general dedication to morality and Torah observance.

Addressing Challenges in Relationships Productively

It is obviously a lot easier to speak positively about others when everything is going well in our relationships. However, our responsibility to speak about others properly includes many situations where our relationships are not going so well, and it is difficult to speak about them properly. We need the commitment to speak about others properly to the extent that we are ready to do so, even when it is difficult.

Relationships often have a certain amount of conflict within them. When conflicts arise, we are often hurt and angry about the past (because we were not treated as we would have liked to have been treated), and we are often afraid about the future (we are concerned that we will not be treated as we would like to be). These feelings often lead us to unproductive behaviors, including speaking to others about the person who is upsetting us.

The *Mesillas Yesharim* (ch. 11) and *Orchos Tzaddikim* (*Sha'ar Hasinah*) both discuss the bad feelings that result when someone hurts us.

The *Mesillas Yesharim* explains that humans are extremely sensitive, and when someone has hurt us, this causes us a lot of emotional pain. This pain does not go away on its own. It is always on our minds. Even when we are not thinking about it consciously, we are still thinking about it subconsciously. Our pain often leads to hatred and a desire to "get back" at the other person.

According to the *Orchos Tzaddikim*, when we are hurt by someone and develop feelings of hatred for them, this often leads to inappropriate desires. We tend to want bad things to happen to the person, and we will do what we can to hurt them. Often, the easiest way to hurt them is with our words, so we will often try to hurt them in that manner. We even learn from this *sefer* that we will "constantly" be thinking about and planning how to cause them harm!

When we are hurt, angry, or afraid, we have a few options concerning how to deal with the situation. We can try to resolve our problems in our own minds through putting things into a productive perspective, thereby addressing our anger, our hurt, and our fears productively. We may be able to help ourselves become less angry, hurt, or afraid, or we may at least be able to manage those feelings productively. Alternatively, we can speak to those we are upset with, inform them how we feel, and try to work out our differences. Or we can complain to others about how evil the other person is.

Obviously, the third way is inappropriate and unproductive. However, the other two ways are difficult and also do not always work so well. That is why we often find ourselves taking the third route even though it is not good for us.

It is important to recognize that the reason why we end up speaking inappropriately about others (and the reason why we act in other inappropriate ways toward others) is that we are hurt, angry, or afraid, and we do not know how to (or we do not want to) deal with these feelings in a productive or appropriate fashion. That leads us to deal with our feelings inappropriately, which often includes speaking about others in negative and critical ways.

Realistically, even if we begin the process of working on our relationships and our feelings in a productive way, it takes time to develop the proper feelings, and in the meantime, we will often be motivated to speak inappropriately about others.

We need to devise a productive game plan to address all the factors that relate to the process of speaking properly about others.

Working on Ourselves and
Communicating Productively

The most productive approach when we are upset, hurt, or afraid is to combine working through our thoughts and feelings in our own minds and hearts with working through the problem with the other person as well.

Within our own minds, it is helpful to find strength and encouragement through our faith in Hashem, remembering that He cares about us, He takes care of us, and everything that He does for us has a purpose. We can also build up our self-confidence by focusing on our innate value as a human being, being proud of our achievements, and appreciating what we have to offer to the world. It is also helpful to focus on understanding where the other person is coming from.

Additionally, it is helpful to work through the conflict by talking it out with the other person to try to reestablish the relationship in a positive way. It is helpful for everyone to empathize with each other's pain, to take some of the responsibility for what transpired previously, to understand where the other person was coming from, to commit to avoiding causing each other harm in the future, and to develop a productive strategy to make that happen (with realistic expectations).

However, while this approach is ideal, there are a few caveats to keep in mind.

We often do not have strong skills in how to work through our thoughts, feelings, and perspectives or how to work through the difficulties in our relationships. It is hard to communicate with others in a productive way when we are upset at them.

It is also difficult because all of us are somewhat selfish, critical, and judgmental of others. We do not care as much about others as we would like to think we do, and we do not have as much respect for others as we would like to think we do. That makes it difficult to get along with others and to communicate with them productively. It is hard to communicate with someone in a manner that will lead to a feeling of camaraderie and closeness when we do not care about or respect them so much. Our thoughts and feelings come through. It does not help to pretend. If we want someone to think that we care about or respect them, our behavior must be genuine, or they will pick up on our pretense, no matter what we say.

It also takes time to work on ourselves to be able to remove or minimize our pain, our anger, our resentment, and our fears. During that time, we will be limited due to all of the negative feelings that we still feel at that time.

Doing Our Best

The reality is that it takes a while to be able to succeed against the challenges in our relationships. It is a process, and even if we start to work on overcoming those challenges, it still takes time. However, if we put in the effort, we will slowly get better. We can only try to do our best.

As we are growing and getting better at working through our internal thoughts and feelings, and as we are getting better at improving our communication, we will still have to deal with our anger, resentment, and pain in the meantime. These feelings will still motivate us to be critical of those we are upset with, and we will be motivated to speak about them in a manner that is hurtful to them. We need to be aware of the challenges and to motivate ourselves to do our best to avoid falling into the trap of speaking inappropriately about others.

When trying to improve a difficult relationship, we will likely face various challenges in our own minds. For instance, when we have been hurt by someone and are upset at them, we often do not want to improve our relationship with them. We do not like them, and we do not want to have a closer relationship with them.

Additionally, when we have been hurt by someone, we often do not think a better relationship with them would be possible even if we wanted it. We think it will be too difficult to overcome our negative feelings, and we have also learned that the relationship is not going to be the type of relationship that we are interested in. It does not seem to be a safe or enjoyable relationship. It is difficult to imagine that the relationship will improve to the extent that it will be enjoyable or productive.

These two factors feed off each other. When we do not think that our relationship will be able to improve, then we are less likely to try to make it improve. Similarly, if we do not feel like we want the relationship to improve, then it is less likely that it will improve.

The combination of these two perspectives can be crushing for a relationship. We think it is a bad relationship, "I do not like the person, and there is nothing I can do about it anyway; therefore, it is not even worth trying."

These thoughts and feelings will usually stop us from working on improving our relationship. They also often lead us to be even more upset at the other person because we have no positive context for thinking about the relationship. We might say, "It is a bad relationship," "It is the other person's fault," "It has caused me harm and pain," and "I am hurt and upset about it."

Feeling this way will also lead us to speak about the other person in a negative and critical manner. We will try to justify our feelings to ourselves and to others, and we will want others to know that it is the other person's fault that the relationship got messed up. We will also want everyone to understand that it is not our fault for not making it better; rather, the other person is such a bad person that there is nothing we can do to improve our relationship with them.

However, self-awareness and a desire to be honest with ourselves, to take responsibility, and to be compassionate can help us rebuild a difficult relationship. When we desire to have a good relationship for our own benefit as well, then we are even more likely to be able to rebuild our relationships.

We should try to recognize that even though we were hurt and are justified in being upset, it does not mean that we cannot have a good relationship with the other person. Realistically, we are not going to change who we are in a significant way, and neither will they, and there will always be problems and complications in the relationship. The same thing that caused the problem the first time might cause the same problem in the future. However, at the same time, there is room for a lot of positive feelings in a relationship.

We need to try to grow one step at a time, try to have a positive and optimistic outlook on the relationship, and try to slowly improve how we think about, talk about, and act toward the other person. That is the best that we can do, and generally, it will lead to a significant improvement in the relationship over time.

Surrounding Ourselves with People Who Do Not Speak *Lashon Hara*

Dovid Hamelech begins *Tehillim* (ch. 1) by describing how fortunate we are when we surround ourselves with people who are acting appropriately. He is telling us that it is extremely helpful for our *avodas Hashem* when we are surrounded by such people.

Chafetz Chaim (6:5) considers the challenges that come from being in a social environment in which people speak about others in a critical manner.

We will face many situations in which there is a lot of social pressure to join in a conversation about others' faults. We will be tempted and even expected to join in. It is difficult to avoid the conversation or to remove ourselves from the conversation because our lack of interest in speaking *lashon hara* is often also viewed as a criticism of the speaker. That will usually make them defensive, and they may ridicule us or at least say something hurtful to us as a means of making themselves feel better. The ridicule does not have to be so overt in order to be hurtful, and even among friends and family, there is often a subtle comment that can really hurt. Sometimes, it is even more common among friends. We constantly criticize our friends. It is much more comfortable to just listen to the *lashon hara* and to avoid the conflict and friction.

Often, it is difficult to avoid being in this situation, and we can only make the best of it once we are there. However, the Chafetz Chaim (*Chafetz Chaim* 6:5) tells us that we are obligated to avoid being in such a situation when this is possible.

Our responsibility is not only to do our best in dealing with the challenges that are in front of us; we are also obligated to set ourselves up for success.

The Chafetz Chaim tells us (*Chafetz Chaim* 6:5) that it is unlikely we will be able to avoid speaking *lashon hara* if we are in a social environment where people are constantly encouraging us to speak in a negative manner about others. Therefore, he says that we often need to change our environment. We may need to choose different friends or at least create boundaries within our relationships that will reduce our temptation to be involved with speaking in a critical manner about others.

The Orchos Tzaddikim (*Sha'ar Lashon Hara*) says that when we have a group of friends we speak *lashon hara* with, the situation often requires extreme measures for us to break out of our habits. We may need to make a drastic change in our environment in order to stay away from the previous problems and to have a fresh start in how we speak.

It is also necessary to develop the strength and the wisdom to be able to not speak *lashon hara* even within a relationship or an environment where there is a lot of *lashon hara*. It is difficult and even inappropriate to run from all of our relationships and environments where there is *lashon hara*, and we need to develop the ability to do the right thing even in those situations.

• CHAPTER 2 •

IDEALS AND VALUES RELATING TO
PROPER SPEECH

THERE ARE MANY MITZVOS IN the Torah that are known as *mitzvos bein adam lechaveiro* (mitzvos between man and his friend). They relate to how we should think, feel, and act toward others. The reason there are so many mitzvos between man and man is that treating others properly is an important value of the Torah. The Chafetz Chaim demonstrates (introduction to *Chafetz Chaim*) that many of these mitzvos govern how we use our words when we communicate about others.

It is clear that the moral and ethical thing to do with our words is to help others and certainly not hurt anyone. The goal of proper speech about others is simple and straightforward: We need to speak with care and respect, and we need to avoid saying anything about others that could be hurtful to them.

However, there are many important matters to clarify in order to understand the proper ideals and values in relation to our speech. For example, what is the reason for caring about others, even strangers? How important is it, and to what extent are we obligated to speak with care, respect, and sensitivity about others? Is it important, and are we obligated to speak with care, respect, and sensitivity about *all* people? Is it only family? Is it only "good people"? Is it only "nice people"? Is it only someone who cares about me, or at least someone who cares about others in general? What about people we do not know? What about people who are not acting appropriately — do they deserve the same sensitivity, care, and respect as anyone else? What about people who have hurt us, or people we do not care about, or others in general?

We interact with many people in many different situations, and there are many situations in which we are not sure what we should be doing or saying. It is important to clarify the appropriate way of speaking for each situation.

Our responsibility to speak nicely about others is much broader than it seems at first glance. It is related to our thoughts, our feelings, and our *middos*. Our true responsibilities are based on having the proper ideals and values regarding matters such as Hashem's role in our lives, respect, love, and human value.

Helping Others with Our Words and Not Hurting Them

Our words are very powerful. They can be used for "life" — to be very helpful to others — or they can be used for "death" — to hurt others. These are the two fundamental goals that we have concerning our speech: to use our words to help and not to hurt others.

A Matter of Life and Death

As Shlomo Hamelech says in *Mishlei* (18:21), "Life and death are in the hands of the tongue." One of the lessons that Shlomo Hamelech is teaching in this *pasuk* is the importance of recognizing the impact our words can have. They can be extremely helpful to others, or they can cause a lot of damage to others. Hashem gave us many great opportunities and many great responsibilities when He gave us the ability to speak. We need to understand both the opportunities and the responsibilities that come along with our ability to speak.

There are many mitzvos in the Torah that relate to our responsibility to help others with our words and to not hurt them. It says in the introduction to *Chafetz Chaim* that the fact that Hashem gave us many mitzvos related to how we speak about others teaches us about the nature of Torah Law, the nature of our responsibilities in life, and the nature of Judaism.

The number of mitzvos related to relationships between people indicates that a significant part of Torah Law, a major part of *Yiddishkeit* in general, and a major part of our job in the world is to focus on being nice to others. Most of *Chafetz Chaim* directly addresses the laws that relate to not hurting others with our words, but the Torah's laws about speech cover the responsibility to help others as well.

One of the most fundamental laws of the Torah is to "Love your fellow like yourself" (*Vayikra* 19:18). This law is relevant to a very broad set of interactions with others, and it is certainly very relevant to the way that we speak about others. We are required to use our speech to help others as much as we possibly can. Just as we constantly try to use our speech to help ourselves out, so too should we constantly try to use our speech to help others as well. This teaches us that we should always be aware of this obligation and avoid saying anything that could hurt someone else in any way.

Another fundamental law of the Torah is to emulate the ways of Hashem in every way possible. The Gemara teaches us that our responsibility to emulate Hashem includes performing acts of kindness and being merciful and kind, like He is (*Sotah* 14a; *Shabbos* 133b). Emulating the ways of Hashem includes using our speech to help others in any way that we can: financially, spiritually, and emotionally. It also includes not hurting others in any manner.

There is also a law that directly teaches us that we are not allowed to hurt others with our words, as the Torah says, "Do not cause pain to others" (*Vayikra* 25:17), and the Gemara explains that this *pasuk* refers to causing pain through our words (*Bava Metzia* 58b).

The laws of *lashon hara* (telling our friend something negative about someone else) and *rechilus* (telling our friend something about someone else that will cause him to dislike that person) specifically apply to hurting others by communicating something negative about them to someone else, but they and all the above laws revolve around broader essential ideals, values, and responsibilities that we have toward others.

It is important to recognize the fact that helping others with our words and not hurting anyone with our words are some of the most important mitzvos!

Opportunities to Use Our Words Helpfully
or Unhelpfully

All people have many needs, interests, and desires. We live in a social world, and our lives are affected by the people around us on a consistent basis. We are generally not self-sufficient, and we often need help from others to fulfill our needs, interests, and desires. They can help us in a significant way, or they can sometimes interfere with us in a significant way. We are also often in a position to be able to help or to hurt others with their needs, interests, and desires.

One of the key tools we can use in order to help others is our ability to communicate through our words. We need to use our speech in order to help others as much as we can. On the other hand, our words can also be among the most dangerous weapons.

Our words can affect others in a practical sense. We can bring others respect, and we can build up their reputations. However, the words that we say about another person can also ruin their reputation, which can affect their business, job, or friendships. Our words can influence other people's livelihoods and many other important matters in their lives. We can help them in these ways, or we can hurt them.

The words we say to others can also be very helpful by communicating respect, care, concern, and empathy. These are universal needs, and it is extremely helpful when we are able to provide them for others. Love, acceptance, and respect are some of the strongest human desires, and we have the ability to make others feel great about themselves. However, our words can also make others feel really bad about themselves. We can communicate a lack of respect, care, concern, and empathy toward others. We can cause them to feel unloved, unimportant, ashamed, isolated, and worthless instead of helping them feel loved, cared for, important, confident, accepted, and valuable.

Becoming Compassionate toward Others

Who we are "inside" is important. It is not just important to not hurt others with our words, but it is important to be the type of person who does not want to hurt others and the type of person who does not think and feel about people in a condescending and critical way. We have to focus on doing the proper actions, and we also need to focus on developing our "inner being" — our thoughts, perspectives, and feelings.

In the introduction to *Chafetz Chaim*, we learn that our job is not merely to do the mitzvos; rather, we are obligated to change ourselves in order to become better people. The Chafetz Chaim quotes a *pasuk* in *Bamidbar* (15:40) that says that our goal is "to do the mitzvos in order to become holy to Hashem." He explains that when we follow the mitzvos (properly), this changes us so that we become holy people.

Becoming a holy person involves acting in the same way that Hashem acts: with kindness, compassion, care, and concern for others. It also includes developing our inner nature to emulate the nature of Hashem. We need to develop our natures to be naturally inclined toward kindness and compassion.

It is not acceptable to walk around thinking negative thoughts and having negative feelings about others. Even if we are somehow able to avoid expressing them to others, it is still inappropriate. Rather, the appropriate goal is to have respectful and compassionate thoughts and feelings about others.

The *Ohr Hatzafun* (vol. 1, p. 52) quotes the Gemara in *Pesachim* (3a) that teaches us the extent of our responsibility to be like Hashem in terms of how to speak about others properly and how to avoid being critical of others.

The Gemara says, "A person should *never* say something derogatory [about another person]." It explains that Hashem speaks about every person with extreme respect, care, and concern. Hashem does not even describe a pig as an animal that is *tamei* (impure) but instead as an animal that is *lo tahor* (not pure). The pig will not be insulted by being described as impure. The reality is that it is impure. The intention is not even to be critical but simply to state the facts of its halachic status. However, Hashem still avoided saying the words that it is impure because it is more appropriate to speak with as much sensitivity as possible.

We are obligated to be like Hashem and to have the sensitivity and compassion toward others to not even want to speak about others in any form of derogatory manner. This principle applies even when we do not intend any harm and even when we are not hurting others with our words.

Chafetz Chaim (10:2) says that the intent to speak critically about others or to hurt them is also a problem on its own, regardless of whether our words actually end up hurting them. The Chafetz Chaim explains further (*Be'er Mayim Chaim* 10) that the main problem with speaking about someone in a negative way in general is not that we caused the unfortunate result that someone was hurt through our words because the reality is that we are not able to hurt anyone. That is in Hashem's control. He determines whether someone will be hurt or not. The only thing that is ever in our control is our thoughts and feelings. Our responsibility is to direct our thoughts, feelings, and efforts to help people and not to hurt people.

These are some of the most basic values of the Torah: to care about others, to respect others, and to try to help them as much as we can. When we truly feel this way about others, then we will not try to hurt them with our words, and we will not speak critically about them even if we know that doing so will not end up hurting them.

To develop the proper thoughts about others, we have to develop the *middos* that lead to positive thoughts and feelings about others and to the desire to help them. We also have to work on managing or changing our *middos* that lead us to negative thoughts and feelings about others or to the desire to hurt them.

It is important to remember that our behaviors affect our thoughts, feelings, and who we are inside.

When we speak in a negative or critical manner about other people, not only are we not acting with compassion, but we are demonstrating that our inner nature is not kind and compassionate enough. If that is the case, we are obligated to try to change it. And in addition to indicating what is inside of us, the way we speak can also affect us, in either positive or negative ways. If we speak in a manner that is critical of others or that harms others, we will become more critical and less caring about others in general.

We can use how we speak about others as a tool to help ourselves improve who we are internally. When we speak about others with respect, sensitivity, and compassion, this can help us develop those thoughts and feelings.

Understanding Proper Thoughts and Feelings

Our speech communicates our thoughts and feelings. The words we use are not an independent function of our existence; rather, our words generally reflect the thoughts that are in our minds and the feelings that are in our hearts.

The people we think highly of are generally not the ones we speak about in a derogatory fashion. We are more likely to be critical of the people we do not respect.

Similarly, the people we like and the people we care about are generally not the ones we speak about in a negative way. Rather, when we are upset at someone or if we do not like them, we are much more motivated to speak about them in a negative way. Certainly, if we were hurt by someone and are upset at them, we are likely to want to get back at them, and that often leads us to speak negatively about them.

We are obligated to be careful about both matters. We need to develop our thoughts and emotions properly: to respect others, care about others, and have positive feelings for them. We also need to use our words properly and communicate in appropriate ways. There are many mitzvos that require using our words properly, and there are also many mitzvos that revolve around the proper thoughts and feelings in relation to others. These mitzvos teach us the proper ideals and values concerning how we should think and feel about others.

Having the proper thoughts and feelings about others is certainly necessary in order to speak properly about them. However, clarifying what the proper thoughts and feelings are that we should have about others itself is a significant accomplishment on its own.

Communicating Our Love of and Respect for Others

The mitzvos of loving your neighbor and emulating the ways of Hashem include most of the ways in which we should think and feel about others. We can break these thoughts and feelings down to their specifics and find many different aspects of care, concern, value, and respect.

Love

We are instructed, "Love your fellow like yourself" (*Vayikra* 19:18), but we may have a few questions with regard to our responsibility to love others. First, are we obligated to love everyone? If so, why? Why should we care about people we do not know or people we do not have a relationship with? Certainly, why should we love someone who has treated us inappropriately? And even if we are obligated to love everyone, how can we develop that love if we do not feel it, especially if they have hurt us? How can we develop feelings that we do not have, and how can we get rid of negative feelings that we do have?

There is another question that these questions are really based on: What is the foundation of love? What does it mean to love someone?

The Torah teaches us that there is a responsibility to love every member of the Jewish people. The Ramban explains what it means to love our friends as we love ourselves. It means that we should want our friends to have everything good, the same way that we want the best for ourselves. We want our lives to be filled with pleasure and comfort. We want to find success and happiness with our families, our finances, and our social experiences. We want the best in both our spiritual and our mundane pursuits. Possibly the strongest desires that we have are to be respected and loved. In the same way, we should want these things for our friends as well. Often, even when we care about others, we still have limitations in how much we really want them to succeed. We do not want to see them succeeding in ways that compete with our success. However, the mitzvah is to develop a desire for them to have as much success and happiness as possible, just like we want for ourselves.

It is really difficult to develop our love for others. There are many

Jews that we do not have much to do with, and generally, we do not have many feelings for them at all. There are others we have more to do with, and often, we do have feelings for them, both positive and negative. It is difficult to develop more positive feelings, and it is also difficult to avoid the negative ones.

The *mussar sefarim* discuss the topic of having mitzvos that tell us what our feelings should be. We feel how we feel. How can we be told how to feel? All the *ba'alei mussar* say that the fact that there are mitzvos about how we should feel means that we do have the capacity to change our feelings. One of the main ways we can do that is through changing our thoughts and perspectives.

It is difficult to change our thoughts and perspectives, but it is our responsibility to develop the proper thoughts, perspectives, and feelings toward our fellow Jews.

Respect

As with love, we may have some questions about respecting all people. Is there really a responsibility to respect everyone? Why? Does everyone deserve respect? Some people do not seem to give us any positive reason to respect them, and based on the behavior of certain people, it would seem that it should be inappropriate to respect them! Further, even if I am obligated to respect everyone, how can I respect someone who I do not have respect for?

There is another question that these questions are really based on: What is the foundation of respect? What does it mean to respect someone?

It is not clear that we have a responsibility to respect every Jew. The Torah says we should love every Jew, but that does not necessarily mean that we are obligated to respect every Jew as well.

The *Ohr Hatzafun* (vol. 1, p. 224) explains that included in the mitzvah to love someone is to give him as much respect as he deserves. However, it is unclear from that mitzvah how much respect each person deserves.

Aside from the responsibility to respect others due to our responsibility to love them, we also have a mitzvah to emulate Hashem's ways.

Throughout the Torah, we are taught how much Hashem respects every person. The Mishnah in *Sanhedrin* (4:5) tells us that Hashem taught us how much value every person has: He created the world with only one man at the time in order to teach us that every person is so valuable in Hashem's eyes that it is worthwhile to create an entire world for his benefit.

Since we know the great extent of Hashem's respect for every person, we must emulate Him and give each person that same respect. Once we see how much value every person has, we realize that it is our responsibility to give each person that degree of respect.

Avoiding Negativity

Criticism is the backbone of our challenges when it comes to respect and love. Criticism relates to how we measure whether someone is good or bad, smart or foolish, talented or not talented.

Shlomo Hamelech says (*Koheles* 1:18), "With more wisdom, there will be more anger." The Midrash explains that he is teaching us an important fact about the reality of humanity: All people are limited in many different ways. We are all far from moral perfection. There are numerous areas of wisdom, and most of us are relatively ignorant in many of them. There are also many areas of talents, and most of us are not so talented in many of those areas.

When we focus on others' limitations, this interferes with our respect and love for them. When we do not think of someone as a good person, a smart person, a talented person, or a capable person, this definitely interferes with our ability to respect or care about them.

Our thoughts and attitudes will often be communicated to others as well. If we do not think highly of someone, we will generally communicate our thoughts in a variety of ways. We will not speak to them with respect and dignity. We will criticize their behavior, their opinions, their philosophies, and any other matter that comes up that we are critical of.

We do not like it when we are not loved and respected. It is hurtful and uncomfortable. This causes us to be upset and to distance ourselves from the person who is not showing us the love and respect that we want.

When we are criticized, it is even worse. It is very painful and uncomfortable, and we lose interest in having a relationship with the person who is criticizing us.

The fact that our critical thoughts about others play such a significant role in our feelings about others, in our general relationship with others, how we speak to others, and how we speak about others means that we have a great responsibility to work on becoming less critical of others and to speak with less criticism!

Developing and Communicating Humility

The biggest factors that determine how we treat others are humility and arrogance. They affect how much we love and respect others, how we speak to others, how we speak about others, and how we treat others in general. We cannot love and respect others and speak appropriately about them unless we have a significant amount of humility.

Arrogance often comes together with an attitude of "I am good, I am capable, and I am important" and an attitude of "I care about myself and my needs." Similarly, it also comes with an attitude of "Other people are not good, not capable, and not important" and an attitude of "I do not care about other people and their needs."

When we are arrogant, these thoughts and feelings will be reflected in our words and actions. We will communicate that "I only care about myself. I think that I am the only good person and the only capable person."

True humility can come with an attitude of "I respect myself, I think that I am a good person, I am confident in my capabilities, I am important, and I care about myself and my own personal needs," but it also comes with an attitude of "I respect others, I think that other people are good, capable, and important, and I care about other people and their needs" as well.

When we are humble, we will respect ourselves as well as others, and we will care about ourselves as well as others. These are also the messages that we will communicate: that we respect everyone and care about everyone.

Generally, people have a certain amount of humility and a certain amount of arrogance, and we therefore do respect and care about others, but we generally do not respect or care about others as much as we should. This is reflected in how we speak about others.

The thoughts and perspectives that relate to our arrogance and humility also affect our love and respect for others.

The Foundation Stones of How We Think, Feel, and Speak about Others

The ideals, values, and responsibilities that revolve around caring about others properly, respecting others properly, and speaking about others in a caring and respectful way are related to a broader set of ideals, values, and responsibilities. The feelings of love and respect for others, which influence how we speak about them, are themselves influenced by many other factors.

A number of core *middos* and perspectives (introduction to *Chafetz Chaim*) influence how much we love and respect others and how we talk about them. Our understanding of how to measure and value people as well as how we interpret and evaluate other people's thoughts, feelings, and behaviors can play a big role in the degree of respect and care that we have for others. Our belief and trust in Hashem affects our thoughts and feelings about others, and this affects how we deal with others. Our humility, our ability to avoid anger, our jealousy, our hatred, our desire to hold onto a grudge, and our desire for revenge all affect how we speak about others.

Measuring Human Value

Our perspective on human value in general certainly influences how much we respect and care about every person. Whether we think that the average person is extremely valuable or worthless plays a major role in how much we respect or care about them.

The respect we have for others is related to our system for determining human value in general: how we understand who we are and our purpose in This World as well as how we define and measure human success and failure. It also relates to how we determine each specific person's individual value and success. In order to respect others properly, we need to have the proper value system for people in general, and we have to apply it appropriately to each person.

Interpreting and Evaluating Other People's Thoughts, Feelings, and Behaviors

We are taught several important messages that relate to how we should judge others. The Torah (*Vayikra* 19:15) and the Mishnah (*Pirkei Avos* 1:6) teach us to "Judge your fellow favorably." The Mishnah also teaches us (*Pirkei Avos* 2:4), "Do not judge others until you are in their place."

Aside from being a responsibility in its own right, judging people favorably is also a necessary component in our ability to respect and properly care about others. Our respect, care, and concern for others are very much dependent upon the way in which we interpret their thoughts, feelings, and behaviors.

We are exposed to a lot of information about other people. Throughout the day, we witness other people's behaviors — we see what they do, and we hear what they say. We also hear a lot of information about others indirectly — people often tell us what they know (or think they know) about other people's thoughts, feelings, and behaviors.

When we process this information about the people in our lives, if we conclude that they are bad people or that they do not care about us or our relationship, that can interfere with our respect and our love for them.

However, very often, we are processing the information incorrectly because the reality is most likely that the person deserves respect and love even though the picture that we see does not demonstrate their worthiness.

The Mishnah in *Pirkei Avos* tells us that we must not judge others until we are in their place. The Mishnah's intention is to tell us:

- We cannot really know the whole story about what goes on in other people's lives;
- If we could know the whole story, we would be less critical of their thoughts, feelings, and behaviors;
- We often jump to conclusions about others and form a negative

opinion about them based on the picture we have about their thoughts, feelings, and behaviors; and

- We should recognize that if we knew the whole story, we would be much less likely to have a negative opinion about the person.

Therefore, we should understand that when we hear a story about someone else, even if the story seems to be true, we should not jump to conclusions about the person because there may be more to the story that changes the whole picture.

Negative Feelings

Our ability to speak nicely and appropriately about others is very much influenced by negative feelings that we have toward them. One of the most common reasons why we speak in a negative way about others is that we feel hurt by them, we are angry at them, and we want to take revenge and get back at them. Alternatively, we speak about them because we are jealous of them, or we feel threatened by them in one form or another.

Therefore, we are obligated to work on our ability to avoid having these negative feelings and to work on speaking nicely to others and about others.

Belief and Trust in Hashem

Belief and trust in Hashem are central elements of our *avodas Hashem*, and they play a significant role in our relationships with others as well. How we think about others, how we feel about others, how we speak about others, and how we act toward others — all these aspects of our relationships are influenced by our belief and trust in Hashem.

The *Sefer Hachinuch* (§241) explains that when someone does something to hurt us, we often think we were affected by the other person's decisions and actions, and that causes us to be upset at them. However, the truth is that Hashem controls everything in the world, and no one can do anything to affect us unless Hashem had decided that we should have that experience. If the result did not come through this person, it would have come through some other means. This perspective helps us to not be so upset at the person who hurt us because we will not think, "I am upset with him because he caused something to happen to me that I am unhappy about."

In general, when we know that Hashem runs the world and we know that Hashem always has our best interests in mind, then we will be at ease, and we will not be upset about the past or nervous about the future. The more we are at ease, the less we will be upset at others.

When our faith and trust in Hashem help us to be at ease and to not be upset about what others have done to us and to not be worried about what others will do to us, then we are much less likely to speak about others in a negative way.

CHAPTER 3

Proper Application of
the Torah's Ideals and Values

The Chafetz Chaim devoted virtually his entire *sefer Shemiras Halashon* as well as the introduction to *Chafetz Chaim* to explaining the importance of avoiding *lashon hara*. However, most of the *sefer Chafetz Chaim* details the specific laws of *lashon hara*.

Knowing the Laws

The laws of *lashon hara* are the guidelines for what we are allowed to say and how we are allowed to say it. The Chafetz Chaim discusses throughout his *sefer Chafetz Chaim* what type of information is considered hurtful, what type of person we are allowed to speak about, the people we are allowed to speak to, and what type of intentions we are obligated to have. He also discusses how much we have to sacrifice in order to avoid speaking *lashon hara*, and he teaches us about the appropriate way to process information in order to determine whether to say something, what to say, and how to say it.

At first glance, it may seem that the laws of *lashon hara* are simple and straightforward. There seems to be a very clear system of morality that relates to how we should speak about others. Most people recognize that it is not appropriate to hurt others with our words, so we are not allowed to speak negatively about others.

However, there are certain scenarios that present moral dilemmas. The reality is that the laws of *lashon hara* are complicated, with many nuances and subtleties to the laws of what is okay and what is not. It is easy to come to the wrong conclusions concerning what is proper and what is not. There is also a lot of room to justify the wrong conclusions in all of these situations. There are many things that we think are okay but are not.

The Chafetz Chaim (introduction to *Chafetz Chaim*) says that one of the reasons why we speak so much *lashon hara* is that we do not know the laws well enough, and we do not understand them clearly. He says that unless someone is educated about the Torah's laws of *lashon hara*, it is likely that he will not develop a true understanding of what is and is not proper of his own accord.

Even if we have general knowledge of the laws, we will still run into a lot of problems if we do not understand them clearly. There are many exceptions to the laws of *lashon hara*, and it is easy to misinterpret and misapply them and end up thinking something is allowed when, in reality, it is not.

Common Misconceptions

There are several common mistakes that people make in applying the rules when they know the "general idea" without knowing them clearly.

It is okay to say it if it is true. One of the most common misconceptions about the laws of *lashon hara* is that it is only inappropriate to say something negative about someone else if it is untrue, but if it is true, then it is not a problem to share the information.

It is universally accepted that slander is inappropriate. It is considered extremely inappropriate to make up stories about others. However, when the information is true, there are different opinions about whether there is a problem in sharing the information. Many people think that if information is true, then there is nothing wrong with sharing it.

This assumption can be based on a number of rationales. We may assume that the person deserves people speaking about them if they have done something wrong or that we should publicize the evil so others will stay away from that type of behavior. (This kind of publicity may sometimes be valid, but that is not usually the case.) We are especially likely to justify speaking about the negatives of those who have hurt us: We think we should be allowed to let people know what they did. We may also assume that people have a right to know the facts about the world. Alternatively, there may be an assumption that if something is true, then it is not negative. Some of these assumptions do not sound so compelling. However, when we make an honest assessment, we will recognize that we do have a lot of these perspectives, and there are many times that we think that we are allowed to say something when halachah actually considers it to be *lashon hara*.

The Chafetz Chaim spends a lot of time in his *sefarim* combating this thought process. He must mention about fifty times in *Chafetz Chaim* (if not more) that *lashon hara* is forbidden even when it is true. Apparently, his feeling is that we have the wrong perspective so ingrained in our minds that it is necessary to repeat the true perspective many times in order to reinforce its truth.

If we are trying to help, then we should be allowed to speak about it. It is true that we are allowed and obligated to speak about other people's limitations when it is necessary to protect ourselves or others or if we are in a situation in which we can help others with our words. In those situations, it is easy to believe that whatever we say is okay because it is justified and appropriate to do whatever we need to do to solve the problem.

However, the Chafetz Chaim (*Chafetz Chaim*, ch. 10) explains that even in situations in which we are trying to help, we are only allowed to say something negative about someone else if we follow a number of different guidelines. Some of the most difficult laws are those that relate to situations in which we are trying to solve a problem, whether it is our own problem with the person or a problem that is only relevant to someone else. The truth is that even though there are times when it is permitted to discuss other people's limitations for the purpose of helping, this has to be done in the right manner.

We may have many ideas about what is and is not a problem, and because the laws are complicated, we often may be mistaken. Therefore, the Chafetz Chaim lays out all the laws of *lashon hara* in a very clear manner. Through studying the *sefer Chafetz Chaim*, we can come to understand what the actual laws are.

If people are likely to have heard the information already, we are allowed to say it. There is some truth in this concept; however, it is not always true. Therefore, we need to make sure that we are applying that rule to the proper situation. Even when it is the proper situation, we have to make sure that the way that we share the information is also the proper way.

It is okay to say something negative if it is not a character judgment. It is also often assumed that it is fine to mention something about someone that may cause them to be looked down upon (e.g., they are short, not smart, slow, or weak) but is not a judgment on their character because we are not criticizing them as a person. However, statements like these are often hurtful anyway and can be problematic.

There are certain people we are allowed to speak about, or to, even if we are saying something negative. The Chafetz Chaim (*Chafetz Chaim*, ch. 8) makes a point out of telling us that *lashon hara* applies even when we are talking *about* family members, and it is also not okay to say whatever we want *to* family members. The same is true when it comes to *rabbanim* and teachers: It is not okay for them to speak about their students indiscriminately, and the same is true regarding the students speaking about them.

In order to avoid these pitfalls, it is necessary and important to study the laws carefully so we will know what is and is not permitted.

Even when we are allowed to speak about others, it is important to keep in mind that one of our primary responsibilities in life is to emulate the ways of Hashem. The ways of Hashem are very much related to kindness and compassion, love, and sensitivity. Striving to emulate these *middos* will motivate us to avoid saying anything that is hurtful to others unnecessarily. Even when we do need to say something, we will be careful to say it properly.

Avoiding Justifications and Managing Relationships Properly

The fact that we are often motivated to speak *lashon hara*, either because we are upset or because we are looking for attention, will motivate us to justify our speaking about others, and we will find a way to back up our justification based on the laws of *lashon hara* themselves!

The justifications and mistakes stem from the fact that sometimes, it is proper to share negative information about others, and it is even our responsibility to share that information. If the rules were the same in all situations — that it is never proper to say anything negative about others — then it would be a lot easier. We would always know what is right and wrong, and our only job would be to overcome our challenges and say nothing negative about others.

The justifications and the mistakes all revolve around the different factors that sometimes make it proper and appropriate to share something negative about others. Since we know there are situations like this one in which it is proper to speak up, we may think that any similar situation is proper as well. We will look at the reason it is okay to speak in one situation and why it makes sense in that situation, and we will think that the same logic should apply to other similar situations.

When we learn the halachos of *lashon hara* properly, we learn the most appropriate and productive way of dealing with life situations.

The halachos of *lashon hara* take into account all the different factors that relate to our potential need to communicate with others about a third party's shortcomings. Therefore, learning these laws also helps us learn the proper way to deal with all these factors.

For example, the laws of when we are allowed to believe what we have heard about others (*kabbalas lashon hara*) teach us how to process information appropriately and productively. We learn about not believing negative information about others without clear evidence. We also learn how to process information in a truthful way. There is so much information that is shared about people, and it is very helpful to learn how to recognize when the information is based on real evidence. Much of what we hear is based on opinions, assumptions, or false information. The laws of *lashon hara* teach us how to identify real evidence, which is extremely helpful in our relationships. People are frequently quoted about things they have said about us that are very hurtful to us. However, they are often quoted without the proper context, and sometimes, the one repeating the statement exaggerates what was actually said. When we believe these stories at face value, we are often incited to be angry and to want to create a fight about it. The fight could have been avoided if the person who was listening had been more careful not to listen to the *lashon hara* to begin with. Even if he heard the report, if he followed the halachos and processed the information properly, he would have been able to recognize that much of the information was not accurate. Following the halachos of *kabbalas lashon hara* properly can protect us from a lot of friction in our relationships.

The halachos of *lashon hara* also teach us how to balance the mitzvah to help others alongside the prohibition of hurting others inappropriately with our words.

This need for balance often arises when someone is looking to have some dealings with someone, whether it is related to a business, social, or marital arrangement. In such a case, they are allowed to find out information about the other person. However, there are a number of factors that need to be considered as they are doing their research. The person sharing the information needs to make sure they only say things that directly relate to the benefit that is needed, i.e., that will help them make an appropriate decision. They also need to make sure that their intent in sharing the information is only for the intended benefit of helping to make a proper decision and not for other motivations. They must try to ensure that the person hearing the information is listening to it with the proper intentions and trying to process it in the appropriate manner. The person receiving the information should not believe it without proper evidence and should only act upon it for the purpose of self-protection. They also have to make sure that there is no other way to accomplish their goal without having to hurt the other person. (The exact halachos are nuanced. These are only some of the general guidelines.)

When someone is able to follow the halachos properly, they will generally accomplish their goal more appropriately and more productively. When the information is accurate and is shared with the proper attitudes, it is more likely that the focus will be to create proper boundaries in the relationship rather than to create a fight.

Another situation in which a person can share negative information about someone else is when he needs guidance (or he needs to vent) about a problem in a current relationship. It is often appropriate and helpful to share the information, but it has to be done properly, including that the goal must be for the purpose of helping and that the information must be stated accurately (without assumptions or exaggerations).

These halachos show us not only the appropriate way to speak but are also the framework for the most beneficial way for us to speak, as well.

It is much better for our psychological and emotional health when we are focused on improving our relationships productively rather than on venting our anger with a goal of criticizing and hurting others. (There may be times when it is helpful to do so, but venting our anger in a vengeful manner is usually not helpful or appropriate.) Similarly, if we make assumptions or exaggerate the problems, we will not be dealing with the true and real situation. We obviously need to work with the reality in order to deal with a situation productively.

• CHAPTER 4 •

THE MOTIVATION TO DEVELOP
PROPER SPEECH

WE ARE GENERALLY MOTIVATED TO be good people, to choose right
from wrong, to act with morality, and to follow the rules of the Torah. As
a result, we are generally motivated to avoid speaking in a negative way
about others because we know that it is inappropriate and forbidden to
hurt other people with our words just as its forbidden to hurt them in any
other manner. It does not fit into our moral and ethical values or into our
dedication to our Torah observance.

However, we are not always fully motivated to avoid hurting others
with our words. There are many levels of additional motivation that we
can hope to reach.

The Chafetz Chaim teaches us that there are many levels of appreci-
ating the importance of speaking nicely about others. Even though we all
know it is important to speak positively about others and therefore try
to be careful, we often do not recognize its full value. Often, we do not
realize how damaging and inappropriate it is to speak negatively about
others. As a result, we are not as motivated as we should be to be careful
about our speech.

Appreciating the Harm of Negative Speech

There are many reasons why it can be difficult to appreciate the seri-
ousness of hurting people with our words. For instance, the hurt we cause
through our words is often not as obvious as it is when we hurt people in
other ways. As a result, we often do not recognize how much we are hurt-
ing others with our words, and it does not feel like it is such a bad thing

to do. We are therefore more likely to hurt others with our words than to hurt them in other ways.

As the Mesillas Yesharim says (ch. 11), most people do not steal from others in clear and tangible ways, but people sometimes steal when it is in less tangible or less direct ways. So too, we will not hurt others in tangible and direct ways, but we are more likely to hurt others with our words because they are intangible, and the effects are indirect, making it much easier to justify hurting others in that fashion.

We would certainly think twice before hitting someone, but we may not think twice before hurting their reputation. However, the reality is that our words can be really hurtful to others as well. They can cause a lot of emotional pain, they can damage relationships, and they can cause a variety of other significant types of loss to others.

One of the ways we hurt others with our words is by hurting their feelings. When someone finds out that we spoke critically about them, they may be insulted because we do not seem to care about them or respect them. It can also be hurtful to think about our reputation being ruined through what people are saying about us. We often underestimate how damaging it is when someone's feelings are hurt. We think, "Sticks and stones will break my bones, but words will never hurt me," but the reality is that words can be even more hurtful.

We also often do not recognize how much our words can hurt others even in a practical sense. When we ruin someone's reputation, it can affect them in many areas of their lives. However, the damage is often indirect, and we underestimate how bad it will be at the time we are speaking.

During a private conversation with a friend, we often discuss a mutual friend. Within the conversation, we may say something negative about the third friend. At the time, we probably do not intend to really hurt our mutual friend. However, we often do not realize how quickly a private conversation can spread, and we often do not think that people will take us so seriously. As a result of the information that was spread (initially by us and later by others), our mutual friend may be extremely embarrassed and hurt. When we underestimate the power of our words to hurt others, we are less careful.

Another reason why we do not appreciate the seriousness of hurting people with our words is that we often feel justified in speaking about them negatively. We think that if someone is a bad person or has hurt us, we are allowed to say what we want about them. This is especially true when combined with the previous factor — the fact that the hurt caused by our words is less direct and less tangible than physical harm.

At times, we also feel justified in speaking about the fact that someone is doing the wrong thing because we want to be helpful. There are times that it is appropriate to speak up in that type of situation, but there is a proper process that we need to follow, and unfortunately, we often do not follow it properly.

Another obstacle is that we do not fully appreciate the importance of being nice to others. We do not realize that possibly the most valuable attribute of Hashem is His kindness, and that kindness may be the most important mitzvah in the Torah.

Furthermore, part of appreciating the importance of being pleasant to others is appreciating how important it is in comparison to other matters in life. This is true regardless of whether it is being compared to other mitzvos or if it is compared to our general needs and interests in life. We often prioritize incorrectly and ascribe more value and importance to other matters than we do to treating others properly.

Finally, the Chafetz Chaim points out (introduction to *Chafetz Chaim*) that hurting others with our words is not generally considered by the world to be a real problem. It is not considered to be a problem morally and ethically, and it is not considered to be a real problem of going against Torah law. He explains that even in circles where it is accepted that *lashon hara* violates the laws of the Torah and of morality, there are so many (perceived) justifications for speaking about other people's shortcomings that societal attitudes become almost the same as if there were no problem with it to begin with. This situation obviously makes it very hard to realize how bad it is when our words cause someone to be hurt.

All of these factors are interrelated, and in combination, they create a strong sense that it is not so bad to hurt others with our words. Since we are not hurting anyone directly or tangibly when we are speaking about someone in a negative way, it is hard to fully appreciate how much we are hurting them. That makes it easier to justify our speech in a situation where we are speaking about someone who hurt us or about someone who is a bad person in our eyes. This is especially true because other people do the same thing as well; therefore, it seems to be a valid justification. What makes the problem more profound is that we never fully appreciated the importance of treating others as much as we should have from the outset.

When we read through *Chafetz Chaim* and *Shemiras Halashon* and get a sense of how important it is to not hurt others with our words, we will recognize how far we are from appreciating the full importance of the matter and how much work we need to do to understand and improve our behavior.

It is important to try to address each of these different factors so that we can come to a greater appreciation of the importance of speaking properly about others.

Hurting Everyone Involved

The Gemara in *Arachin* (15b) teaches us that *lashon hara* kills three people: the speaker, the listener, and the one who is being spoken about. This teaches us three goals we should have when we are speaking: to be careful not to hurt ourselves, the person we are speaking to, and the person we are speaking about.

Lashon hara certainly hurts the person we are speaking about, but it can also be hurtful to everyone else who is involved because it can lead to people fighting with each other. Feelings get hurt, people become angry with each other, and they get involved in a battle of insults that causes everyone to hurt each other's feelings and their reputations.

The most obvious person who is hurt through our *lashon hara* is the person we are talking about. We often cause a lot of pain without really intending to do so.

Sometimes, when we are critical of others with our words, our comments end up getting back to them. When they find out that we are ready to tell others about their limitations and apparently do not respect or care about them, it can be very painful. Most people are sensitive about how people think and feel about them, and it is hurtful to find out that others were speaking about them in a negative way.

We do not like it when people talk about us in a critical way, and when we find out that someone did speak about us, we are hurt, and we usually get upset at them. That generally leads to all kinds of criticism and fighting between the two people. The person who had initially heard the *lashon hara* often also gets involved in the arguments and fighting as well.

Emotional Pain

Most of us have a tendency to diminish the significance of our feelings or other people's feelings. We think of physical pain and emotional pain differently. We recognize that physical pain is real, it can be very hard to deal with, it does not just go away, and it should create a sense of empathy among friends and loved ones. We understand that we should do our best to not cause others to have that pain.

However, we often think of emotional pain differently. We think it is "made up" or at least exaggerated, it should be easy to deal with, it should be easy to "get over," and it does not always warrant sympathy. Therefore, we often do not have such a strong commitment to not cause others emotional pain.

When we recognize the true nature of emotional pain and the damage that it causes, we will be much more motivated and committed to not causing others emotional pain.

Our words make a big difference to the people we are speaking to or the people who we speak about. Shlomo Hamelech (*Koheles* 4:4) teaches us that generally, human efforts are motivated by peer pressure and the desire for honor and respect. We all really want to be cared for and respected. We want to know that people think highly of us and that they have our best interests in mind. Shlomo Hamelech's words certainly give us a sense of how important it is to not hurt people's feelings and reputations!

Words can communicate respect and caring for a person, or they can reflect the opposite. When we hear the former, we are very happy, and when we hear the latter, it is upsetting and hurtful. When we find out that someone criticized us to someone else, it is even worse, because that means that multiple people are demonstrating lack of care and respect for us!

The reality is that hurting someone's feelings, their reputation, or their relationship with others can be extremely damaging. Many of us would prefer to be physically hurt than to have our reputations ruined. We work so hard to receive honor and respect from others because it is so important to us to receive that honor and respect.

The Victim's Self-Image

What we think about who we are, which can be referred to as our self-image, is affected by our self-respect, which refers to the degree of respect we have for ourselves. Our self-respect affects us in many ways. When we respect ourselves and approve of the picture that we have of ourselves, then we will "accept ourselves." However, when we do not respect ourselves or approve of what we see in ourselves, then we will "reject ourselves."

Our self-respect and self-image are very much affected by the messages we hear from others.

We are often taught to think about ourselves as being either good people or bad people. We are taught to think about ourselves as being capable and competent or as incapable and incompetent. We are either taught to think of ourselves as religious, moral, smart, handsome, strong, funny, tall, etc., or the opposite. We are also taught how to judge each aspect: If we are not religious, then we are bad; if we are not smart, then we are stupid; and so on.

There are times when we hear messages such as these: "You should be ashamed of yourself," "You are a troublemaker," "You are a lazy kid," "If you want to be successful, you need to change who you are," "If you want to be a good person, you need to change who you are," "You do not deserve to be treated with respect," or "You need to change if you want someone to love you."

When we hear these or similar messages from others, especially when we hear them from those we love and respect, it affects us in two ways: We do not like it when others look down on us, and these messages also teach us to look down on ourselves. We may start to believe that we are bad or foolish. At a certain point, if we think that we are bad or foolish and have little self-respect, and our self-image is very low, then it is likely that we will eventually not approve of ourselves and therefore reject ourselves.

At first glance, the messages do not necessarily seem to be so bad. They may be interpreted as an innocent way of saying, "You need to take responsibility for your actions, and it is important for you to try to improve." That is an important message that we need to hear and take to heart. Without being aware of our limitations and without taking responsibility for our behavior, we will not lead a productive and appropriate life.

However, when we think about these messages more carefully, we may have a different attitude about them. For example, when a child is told by his parents or teachers (or both) that he should be ashamed of himself because of the way he behaves, that without changing, he will never be worthy of respect, and that without changing, he will never be successful, then this will be how he will think about himself.

When we think that we are unworthy as we are and unless we somehow make a significant change in who we are, we will remain that way, and then, we will likely think that we are stuck in a hopeless situation — because we will not think that we are really going to change.

When we have these thoughts about ourselves, this often leads to extremely unproductive behaviors. We may think that since we will never be able to become a "good person," we might as well do whatever we want. Alternatively, we may think that the only way to not be doomed to failure is to be perfect, so we may try to act in a manner that is very extreme. That is often not good for us. We need to behave in ways that are appropriate and productive for who we are.

When we speak *lashon hara*, we are not only hurting the intended victim, but we are also hurting ourselves in a significant manner. We will discuss this concept in more detail shortly.

The Power of Indirect Messages

The messages we receive from others about who we are and what we should think about ourselves sometimes come directly from others (as above). However, other messages come in a more indirect form.

In one type of indirect message, someone might share their perspective about the world, and based on that perspective, we infer what we should think about ourselves. For example, someone may say that anyone who does not *daven* properly is a terrible person. If we know that we do not *daven* properly, then we may conclude that we are pretty terrible. The fact that even our indirect messages can hurt others tells us that we really have to watch what we say.

Another type of indirect message that can really hurt others is when we are speaking *lashon hara* and saying something negative about someone else. We often know that it is not proper to do so, but we think that it is not such a big deal. However, at times, we may give someone the impression that the person we are speaking about is "a bad guy, and he should be ashamed of himself." We may also convey the sense that he will never be able to change, and he is doomed to be a bad guy for the rest of life. These messages often get back to the person we were speaking about, and not only is he hurt but he may also believe that the messages are true, leading him to many unproductive thoughts, feelings, and behaviors related to shame, hopelessness, and a lack of self-acceptance.

The content of the story is also sometimes very damaging to the person we are speaking about. Our words can affect other people's reputations, jobs, friends, family life, or many other aspects of their lives. That is a major problem of its own, and it can certainly lead to a battle of people hurting each other in other types of practical ways.

There is often much more damage that can come from speaking *lashon hara* than we intend. If we hurt someone's reputation, this can sometimes lead to long-term damage. Our words can cause hard feelings between a husband and wife, between parents and children, between neighbors, friends, coworkers, organizations, communities, etc. At times, these fights can result in long-term pain, suffering, and dysfunction.

The Need for Love and Respect from Others

The reason why our words can cause others so much pain is that we all desire love and respect from others, and it really hurts us when we do not receive love and respect. The fact that we are so needy of that love and respect makes us vulnerable to be hurt when we do not receive it.

The *Ohr Hatzafun* (vol. 1, p. 224) refers to the Gemara (*Kesubos* 111b) that says that giving someone a smile is more helpful to them than taking care of their physical needs. A genuine smile reflects the feeling, "I am happy to see you — your existence is important to me." This usually includes a statement of respect and care. The Gemara is teaching us that it is crucial to each of us to receive respect and love, which means it is important to communicate love and respect with our words as well. The Gemara is also teaching us that we all have the capacity to really help others by sharing positive feelings toward them. We sometimes underestimate how much we can help others by caring about them and communicating that feeling to them.

We also often underestimate the damage that words of criticism can cause. When people are hurt through other people's words, we often have a hard time understanding the extent of the problem with that.

When we recognize the true damage that we are doing to others with our words, we are less likely to justify it to ourselves — the same way that we are not so quick to justify physical assault.

The Value of Speaking Positively About Others

Everyone knows that it is a nice thing to do to speak positively about others and that there is a prohibition against hurting others with our words, but most people do not begin to understand and appreciate the full value of kindness and compassion. In order to appreciate how important it is to show kindness and speak positively about others, we need to learn its importance from the Torah's perspective.

We know how careful we try to be to avoid eating something that is not kosher. We would go hungry for hours and put ourselves through uncomfortable social experiences in order to avoid eating nonkosher food.

If we try to think about *lashon hara* in the same way, then we will be able to have the same type of dedication to avoiding it.

There are a number of reasons why it is so important to speak nicely about others and certainly not to speak critically about them.

The true greatness of Hashem, and the true greatness of a human being, relates to treating others well, helping them, and caring about them.

Hashem created the world for the benefit of each individual person, and He gave each of us a very important mission. It is our job to figure out what Hashem wants from us and to do our best to fulfill our responsibilities. Our ability to speak plays a significant role in our ability to accomplish our goals. Hashem gave us this ability as a gift to help us accomplish our goals in the most productive way. However, we can also use our speech in ways that are not appropriate or productive. It is our responsibility to take advantage of the opportunity Hashem gave us and to use our speech properly and productively.

Chafetz Chaim and *Shemiras Halashon* teach us that speaking positively about others and avoiding speaking negatively about others are two of the most important responsibilities in the Torah. They are crucial to our relationship with Hashem and a significant part of our development as human beings!

These *sefarim* show us how many mitzvos there are that instruct us to be careful about how we speak about others. They list all the mitzvos in the Torah that instruct us to be careful about how we speak about others, and the Chafetz Chaim says (introduction to *Chafetz Chaim*) we should see this fact as a lesson in how important it is to be careful about these matters. He also quotes the words of *Chazal* to support the importance of proper speech and gives many reasons for why it is so important to speak positively about others.

We are generally motivated to fulfill our Torah responsibilities and to be righteous Jews, and the fact that so many mitzvos revolve around speaking nicely to and about others is itself a significant reason to be careful with our speech — to avoid *aveiros* — and it also signifies how important it is to speak properly. A major part of *avodas Hashem* is being pleasant to others! Possibly our greatest responsibility is to emulate the ways of Hashem, as the Ohr Hatzafun says many times in his *sefer*, and possibly the most significant aspect of Hashem's *middos* is the *middah* of *chesed*. Speaking critically about others is certainly not in line with the *middos* of Hashem.

We are also motivated to have a close relationship with Hashem. We learn from the *Ohr Hatzafun* that a big part of having a relationship with Hashem includes understanding and appreciating His ways, and as a result, wanting to live a life dedicated to following in the ways of Hashem. The *Ohr Hatzafun* also teaches us that the ways of Hashem all revolve around kindness and truth. This means that our relationship with Hashem includes understanding and appreciating Hashem's kindness, developing a desire to emulate Hashem's kindness, and living a life that is dedicated to kindness.

It follows that if we want to have a relationship with Hashem, we cannot be involved in hurting other people with our words or in any other manner. Rather, we need to focus on caring about and helping others however we can, including with our words. According to this way of understanding what our relationship with Hashem is all about, the responsibility to not hurt others with our words is a fundamental part of our whole relationship with Hashem.

The *Ohr Hatzafun* (vol. 1, p. 7) uses the same principles to teach us how we can understand and relate to Hashem Himself. We cannot really understand who Hashem is; however, we are taught that we should try to relate to Hashem through an understanding of His *middos* and how He interacts with the world. The *middos* of Hashem are best described as the *middos* of kindness, and by extension, the best way that we can relate to Hashem is as a Being of kindness. This understanding of Hashem can give us a sense of the importance that Hashem places on not hurting others.

We also learn from the *Ohr Hatzafun* (vol. 1, p. 243) that this understanding about who Hashem is, what His ways are, and what is important to Him carries over to an understanding of what all of the mitzvos are about as well. The *sefer* shows that all of the mitzvos revolve around kindness. Some are directly related to kindness, and some are indirectly related to kindness. The *Ohr Hatzafun* explains that our job is to emulate the ways of Hashem, which means being kind, sensitive, caring, loving, etc. just as Hashem is. This understanding of what our role is in This World also gives us a different way of thinking about hurting others. It is against our whole purpose in This World!

Most of us want to develop our moral and ethical character. We want to be moral and ethical, and we want to think of ourselves as moral and ethical people. That is what defines the greatness and the dignity of a human being. Not hurting others with our words is certainly a significant part of living moral and ethical lives.

Hurting the Speaker

One of the most damaging aspects of *lashon hara* is the damage that happens to the speaker. The Chafetz Chaim, in his introduction to *Shemiras Halashon*, refers to the statements of Dovid Hamelech and his son Shlomo, who warn us that our words can be extremely damaging to ourselves. He also devotes an entire section of this *sefer* (*Sha'ar Hazechirah*) to explaining how damaging *lashon hara* can be to the speaker.

Dovid Hamelech says in *Tehillim* (34:13–14) that if we want life (*chafetz chaim*), we need to make sure that we do not hurt ourselves by speaking in the wrong way, and Shlomo Hamelech says in *Mishlei* (21:23) that if we want to be protected from painful experiences in life, we need to make sure to not hurt ourselves with our words. They are both teaching us that our negative words can be a source of personal harm for ourselves.

There are many practical ways in which we can hurt ourselves when we get into fights with others or when we speak in a negative way about others, but even more importantly, when we speak in a way that is not appropriate, we are hurting our spiritual selves.

When we speak *lashon hara*, we are acting without sensitivity to others. This is not the way that we are supposed to live our lives. Our behavior also affects the type of people we become. We do not want to become more arrogant, hateful, or critical by focusing on other people's limitations and problems and putting ourselves "above" them.

The greatest aspect of human dignity and human achievement is our kindness and our integrity. Even though the messages of the world generally define achievement and success based on things like having a good job, making money, being smart, being fit, looking good, or having power or prestige, the truth is that we can only have real dignity and achievement when we act with the proper *middos*.

The greatness of Hashem is described as the *middos* of Hashem, such as His kindness and integrity. The *Ohr Hatzafun* (vol. 1, p. 270) describes human greatness in the same way: Our true greatness and success lie in our ability to act with the *middos* of Hashem, with kindness and integrity.

When we develop love and respect for others, we are developing true greatness within ourselves. So too, when we speak to others and about others with love, respect, and dignity, we are demonstrating our own dignity and achieving the greatest accomplishment. On the other hand, if we speak in a manner that is hurtful to others, we are hurting ourselves: We are acting in an undignified manner, and we are distancing ourselves from our true greatness.

Reward and Benefit

The Chafetz Chaim teaches us how much reward Hashem gives us for speaking properly and how much punishment we will receive as a result of not speaking properly. He explains (throughout *Shemiras Halashon*) that the reward and punishment related to proper speech are significant both in This World and in the Next World.

Most Jews who follow Torah law understand the ramifications of not doing so. We would be concerned about the ramifications (both in This World and the Next World) of eating something that is not kosher, eating on Yom Kippur, or not following the laws of Shabbos. However, most of us are not concerned about the ramifications that we will face if we speak *lashon hara*.

The Chafetz Chaim says (introduction to *Chafetz Chaim*) that we often underestimate the significance of the sin of hurting others with our words. On an individual level, when we speak *lashon hara*, we can be punished in a significant way, both in This World and in the Next World. On a national level, the Gemara (*Gittin* 56a) says that one of the reasons for the destruction of the Beis Hamikdash (and possibly the main reason) was that the Jews of the time spoke a lot of *lashon hara*. The Chafetz Chaim also says the fact that we still do not have a Beis Hamikdash may be due to the situation that as a nation, we still speak too much *lashon hara*.

When we recognize that Hashem considers *lashon hara* such a serious problem and that He awards so much reward and punishment based on it, we will be extremely motivated to avoid speaking *lashon hara*. We will also develop a sense of fear that will be associated with hurting others with our words because the ramifications of speaking *lashon hara* are really quite serious.

It is not so easy to change how we think about the mitzvah of speaking nicely about others. However, if we try to change our perspectives and recognize the importance of speaking nicely, we will become much more dedicated to keeping the laws properly. The more we learn about the major role of acting with kindness and sensitivity toward others in the Torah, the more we will appreciate the importance of being careful about those laws.

Kindness to Others versus Other Important Aspects of Our Lives

When we measure the importance of any matter, we need to compare it to the importance of other matters that compete with it for attention.

The Mesillas Yesharim (ch. 4) says that it is important to recognize that closeness to Hashem is good and that everything else is meaningless. He is teaching us that it is not good enough to realize that closeness to Hashem is good; rather, we need to also recognize that everything else is not meaningful. Both of these realizations together will create a powerful motivation for us to focus on developing our closeness to Hashem properly.

So too, in order to appreciate the true importance of speaking positively about others, we need to recognize that aside from the fact that it is independently important, it is also very important compared to other important things in life.

For example, we might think that even though it is important to not hurt others with our words, making money and supporting my family is more important; therefore, if I need to hurt others with my *lashon hara* in order to make money to support my family, that should take precedence. However, the halachah is not that way. In most situations, we are not allowed to hurt others with our words in order to make money. If we are in a situation in which we would have to give up our job if we do not speak *lashon hara*, the halachah is that we have to give it up! Similarly, if we think it is more important to be in shul on time or to learn Torah than it is to not hurt others with our words, then we may hurt others with our words in order to make it to shul on time or to learn Torah. However, the halachah generally does not allow us to do so.

Overriding Our Justifications and Addressing Our Biases

When we appreciate the importance and true value of not speaking *lashon hara*, we can begin to remove our justifications and our biases for speaking *lashon hara*.

Our biases are based on the idea that we will be better off by sharing the information about the other person; therefore, we are motivated to convince ourselves that it is worth it to share the information. Similarly, we are often motivated to convince ourselves that it is proper and appropriate to share the information.

However, when we have a clear understanding of the importance and benefits of avoiding *lashon hara*, then we will not be so inclined to convince ourselves that it is a good idea to say the *lashon hara*.

Even though we all know that we will be better off only speaking positively, if we do not fully appreciate how important this is, we may still feel (at least subconsciously) that we will gain by speaking *lashon hara*. Therefore, we will be motivated to find a justification for why it should be permitted. The more we recognize that it is better for us to only speak nicely about others, the more likely it is that we will avoid any justifications for not doing so.

Overcoming Pressure to Speak *Lashon Hara*

Several problems result from the fact that society seems to teach us that it is acceptable to speak about others. First, our moral and ethical code is often affected by the perspectives and behavior of those around us, and we will often come to think that this behavior is acceptable. Second, when people in our social group speak about others' problems, it creates a social pressure to speak in the same way. Speaking about others is considered to be normal behavior. Third, one of the things that generally protects us from sin is positive peer pressure that holds us accountable to keep up with the standards that are expected from us. Peer pressure holds us back from many *aveiros*. Since *lashon hara* is so widely accepted, it is hard to feel pressure to avoid it.

In the relationships that people have with family or friends, there is a powerful need to have others agree with them, and people also have a powerful need to have others empathize with them as well. These needs often create strong peer pressure and a strong compulsion to get involved in conversations about others. When someone shares their criticism about a third party, it is difficult to avoid giving them the reassurance that we agree with their perspective. This is especially true when they are looking for us to empathize with them. The same is true when we are the one who is looking for empathy regarding a matter that relates to a difficulty that we are having with someone else. We will want to share our frustration with that person with a third party in order to receive validation and empathy. In this process, we will often speak a lot of *lashon hara*.

It is important to have a plan to counter these influences that we receive from our society. Being educated properly about the magnitude of our responsibility to avoid *lashon hara* is one of the keys to enable us to counter the influences and pressures. We also need to attain the confidence to stand up for what is proper even when it is not socially accepted. We also need to develop the self-motivation to do the right thing on our own, without relying on outside pressure to do the right thing.

There is a way to discuss frustration in our relationships with a third party without it being considered *lashon hara*; however, it must be done in a very specific manner, and we often do not know how, or we are not interested in doing so.

Closing Blessing

Dovid Hamelech tells us that whoever truly desires life should be careful about what they say about others. The Midrash (*Vayikra Rabbah* 16:2) describes avoiding *lashon hara* as the "potion for life." Speaking properly about others is a great merit for life in This World and the Next World!

We should all be blessed with the awareness to recognize how important it is to avoid speaking *lashon hara,* and we should dedicate ourselves to avoid speaking it as much we can.

– PART 2 –

RESPONSIBILITY IN RELATIONSHIPS

Introduction

It is important to remember a few principles regarding our responsibilities in our relationships:

- It is up to us to do our best to make our relationships productive.
- We will live with the effects of our actions.
- We are defined by the choices that we make.

These principles play out in all of our relationships, and it is important to recognize that they are true and to focus on them throughout our lives.

Our success in life and the legacy that we leave are defined by the nature of the choices that we make throughout our lives. If we have made productive and appropriate choices, then we can certainly be proud of what we have accomplished, and the opposite is true as well.

We make many choices in life. We need to choose which goals to pursue and what we will put into pursuing them. Many of these choices relate to choosing between right and wrong. Each of the choices that we make affects who we become as a person, what we make of our lives, and which goals we are going to accomplish.

Most of us have many goals, desires, values, and ambitions in life, including the goal and desire to be "good people" and to live a moral and ethical life. It is all our choice. What we get out of life will be what we put into life. It is an obvious concept, but we often do not focus on it, and we do not live with that clarity.

It is true that we do not have control over the results of our actions. Even when we make good choices and put in the proper effort, we do not always get the results that we were hoping for. However, when we choose to do the right thing and we put in the effort to achieve the proper results, we did our part. That is all we can do, and it is all we need to do. True success in life is defined as doing our best to be a good person.

Relationship Goals

Two central goals that we have within our relationships are to be as helpful as we can be to the other person and to receive the benefits that come from a loving and caring relationship.

In order to achieve these goals, we often set out to do our best to help the other person with their physical, financial, emotional, and spiritual needs and interests. However, we are faced with many choices about how dedicated we will be to helping the other person.

When we choose to dedicate our lives to being the best husband, wife, mother, father, son, or daughter that we can be, and we choose to be kind, compassionate, and encouraging to our spouse, child, or parent, this has a huge positive impact on who we are as a person, and it contributes significantly to the likelihood that we will have a loving relationship.

We do not have complete control over the success of our relationships. We may face difficulties in our relationships, and even when we make good choices and put in the proper effort, we do not always get the results that we were hoping for. However, when we choose to do the right thing, and we put in the effort to achieve the proper results, we did our part. That is all we can do, and it is all we need to do. Our efforts define true success as a parent, child, spouse, friend, or fellow human being: doing our best to make the proper choices.

Putting in the Work

When we think about our relationships idealistically, we would all like to be nice and kind to everyone, especially to our family and friends. Who does not want to be a great mom or dad? We want to be nice and kind both for idealistic reasons and for our own selfish benefits. When we treat others well, it makes it more likely that our relationship with them will be productive, and that is certainly beneficial for everyone.

However, it is important to recognize that relationships are difficult, and even when we want to be the best spouse, parent, or child, it is difficult to always treat others properly. It is even hard to always be dedicated to being the best person that we can be in our relationships.

We want to and we are obligated to develop and maintain good relationships. However, in order to do so, we need to treat others with sensitivity, love, and respect — and that is often a very difficult thing to do.

In order to fulfill our responsibilities and have productive relationships, we need to identify and develop a number of thoughts, attitudes, skills, and perspectives:

- knowing what our responsibilities are, how far they go, and the degree of our responsibility to fulfill them;
- finding value in our responsibilities;
- being motivated to fulfill them;
- accepting and embracing our responsibilities;
- knowing how to balance our own needs and those of others;
- following through with carrying out our responsibilities; and
- identifying the challenges that stand in the way of our ability to accomplish these things and knowing how to overcome these challenges.

The objective of this section of the book is to help us develop a proper sense of responsibility in all of our relationships. It will focus on the first four of the aspects that we just mentioned. We will use the guidance of the Torah to understand our responsibility to commit unconditionally to being helpful and kind to others, especially family members, to the best of our ability in all situations.

All of the above aspects are significantly affected by our understanding of the basis of our responsibilities; the true context of our responsibilities; and the ideals, values, and perspectives that are the foundation of our responsibilities. When we have a proper understanding of these matters, we will realize that our responsibilities were placed upon us in a fair and appropriate manner. We will be able to clarify what they are, why they are important, and how to balance our needs with our obligation to helping others. We will also appreciate the benefits of fulfilling our responsibilities.

All these matters are also affected by an understanding that pursuing our pleasures and temptations will not lead us to the degree of happiness and success that we may be hoping for.

CHAPTER 1

THE SOURCE AND IMPORTANCE OF
OUR RESPONSIBILITIES

SOME OF THE MOST IMPORTANT responsibilities and commitments that we have in our lives are related to our relationships. Being a spouse, parent, teacher, rabbi, or child comes along with significant responsibilities.

Every relationship has its own set of responsibilities and commitments. In family relationships, people generally feel obligated to visit each other from time to time and to share life events. In addition, every family has their own way of defining, for themselves, what their family responsibilities are.

However, our commitment is not merely to have the relationship and to fulfill our "family responsibilities." It is just as important to commit ourselves to being helpful and courteous to each other in our day-to-day interactions within these relationships. We need to accept the responsibility to do our best to help each other and care for each other throughout the relationship.

Our responsibilities include helping each other in any practical way that we can, caring about each other, and giving each other the emotional support each person needs.

When we have a child, we take on the responsibility of giving much of our time, energy, and resources to take care of the child's needs. Parents wake up at all hours of the night to take care of their infants, they change thousands of diapers, and they spend most of their waking hours (for decades) working to support their families. There are years filled with homework, reports, and soccer games to stay on top of. Doctors, dentists, and karate practices are part of our routine.

These are only the responsibilities we have when everything is going well. When children are sick, parents can spend countless sleepless nights with their child and may even sleep in a chair in the hospital in order to be there for a child who needs them. Which parent would not go to the end of the world for the sake of their child?

To a lesser degree, the same types of responsibilities sometimes fall on children as well. As parents age, they are less able to care for themselves, and the burden often falls on the children to care for their parents' physical, emotional, and financial needs. These needs are often very extensive, and it can require a real commitment from the children to properly make sure that their parents are taken care of in their elder years.

When a young couple stands under the *chuppah* on their wedding day, they look at each other and commit to each other: "I will be there for you through all of the highs and lows of life." We commit to love, respect, and cherish each other in all situations, no matter what our financial state or our health will be at the time.

Some relationships involve these moments when we think consciously about what we are committing to and about what our responsibilities are going to be in the relationship. However, in many other relationships, we do not always stop to think about what our commitments should be and what our responsibilities are.

It is important to figure out the extent of our commitments and responsibilities within our relationships. What do they include? What are the limitations of our responsibilities? How important are they, and why?

The Extent of Our Responsibilities and Commitments

It is important to understand the extent of our responsibilities, including any conditions or limitations.

We all know the "golden rule": treat others the way that you would want to be treated. It is important to determine whether there are any limitations or exceptions to that rule.

Many of us tend to "promise the world" — especially to our spouse under the *chuppah* or to our child when we hold them for the first time in the maternity wing. We commit to always treat each other with the golden rule: to always treat the other person with sensitivity, love, care, and respect, just like we want to be treated. We commit to never be insensitive or treat them without love, care, or respect. We commit to think about them positively, to avoid speaking to them in an insensitive manner, and to not hurt them with our behavior in any way.

However, are we supposed to promise the world? Are we obligated to take care of every one of our children's, parent's, or spouse's needs? Are we obligated to make that commitment? Is it realistic for us to live up to that commitment?

As life goes on, we usually find out that our commitments do not play out the way we may have expected. We often do not end up following through on our commitments as much as we would have wanted to or as much as we would have expected to. We often find ourselves not treating others with sensitivity, love, care, and respect. We find ourselves thinking negatively about others, and we often say or do things that are hurtful to others.

When we find ourselves not living up to the commitment of always being nice to each other, we may think that our responsibilities should be limited. We may think, "I cannot help," "It is hard for me to help," "I do not want to help," or "I should not be obligated to help."

Are these thoughts and feelings understandable, proper, and productive, or are they inappropriate?

Limitations in Our Responsibilities

Our responsibilities in our relationships are certainly limited based on our personal limitations. We obviously cannot be responsible for doing better than our best.

We cannot always help our parents, children, or spouse with everything they may want or need. When we are able to help, we are obligated to do our best; however, we are obviously only responsible for helping when we are able to do so.

It is natural to sometimes want to help and other times not want to. When we do not want to help, it is hard to be helpful, and it is hard to even try to do our best. However, we can do the best that we can in the situation, and we may even be obligated to work on ourselves so we come to want to help. The same is true of situations where it is difficult to help. We can still do our best in that situation, and we are obligated to work on the factors holding us back so that it can be easier to help.

When we are limited in terms of how much we can do to help, either because we do not have the time or the resources or because we have other responsibilities that conflict with our availability to help, then we obviously cannot do better than our best. But when it comes to situations in which we are theoretically able to help but we do not want to or it is hard for us, does that affect whether we are obligated to help or not? Are we always obligated to give as much as we can? If we do not have any specific conflict and we are able to help if we want to help, do we always have to help? How much do we have to help?

Answering these questions involves knowing how we are supposed to balance our own needs and interests with our responsibility to help others. How much are we obligated to put aside our own needs, interests, desires, and assets in order to help others?

Three key factors seem to affect our responsibilities within relationships:

1. The degree of our relationship with them is relevant. Are the people we need to help family members, friends, or neighbors? It may seem that our responsibility should be based on what our relationship is with them.

2. The degree to which they deserve to be treated well is important. It may seem that we should be obligated to be pleasant to good people, but if they are not good people, then there is much less of a reason to go out of our way for them.

3. The degree to which they have treated us well is another consideration. When someone treats us well, then it may seem that we are much more obligated to treat them well in turn.

We all think that there are exceptions to the golden rule, and we think there are situations in which we are not obligated to try our best to be nice to the other person.

We may think that we should not be obligated to care about strangers because they are not our responsibility. Or we say things like, "Anyone who acts like him does not deserve to be treated nicely!" "Why should anyone be nice to him after what he has done?" or "Why should I help him, when he does not help me?"

All of these sentiments reflect a mindset that only certain people deserve to be treated in accordance with the golden rule.

The Source of Our Responsibilities

The determination of the parameters of our responsibilities is really based on what the reasons are for being nice to others. Why should we be nice to others? Why should we avoid doing things that could hurt others? When we determine the source of our responsibilities, then we can examine what that source tells us about how to apply the responsibilities to each situation.

In some situations, regardless of the source for our responsibility, it is clear that we are responsible. However, in some situations, the degree of our responsibility or the level of importance that is attached to our responsibility may be different depending on where our responsibilities come from.

If we understand the source and application of our responsibilities toward each other, we can determine how to balance our own needs and interests against our responsibilities to others. Knowing the source also allows us to determine what the potential limitations are within our relationships, such as how much we are obligated to help strangers, people who seem to be bad people, and those who have hurt us. Determining what our responsibilities are in any given situation depends on identifying the source of and reason for our responsibilities.

The Torah is the proper source for us to use to be able to determine the extent of our responsibilities toward others and how to balance them with our own needs and limitations.

What Our Responsibilities Include

As we mentioned above, we have many different relationships in life, and each type involves a different set of responsibilities. In each type of relationship, there are certain basic responsibilities that are generally accepted, but there is also a lot of room for different people to have different ideas about what each person's responsibilities are. There is also a lot of room for different perspectives on how important it is to fulfill various responsibilities.

The Extent of Our Responsibilities

There are many things that need to be taken care of in any family, and they require a lot of work. These "chores" are often divided among the different family members. At times, everyone is happy with the chores they have, and everything gets taken care of properly and productively. However, it is very common to have conflict within families about how many chores each person should have and about which chores each person should do. Husbands and wives often argue about how they should divide their responsibilities, and parents and children argue about how they should divide their chores and responsibilities.

There are many thoughts, perspectives, and philosophies that go into determining how to divide family responsibilities. Gender roles and parental responsibilities shape many of our ideas about how to divide jobs within the family. Expectations about each person's roles often depend on social, societal, and religious backgrounds.

It is important to define and understand what our responsibilities really are so we can appropriately do what we are supposed to do and avoid many conflicts. Like the extent of our responsibilities, this will depend on a proper understanding of where our responsibilities come from. Why should we be nice to others? Why do we need to work hard to help others?

When we determine the source of our responsibilities and the reason why we should be obligated to help others, then we can examine logically what that source tells us about what our responsibilities should be. We will recognize that there are certain times when there is an objective right and wrong about what the responsibilities should be. There will also be times when the subjective factors in the situation will make it clear what the right application of the responsibilities should be in that given situation. There will also be times where there is no specific way to determine what the exact responsibilities should be in that situation.

The Importance of Our Responsibilities

The importance we attribute to the responsibilities in our relationships affects our commitment to fulfill them. Therefore, it is important to analyze how much importance we attribute to our responsibilities to explore what their true importance should be and then to try to align our current perspectives with the proper perspectives.

There are some responsibilities that we consider very important. For example, most of us would consider our responsibility to care for our parents, our children, or our spouse to be extremely important. However, it is still important to consider whether we value our responsibilities enough, and even if we do, whether we have a proper understanding about what our responsibilities are and when they are relevant.

The way in which we determine how important our responsibilities are also depends on what the source of our responsibilities is and what the logic is for why we should be responsible. When we determine what the source of what our responsibilities is, then we can examine what that source tells us about how important the responsibilities are and how much we should prioritize them compared to other responsibilities.

Our perspectives about what our responsibilities are and how important they are will play a big role in determining how we carry out our responsibilities. It will affect what we are ready to do, how motivated we are to fulfill our responsibilities, and how much we prioritize them.

Identifying the Source of Our Responsibility to Be Kind

One way to look at the source of our responsibility to be nice to others is that it comes from a social agreement — either an expressed agreement between two people (such as in a marriage) or through understood societal expectations about how people should treat each other in a relationship.

If this is the source of our responsibilities, then the logic is related to the concept of integrity. It is appropriate to honor the agreements and the commitments that we have made.

A second source of our responsibilities in our relationships may be our responsibility to follow the laws of morality. The laws of morality include how we should behave as a moral person on our own (be nice to others and do not hurt others) and how we should behave in relation to what the other person deserves (people deserve to be treated nicely and to not be hurt by others). The responsibility to be a moral person is both the source of and logic for our being nice to others.

A third source of our responsibilities in our relationships is the Torah. The laws of the Torah may include how we should act according to who we are as a person (the Torah teaches us that we should help others and not hurt them) and how the other person deserves to be treated (people deserve to be treated well and to not be hurt by others). In order to clarify what the Torah teaches us, both about the laws and the logic of our responsibilities to help others, we have to see what the Torah says about them.

Social Agreement as the Source of Our Responsibilities

When the source of our responsibility is an agreement between two people (such as husband and wife) or a societal agreement, then the responsibility is defined by and limited to whatever the agreement is. The terms and context of the agreement will determine what we are obligated to do for each other and in what situations as well as how important those responsibilities are.

For instance, in general, when we enter into an agreement, it is understood that each person only commits to be pleasant to the partner when the partner is pleasant to them and when the partner deserves that respect and care.

Therefore, if we determine that our spouse is not treating us properly, and we interpret their actions as demonstration that they do not care about us, we will often think that we should not need to be nice to them.

This is certainly true if we determine that their actions are an indication that they are not a good person, and as a result, we do not have to treat them with respect and compassion.

In a broad sense, there is an understood societal agreement that most of us accept upon ourselves to be helpful and kind to others. The "terms" of the societal agreement may depend on our specific social circles, but it usually includes a responsibility to treat others well even if we have not made a direct agreement with them. However, there are usually built-in limitations to our responsibilities that most societies agree to. It is usually understood that we have limited responsibility toward strangers, "bad people," and to people who have not treated us well. Even the responsibility we do have to be helpful is usually very limited. We are not generally expected to have unlimited time, money, energy, or compassion for others.

Many of our close relationships rely on understood agreements. We do not make a specific agreement with our children when they are born, but when we become parents, it is understood that we are accepting the responsibility to take care of their needs. Even in a marriage, where our responsibilities are based on an explicit agreement that we have made, we often do not spell out what our exact agreement is — we rely on an understood agreement to define our responsibilities.

When we make an agreement, we usually attempt to figure out what the appropriate degree of responsibility should be, and we commit to uphold that. We also try to figure out what is important to us, and we expect the other person to commit themselves to give that to us as long as we commit to give them what they want.

At first glance, it seems that this would be a good recipe for marriage or for any relationship because each person would get what they want and would give the other person what they want.

However, if our responsibilities are limited to what we were ready to commit to, then there will be many limitations. Relationships often require a significant amount of commitment, and while we might be ready to commit to a lot of responsibility, we also often have many strings and limitations regarding how much we are really ready to commit to do.

When our responsibilities come as a result of our commitment, then the importance that is attached to our commitment is only as much as we had committed to. If we had in mind that we would be committed to prioritize our relationship more than anything else, then that would be the amount of responsibility that we would have.

However, if we had in mind that we are ready to make a significant commitment to our spouse, parent, or child, but we are only ready to commit to prioritize our responsibility to them to a certain extent, then the commitment will be limited to the extent that we had intended and communicated.

Moral Obligation as the Source of Our Responsibilities

When the source of our responsibility comes from our moral obligations, then the responsibility is defined by and limited to whatever is considered to be morally appropriate in a given situation. However, where do we get our moral code? Where do we get our ideas about what is right and what is wrong?

If our moral obligations are not determined and defined by any specific objective source (such as the Torah), then it will be unclear what our moral obligations are and how far they go. We will have to rely on a subjective determination of what is considered to be the proper moral code. These ideas often come from a combination of the messages that we receive from those around us (including our parents, teachers, friends, neighbors, and everyone else in society) together with our own inner sense and intuition.

Therefore, the parameters of our moral code are mostly dependent upon the messages that we have received over time, together with what our intuition dictates.

How far do we think and feel that those responsibilities should go? Which people are we obligated to help? Do we have to spend our resources to help others? How much should we be obligated to treat a person well when they are not treating us well? Does the other person deserve respect even though they are acting inappropriately?

Fortunately, most of us live in a society where there is a strong moral code that requires treating others properly. We are strongly encouraged to be pleasant to others and not hurt them. Often, our intuition will tell us, and it is generally accepted, that even when the other person is not treating us so well, we should still try to be "the bigger person" and be nice to them.

However, even though most people would say that we are obligated to treat every human being properly, the moral code of most societies would consider the extent of a person's responsibility to help a stranger to be relatively limited.

Most people would also say that at some point, we would not think that we are morally obligated to be nice to others when they are not being nice to us. There is a strong tendency to think that when others are not treating us well, there is no responsibility for us to treat them well.

There is also a strong tendency to think that we are not obligated to be nice to others if they are not acting as good people themselves.

Our true responsibility to be pleasant to others is based on what the Torah tells us. Therefore, we need to study the Torah so we can discover what the Torah teaches us about our responsibilities.

• CHAPTER 2 •

OUR RESPONSIBILITIES
ACCORDING TO THE TORAH

HASHEM GAVE US A SET of responsibilities about how we should treat others. He did not leave it up to each of us to figure out appropriate moral guidelines. Rather, He gave us the Torah as a guide and a rulebook to teach us right and wrong, and many of those rules and guidelines teach us about how we should act in our relationships.

Most of us have our own ideas about morality, and we may think there is no need for us to learn more about what the proper moral code is. We may not think there is any objective right and wrong, and morality is defined by whatever we determine should be right and wrong, or we may think that even if there is an objective right and wrong, we are the ones who have discovered it, and we do not need further insight.

The Ohr Hatzafun (vol. 1, p. 230, 242) teaches us that even though most people are convinced that they already understand morality, they are often far from the truth. They do not really understand how important it is that we help others, and they do not realize how much we are responsible for helping them.

He also explains that there are objective rights and wrongs when it comes to our responsibilities and that it is important for us to follow the proper guidelines. Hashem gave us the Torah as our guidebook so that we can study it in order to learn about the true objective morality.

There are many laws in the Torah that teach us about our responsibilities to others. They teach us about how we are expected to treat people in general, and they also teach us about how we are expected to treat the people we have a close relationship with.

The Torah provides us with an understanding of the true value of helping others and treating others properly. Torah law includes more responsibilities than we would have thought, and it assigns us responsibilities to more people than we would have thought. Torah law requires us to be nice even to strangers, to be nice even to people who are not such "good people," and to be nice even to people who are not so nice to us.

The Torah's Unconditional Golden Rule: "Love Your Fellow Like Yourself"

According to the *Ohr Hatzafun* (vol. 1, p. 230), the Torah teaches us that our responsibilities to care about others and to help them are much greater than we tend to think (based on our own understanding of what our responsibilities should be), in a number of ways.

The ideals and values that the Torah's responsibilities are based on are different from the ideals and values that we would have without the Torah. These differences lead to a large set of rules and responsibilities. We will now discuss some of these matters.

The Extent of Our Responsibility to Care About Others and to Help Others

Everyone knows that there are certain basic responsibilities to care about and help others. However, when the Torah teaches us about our responsibilities to others, it is much more extensive.

The Torah expresses our general responsibility by instructing us, "Love your fellow like yourself" (*Vayikra* 19:18) and treat them accordingly. Everyone knows this as the golden rule, and we all aspire to live in that manner. However, most people understand this concept in a manner that is different from its true intention.

Most of us would say that our general responsibility to treat others well includes responsibilities such as helping people with their essential needs (like food, clothing, or shelter) and not causing them any physical, emotional, financial, or other harm.

However, when we consider the Torah's full intention when it says to love others as we love ourselves, we will recognize that the Torah is giving us a great responsibility! To love others the same way we would love ourselves means having the same thoughts, feelings, and perspectives about others that we would have for ourselves and to help them in whatever ways we would help ourselves. We are obligated to give to others what they need and whatever we would want to receive if we were in their shoes.

We spend our days thinking, dreaming, planning, and worrying about how we are going to fulfill our needs, desires, and interests. We also spend our time, money, and energy pursuing these needs, desires, and interests. The Torah requires us to care about and to pursue other people's needs, desires, and interests the same way that we would our own.

The Torah does give us a number of guidelines that teach us how to balance the fact that we have limited resources, and we have many responsibilities. We are primarily responsible for caring for ourselves and our families; however, we also have a significant responsibility to help others to the best of our ability. The Chafetz Chaim's *sefer Ahavas Chesed* is dedicated to both teaching us about our extensive responsibility to help others and explaining the guidelines on how to balance our different responsibilities properly.

The Ohr Hatzafun (vol. 1, p. 230) explains that the Torah is teaching us a number of new aspects in our responsibilities that are included in our job of loving others as ourselves.

The Types of Needs That We Are Obligated to Help Others With

We learn from the *Ohr Hatzafun* (vol. 1, p. 230) that we often think our responsibility to help others is limited to whatever needs are considered to be the standard, basic, fundamental needs of survival. When someone is having a hard time fulfilling those needs on their own, then we feel obligated to help them.

However, we generally do not feel responsible for helping other people to fulfill their other needs, interests, or desires. Once we determine that it is not a standard fundamental need, then we often feel that it is not our responsibility to help them.

The *Ohr Hatzafun* quotes the Gemara (*Kesubos* 67b) that says that the mitzvah of *tzedakah* includes the responsibility to help anyone who is missing something that they would really want. This could even include matters that are not standard essential needs. What a person needs for his happiness is a subjective matter, and the Torah teaches us that even the needs that are not essential are also important. We are even responsible for helping others with their needs that would be considered luxuries for most people.

For example, perhaps a man was accustomed to a luxury lifestyle, and it was important to him to have horses running in front of him. If he is no longer able to afford that luxury, it is our responsibility to help him access it. The Gemara brings an example of Hillel, who provided this service for a man who had that need. He ran in front of the man's horses himself!

The Gemara explains that this was Hillel's responsibility because the responsibility of charity is not measured objectively; rather, it is determined based on a subjective standard of what this specific individual needs. The fact that most people would not feel any significant loss when they do not have a given item does not mean that we do not need to be concerned about this person's needs or interests. If this person feels pain when he is missing the luxury item, it is considered to be a real need, and we are obligated to help him fulfill his needs. We learn this from the fact that the Torah says we must provide "sufficient for his lack that he is missing" (*Devarim* 15:8), which means that our responsibility is to help with anything that is a loss to him individually.

The Ohr Hatzafun also explains that many people would not consider it to be anyone's responsibility to be concerned about someone else's spirituality. First, we often do not consider it to be a fundamental need. In addition, we do not feel obligated to motivate, inspire, or convince others to change their ideals or values. When someone is convinced that their values are correct, they are not looking for anyone's help to get them to change their ideals, and we often think that we are not responsible for helping someone who is not interested in our help. However, the Torah teaches us that in a situation where we can help someone to learn more appropriate ideals and values, we are obligated to teach them even if they were not looking for the help. One of the responsibilities to help others in this manner is seen in the *pasuk* that says, "You shall surely rebuke your friend" (*Vayikra* 19:17).

According to the *Ohr Hatzafun*, our responsibility to help others even includes helping them in ways that the receiver would never have expected. Avraham Avinu prepared a feast that was worthy of royalty for random travelers he had invited into his home. They certainly did not expect that! The Ohr Hatzafun (vol. 1, p. 224)) quotes the Gemara (*Berachos* 14a) and the *Reishis Chochmah*, where it is spelled out even more clearly that we are responsible for treating all Jews in a similar manner — as royalty!

Strangers

The mitzvah to love others the same way just as we love ourselves applies to all Jews. This mitzvah teaches us that we are obligated to care for strangers.

Everyone knows we have certain responsibilities toward all other people. However, even though we know that we are not allowed to hurt others, we generally do not think that there is any reason to care about strangers or to help them in any significant manner.

However, the Torah teaches us that not only are we responsible for treating everyone with a degree of sensitivity, but we are even obligated to love them as ourselves. We are responsible for treating others with sensitivity, love, care, and respect and certainly for avoiding being insensitive and acting without love, care, or respect. We are obligated to think about others in a positive manner, to avoid speaking about them in an insensitive manner, and to avoid acting in a hurtful way toward others.

People Who Have Hurt Us

The Mesillas Yesharim (ch. 11) explains that the Torah's laws that prohibit us from taking revenge or even bearing a grudge give us a context for understanding how far our responsibility to love others goes.

He explains that when someone hurts us, we are often upset at them, we may hate them, and we may want to hurt them. We certainly do not feel like we love or care about them or want to help them. He also explains that if we do try to improve our relationship with them, our goal will usually be limited to trying to be less upset at them, not to hate them as much, and not to hurt them. We may even have a goal of trying to care about them somewhat and even to be interested in helping them to some extent. However, the Mesillas Yesharim says it is very unusual to even try to bring a relationship back to the way it was before we were hurt. The way we act toward the other person will usually be with less positivity, and our feelings will certainly be less positive.

However, even though it is very difficult to do, the Torah holds us accountable for doing our best to bring our relationship back to the way it was before the hurt. We need to even work to bring ourselves further than that — to have a true feeling of "love your fellow like yourself" toward that person. That includes a true interest in caring about the other person as much as we care about ourselves and helping the other person as much as we would help ourselves.

The *Mesillas Yesharim* is clarifying that our responsibility to do our best to help others is unconditional. Regardless of who the other person is and regardless of what they have done to us, we are always obligated to do our best to care about others and to help others!

The fact that we are obligated to act with respect, care, and concern even toward those who have hurt us does not mean that we are supposed to let others hurt us and take advantage of us.

The Gemara in *Sanhedrin* (73a) teaches us that we are allowed to and even obligated to protect ourselves from being hurt by others. There are times when we may to even cause harm to the aggressor in order to protect ourselves from being hurt by them. Certainly, we need to create the proper boundaries in our relationships that enable us to be protected from being hurt.

Ideally, even when we are protecting ourselves from harm, we are still obligated to have kindness in our hearts toward the aggressor and we must act toward the other person with as much compassion as we can. In some relationships, this is very difficult to accomplish, but it is important to work toward this goal.

The process of dealing with pain within our relationships can be very complicated, and it is important to get the proper advice and guidance in order to deal with the issue appropriately.

At Our Own Expense

Most people would assume that we are not responsible for giving up much time, money, or energy in order to help others. Helping others is often understood to be necessary only when we have a surplus available to give them. However, we often do not have a surplus of any of these resources; therefore, we assume our responsibilities are limited.

However, the Torah holds us accountable for helping others even when we do not have much of a surplus. The responsibility to give *ma'aser* is one example. Outside of the Torah-observant community, almost no one feels obligated to give a tenth of their earnings to *tzedakah*!

The How of *Chesed*

Throughout Torah literature, we are taught that the way in which we perform *chesed* is significant. The act of helping others is an accomplishment, but the thoughts, feelings, and motivations that go along with the *chesed* are also important. We are obligated to care about and respect others. We are also responsible for sharing in their happiness and in their pain.

When we are helping others, it should be accompanied by positive thoughts and feelings. We should be helping them because we care about them and want to help them. That is a much greater accomplishment than the act of helping alone.

We see from *Chovos Halevavos* (*Sha'ar Habitachon,* ch. 4) that when we help others, our motivation should come from the fact that the Torah gives us a responsibility to help them and not from our own personal interest. *Chiddushei Halev* (*Vayikra* 19:18) explains that the intention of *Chovos Halevavos* here is that even the love we have for our family and friends should not be self-serving; rather, it should be motivated by the fact that the Torah teaches us that we are obligated to love others.

The way we give to others also affects the person who accepts the favor, such as whether they will feel bad about receiving the gift or not. The Rambam (*Hilchos Tzedakah*, ch. 10) teaches us that it is important to do our best to help others in a manner that will help them will feel good about receiving our gift.

Our Great Responsibility to Our Families

Tanna D'vei Eliyahu (27) quotes a *pasuk* in *Yeshayah* (58:7) that says, "From your own flesh you shall not hide (hold back your kindness)." The Midrash explains that the Torah is teaching us that we have a greater responsibility to act with kindness toward those who are closest to us. The fact that we have a significant responsibility to act with kindness to any stranger indicates that we are extremely obligated to act with kindness to our own families.

We are instructed, "Honor your father and your mother" (*Shemos* 20:12). Our responsibility to our parents is discussed in the Ten Commandments themselves! The Torah also gives us a specific mitzvah to tell us that we have a responsibility to revere our mother and father (*Vayikra* 19:3).

The Gemara (*Sanhedrin* 76b; *Yevamos* 62b) teaches us that a husband has a responsibility to give a lot of love and honor to his wife — to "love her as much as himself and to honor her more than himself." His responsibility is to love her as much as himself and to respect her even more than himself!

We have a responsibility to teach our children about the Torah and mitzvos and to help them keep the mitzvos as much as possible. The Chafetz Chaim tells us in *sefer Chomas Hadas* ("*Chinuch*") that doing what we can to make sure that our children keep the mitzvos is a greater mitzvah than almost any other mitzvah, including learning Torah and *davening* to Hashem.

The Importance of Our Responsibility to
Treat Others Well

The significance of our responsibility to help and care about others is a result of the fact that these are very important Torah values.

The Chafetz Chaim begins *Ahavas Chesed* with a quote from the Gemara in *Sotah* (14a) that shows us how much the Torah values kindness. The Gemara highlights the fact that the Torah talks about kindness at the very beginning (when Hashem clothes Adam and Chavah [*Bereishis* 3:21]) and at the very end of the Torah (when He buries Moshe Rabbeinu [*Devarim* 34:6]) in order to teach us the importance of *chesed*.

The Chafetz Chaim adds (introduction to *Ahavas Chesed*) that throughout the Torah, there are consistent messages about our responsibility to act with kindness. One example of *chesed* that stands out is seen in Avraham Avinu's decision (at the beginning of *Bereishis*, ch. 18) to interrupt his private meeting with Hashem in order to help out strangers who were in need. The Torah relates that Hashem had come to "visit" Avraham Avinu, but during the "visit," Avraham Avinu saw a few people who needed his help. Avraham Avinu "left Hashem's Presence" in order to help the people who were in need. Avraham Avinu apparently recognized that helping others is even more important than speaking to Hashem in an intimate manner! The Gemara (*Shabbos* 127a) learns from here that the mitzvah of caring for guests is, in some ways, more significant than speaking to Hashem! This would seem to be an indication that kindness is (at least one of) the most important thing(s) in the world.

In that situation, Avraham Avinu helped his guests in a number of different ways. Not only did he make sure that their essential needs of food and shelter were provided, but he was also personally involved in caring for their individual needs. This really highlights the importance of *chesed* — that it is important to make sure the person's needs are taken care of, and it is also important to be involved in *chesed* ourselves. It is apparently also important to be involved in seemingly mundane matters. We see that Avraham Avinu placed significant value on catering to other people's eating, drinking, and sleeping needs! We might consider these to be menial tasks, but to Avraham Avinu, this is the purpose of life.

Almost every *parshah* of the Torah has examples of the importance of *chesed*. This further proves that kindness is certainly one of the most important principles of the Torah!

There are many mitzvos that obligate us to treat other people properly. These mitzvos regulate every aspect of how we relate to and interact with others. There are laws that regulate our speech, our actions, our thoughts, our finances, and every other area of our lives that affects others. These laws dictate how we should deal with these matters properly.

The Many Mitzvos That Relate to Treating Others Properly

The *Sefer Hachinuch* lists many mitzvos that relate to the way we treat others, such as:

- §33: Honor your father and mother.
- §34: Do not kill.
- §35: Do not act inappropriately with someone else's wife.
- §36: Do not kidnap.
- §37: Do not testify falsely.
- §38: Do not desire that which belongs to your friend.
- §42–45: Treat a Jewish maidservant properly.
- §46: Take care of your wife's needs.
- §63–65: Treat converts, orphans, and widows with sensitivity.
- §66–68: Lend money to those who need it and treat the borrower with kindness.
- §168–177: The laws related to *lashon hara* and *tzara'as*.
- §220–222: Help the poor.
- §224–230: The various laws concerning dealing honestly with money.

These are just a few of the many laws that relate to the importance of treating others with honesty, kindness, and respect. We see that the Torah really values the importance of caring and compassion for others. As we mentioned above, the concept of a requirement to give one-tenth of our income to *tzedakah* certainly highlights to us how important kindness is.

Every interaction with others is regulated by the mitzvah to love others as we love ourselves because the mitzvah is to give them as much as we can. However, the Torah gave specific mitzvos for many of the individual aspects of interpersonal interactions. This emphasizes the importance and significance of each aspect of kindness.

The fact that the Torah gives us so many rules, regulations, and responsibilities related to how we treat others indicates how important these matters are to Hashem and how essential their role is in Torah observance. Some of our responsibilities to treat each other properly were even included in the Ten Commandments!

CHAPTER 3

THE FOUNDATION OF OUR RESPONSIBILITIES IN OUR RELATIONSHIPS

THERE ARE MANY VALUES, IDEALS, and perspectives that relate to the underlying factors that determine what we should be obligated to do to help others. They also determine the degree of importance we should attribute to these responsibilities. Therefore, it is important for us to clarify what the appropriate values, ideals, and perspectives should be.

As we mentioned in the previous section, there are many rules and guidelines in the Torah that relate to our responsibility to help others. They are all based on the Torah's value system. The Torah teaches us about the proper attitudes, perspectives, and values through its stories and halachos. They are the source of why we are obligated to help others and they are the reason why helping others is so important. These Torah values also shape the guidelines of how we are supposed to apply our responsibilities.

Many of our thoughts, attitudes, perspectives, and *middos* also influence our ability to carry out our responsibilities productively. The Torah teaches us about what the proper *middos* and character traits are. When we develop them properly, they will help us carry out our responsibilities properly.

We learn from the Chafetz Chaim's *Ahavas Chesed* (Introduction) and the *Ohr Hatzafun* (vol. 1, p. 243) that most of us think we know all there is to know about *chesed*, so all we need to do is motivate ourselves to act with kindness more often.

In the *Ohr Hatzafun* (vol. 1, p. 243), we are taught that even though everyone believes it is a nice thing to help others, most people consider it to be "beyond the letter of the law" rather than a fundamental responsibility. The Ohr Hatzafun would probably agree that most people do consider it to a fundamental responsibility to treat others with kindness in some situations, such as when it is easy for us to help, and we have no strong reason not to. Certainly, it is forbidden for us to hurt others when we do not have what we would consider to be a good reason to hurt them. However, in a situation where the kindness is difficult for us, or if we think that we have a reason to hurt others, most of us would consider it to be beyond the letter of the law to treat them with kindness.

However, both the Chafetz Chaim and the Ohr Hatzafun explain that our understanding of the importance of helping others is generally very limited, and we also generally do not recognize how far our responsibilities go. This causes us to not value *chesed* properly and to not apply it properly.

They explain that the only way we can understand the true extent of our responsibilities and appreciate the full value of helping others is through studying the Torah. The Torah teaches us the rules and guidelines of how far our responsibilities go. The Torah also teaches us about the context of why we should be helping others. When we understand this context, we will recognize the value of helping others, and that will lead us to be motivated to fulfill our responsibilities to the best of our ability.

The Basis of Our Responsibilities to Treat Others Well

The *Ohr Hatzafun* explains that the Torah teaches us three reasons why it is proper and appropriate to treat others with love and respect:

1. *Chesed* is objectively good.
2. People are special and deserve to be treated properly.
3. It is beneficial for us to treat others properly.
4. Even without a Torah perspective, we would still be aware of all these factors. Everyone agrees that we have a moral responsibility to act with kindness. We also know that people are special and should therefore be treated properly. We also know that it is often beneficial to treat others properly.

However, each of these reasons has a limited reach without a Torah perspective. The Torah teaches us how great *chesed* is in a manner that we could not know or understand without the Torah.

The Torah also teaches us that humanity is far greater than we may realize; therefore, every person deserves to be treated with much more respect than we might think.

We also learn from the Torah that it is much more beneficial for us to act with kindness and compassion for others than we might think.

Each of these aspects of *chesed* is affected by our understanding of the following:

- Who Hashem is, what His greatness is, and what His values are;
- what Hashem's purpose was in creating the world and creating the people in it;
- a human's nature, value, purpose, and mission in This World; and
- what it means to be a good, moral, and ethical person.

The Nature and Greatness of Hashem:
Traits of Kindness

After the Sin of the Golden Calf (*Shemos* 34:6), Moshe Rabbeinu asked Hashem to let him understand Him better. As a result, Hashem revealed His attributes to Moshe Rabbeinu, and what Moshe Rabbeinu "saw" and understood about Hashem was Hashem's attribute of *chesed*. Our best understanding of Hashem and His greatness is that He is a Being of *chesed*.

We are taught (*Tehillim* 89:3) that everything in This World was created by Hashem for the purpose of Hashem doing kindness to His creations. There is no limit to the amount of *chesed* that Hashem does.

We can learn how to understand and relate to Hashem from the Gemara's description (*Shabbos* 133b) of our mitzvah to be like Hashem. The Gemara explains that what being like Hashem means to recognize that Hashem is a God of kindness; therefore, to act with the *middos* of Hashem means to act with kindness.

In *Ahavas Chesed* (Introduction), we learn that the fact that Hashem's essence is kindness and compassion has many ramifications. If we value and pursue kindness and compassion, we are respecting, embracing, and emulating Hashem's ways. He also describes closeness to Hashem as valuing *chesed* and being dedicated to following that path. The opposite is true as well: If we do not value and pursue kindness and compassion, we are disrespecting and rejecting Hashem and His ways.

When we have these perspectives about *chesed*, we will recognize that acting with kindness is one of the ultimate achievements in life. We will also recognize that there is no limit to the kindness that we should do. The same way that Hashem's *chesed* is infinite, so too, our *chesed* should be as much as possible.

The Importance of Every Person

The Ohr Hatzafun says (vol. 1, p. 271) that the way that we treat others is commensurate to the extent that we value them. We generally do not treat the CEO of a company the same way that we would treat the average employee.

The Torah teaches us that we should attribute infinite value to every person. We are each created in the image of God (with a *neshamah*) and with an important mission in life. This teaches us that every person we have a relationship with should be treated with dignity and kindness.

The Tremendous Accomplishment of Caring About Others and Treating Them Well

As mentioned above, we are taught that our responsibility in life (our purpose and mission) is to emulate the ways of Hashem, and the ultimate achievement in life is to "be like Hashem," i.e., to act with His *middos*.

When we apply these fundamental Torah principles about *chesed*, we can realize that the Torah's perspective about the value of *chesed* and the guidelines relating to *chesed* will be very different from secular humanistic values of *chesed*.

From the Torah's perspective:

- Hashem's "essence" and His greatness revolve around kindness.
- The entire world was created by Hashem as an act of His kindness

and for the purpose of bestowing kindness upon the world.

- Our mission (and the measure of our success in life) is to act with *chesed* and to enjoy the benefits of having acted with *chesed*.
- Everyone is created in the image of Hashem, with an eternal soul, and deserves to be treated with a lot of respect.

When we contrast this Torah perspective to the perspective that most of the world has about *chesed*, there is a very significant difference that affects both the importance we ascribe to *chesed* and the guidelines relating to *chesed*.

When our perspective about kindness is not coming from the Torah, then we often will not really appreciate the value of a human being in a significant way. We also do not think of helping others as an important part of our goal, mission, and purpose in life.

Therefore, we will often conclude that even though it is proper and appropriate to help others, our responsibility is very limited. We will think that people are generally important enough that we should be pleasant to them when we can help without much difficulty. However, sometimes, people can be annoying, or they can do things that are hurtful to us, and if we do not recognize the true value of the person, we will not think we are still responsible for treating them properly.

From the Torah perspective, it is clear that there is an enormous value to *chesed*, and we have a great responsibility to act with kindness and compassion. Each person has an eternal soul, and we must treat them accordingly, which means that our responsibility to be nice to others has no limits (other than our limited resources). We should help anyone and everyone as much as we can, no matter who they are and no matter what they have done to us, in any situation.

The *Ohr Hatzafun* (vol. 1, p. 273) teaches us that we are obligated to even treat a person who has done many bad things with kindness and dignity. This is because even such a person still has a *neshamah*, which will always have a lot of value and significance.

When we think, "Why should I be nice to this person if he is not nice to me?" or "Why should I be pleasant to this person if he is not a good person?" we are not thinking about our mission in life and our success in life properly.

Helping others often interferes with the needs, interests, desires, and goals in our lives. It often gets in the way of our pursuit of pleasure and comfort. That often causes us to think of helping others as annoying and as an interference with our happiness and success.

We want our days to be relatively easy and free of stress — any person we interact with who causes us hardship or stress is interfering with our needs, and we will resent that. If we want our spouse or child to be a certain way, then we will be distressed if we see them acting differently than we want them to.

We often pursue pleasure and comfort because of our perspectives about happiness and success. However, if we recognize that our mission and purpose in This World require us to become better people and develop our good *middos*, then we will see that our greatest accomplishments are related to the kindness that we are able to do for others.

When we have this perspective, we can approach the question of "Why should I help you?" differently. We will want to help. We will see that it is in our own best interests to help. Helping others is the vehicle through which we can achieve our goals of being good people and fulfilling our purpose in This World rather than a nuisance that gets in the way of our ability to accomplish our goals.

From a secular humanistic perspective, even if people realize that there is a concept of acting in a moral and appropriate manner, acting with morality is far from the goal of life and is not the main determination and definition of success in life. Therefore, according to this view, it would not make sense for our dedication to others to be a high priority in our lives.

In a situation in which helping others requires us to use our own resources, such as our time, money, or energy, we often consider that we are giving up something of our own in order to help others. We also think giving up something of our own for others interferes with our own success. Therefore, even though we are often willing to give something up to help others, we do not always feel good about it. We are also likely to limit how much time, money, and effort we are ready to sacrifice in order to help others, because we do not want it to interfere with our own success and happiness.

However, from a Torah perspective, caring about others and helping others is good for us as well. When we are helping others, we are really helping ourselves. We are succeeding in fulfilling our mission in life, we are making ourselves into better people, and we are investing in our eternal rewards program.

We are taught by the Midrash on *Rus* (*Rus Rabbah* 5:9), "The poor man does more for the wealthy man than the wealthy man does for the poor man." The Midrash is teaching us that when we help someone, we are actually helping ourselves. The giver benefits more than the recipient.

When we recognize this is true, we will be much more motivated to give our time, money, and energy to others, and we will feel much happier when we do so. However, we can only appreciate the true value of *chesed* when we have the perspectives of the Torah. We will see that our purpose, mission, and success in life are all related to *chesed*. We will also recognize that *chesed* is the description of Hashem's greatness, it is the greatness of humanity, and it is the essence of the Torah.

Hashem Runs the World

Our *emunah* and *bitachon* (in the fact that Hashem created the world and controls everything in it) affect our understanding of our responsibility to help others. This affects how we see the importance of our responsibilities to help others, the guidelines of our responsibility to help others, and the perspectives underlying our responsibilities as well.

Giving without Losing

We learn from the *Kli Yakar* (*Vayikra* 19:18) that many of our decisions about how we treat others relate to how we determine the value of our own physical, emotional, or material needs compared to the importance we attribute to our obligation to care for others. When we think about helping others, we often think, "My time, money, and energy belong to me.

I do not want to give away my resources. I want to use them for myself."

Even though we do feel like it is important to help others, we usually have more value for our own needs and feel it is more important to keep our resources for ourselves than to give to others.

However, the Kli Yakar explains that from a Torah perspective, when we compare the importance of being kind to others to the importance of any material possessions, we will recognize that it is important to prioritize kindness over our other personal needs.

The reality is that all our resources were given to us by Hashem. Therefore, if Hashem tells us to give up our resources for the sake of others, He is entitled to do so. It is important to remember that "our money" is really Hashem's money!

According to the *Mesillas Yesharim* (ch. 22), there is another step that is beyond this basic point. Everything we have was given to us by Hashem, and Hashem had a specific purpose for everything that He gave us. Hashem told us that many of the resources that have been given to us were specifically given to us for the purpose of sharing them with others. From that perspective, it is a lot easier to use our time and money to help others.

The *Mesillas Yesharim* explains further that even after Hashem gives us the resources, even though they are in our possession, in many ways, they are still owned by Hashem, and we are merely guarding them. Therefore, we are not really giving away our own resources — they are really Hashem's.

We also see in the *Mesillas Yesharim* (and *Tur, Yoreh De'ah* 247) an analogy of a situation where a homeowner hires people to help around the house or an employer hires people to help at their company, and he gives them assets of his to use in order to complete the job. It is clear that the employee needs to use those resources in order to fulfill his job. It is not even an act of righteousness for him to not use the resources for his own benefit alone. That would obviously be criminal!

Hashem owns everything in This World, and even though we have ownership over our resources and how we use them, we are really just managers of the money, power, fame, and whatever else Hashem gave us, and our job is to use them in the manner that Hashem intended. Hashem tells us through the mitzvos in the Torah that He wants us to use His resources, which we are managing, in order to help others. With this perspective, it is easier to be able to share our resources with others.

Hashem gave us the responsibility to help others. The reward that we receive from Him for fulfilling our responsibilities will certainly be greater than whatever we are giving up in This World. Therefore, we never lose when we give up something of our own to help others. Hashem promises to reward us both in This World and in the Next World. The eternal benefits that we will receive are much greater than anything we are "giving up" through our *chesed*!

The Torah teaches us that when we give our money to others who are needy, we will not even lose out financially. The Gemara in *Ta'anis* (9a) derives from a *pasuk* in *Devarim* (14:22) that Hashem guarantees us that when we give *ma'aser*, not only will we not lose out, but we will actually gain financially (see *Tur, Yoreh De'ah* 247).

From the Torah perspective, when we give our time, money, or resources to help others, we are not losing out. Rather, giving is the best investment for our growth as human beings, for our service of Hashem, and for the benefits that we will receive in both This World and the Next World.

How to Treat Those Who Have Hurt Us

It is common to think, "Why am I responsible for being nice to a person who has caused me so much harm?" We may think that our lives would have been much better if the other person had not done what they did. Therefore, it would seem justified to hold a grudge against a person who has hurt us.

We also often think, when we find ourselves in a difficult situation, that we should not be obligated to deal with it. These thoughts can come in different variations. We may think, "Why am I responsible for the situation that I am in? I did not create this mess!" We may think it is too hard; we may not be interested in dealing with the situation; or we may doubt our ability to address the situation successfully. In all of these situations, we may be thinking, "I would be ready to work hard to make the best out of the situation if I had chosen it, or if I thought that I could succeed, or if I thought that it was a good situation to be in, but since that is not the case, I am not interested, and I am not responsible."

Trust and Faith in Hashem

When we have the proper faith and trust in Hashem, then we will have a different perspective about all these matters.

The reality is that nobody's actions can affect us. Whatever happens to us was dictated by Hashem. If we are hurt in any manner, it means that Hashem determined that we were supposed to be hurt. The fact that this specific person hurt us does not mean that we would not have been hurt without him. Once Hashem determined that we should be hurt in this manner, it was going to happen to us regardless.

This perspective will make us less likely to feel justified in hurting someone who hurt us. Rather, we will be able to focus on the reality that Hashem determined that we should be in this situation for a reason. We should try to figure out why Hashem gave us the situation and think about what our responsibilities are.

Whatever situation we are in, at every stage of our lives, we should realize that Hashem put us into the specific situation because it is the best situation for us. Everything that happens in our lives is there for our benefit and to further our spiritual success. Therefore, we have no reason to say that because it is hard or because we did not choose the situation, we have no responsibility. Rather, Hashem gave us this situation, and He gave us the responsibility to do our best in this exact situation! Therefore, we can always say that in reality, "This mess is actually the best thing for my success, and this mess is my responsibility."

The *Middos* That Relate to Our Responsibility to Treat Others Well

The Orchos Tzaddikim describes the appropriate character traits that we need to develop, and he also describes the character traits that we need to avoid or at least control.

He teaches us to develop the *middos* of trust and faith in Hashem, humility, generosity, love, compassion, happiness, zeal for good things, honesty, fear of Heaven, and more. He also teaches us to avoid negative *middos*, such as selfishness, arrogance, anger, hatred, not caring about others, jealousy, laziness, stinginess, dishonesty, hurting others with our actions or our words, and a lack of trust, faith, and fear of Hashem.

Each of these *middos* can be broken down into many different specific aspects. For example, someone who is arrogant will often be self-centered, self-righteous, critical of others, and antagonistic toward others.

All of these *middos* play significant roles in our relationships in many ways. Many of them affect what we think about our responsibility and our ability to fulfill our responsibilities to be pleasant to others in our relationships. Developing the positive character *middos* and avoiding the negative ones helps us to feel more obligated to be nice to others.

When we ask, "Why should I treat you well if you do not treat me well?" or "Why should I be nice to you if you are not a good person?" we can answer the question by saying to ourselves that the reason to treat others well is that we want to act properly.

When we dedicate ourselves to trying to be pleasant to others as much as we can, we will need to act with the proper *middos*.

The way we relate to our experiences in life affects how we relate to our responsibilities and how we develop the proper *middos* in our relationships. Our trust and faith in Hashem affect our perspective and our attitude about our responsibilities in all our experiences in life. The *middos* of humility vs. arrogance also have significant effects on our attitude toward our responsibilities in our relationships.

Humility vs. Arrogance and Selfishness

In some cases, we may think, "Why is it my job to help them? If anything, they should be helping me," or, "If they do not listen to me, why should I go out of my way to help them?" These attitudes often stem from arrogance: We think we are "above" the other person and therefore should not be obligated to help them — certainly not when they are not treating us properly. Parents or teachers can certainly have these thoughts about their children or their students. The fact that parents and teachers deserve respect from their children and students is often interpreted in a manner that makes them feel entitled to treat the children and students badly. The attitude of entitlement can make authority figures think they are not responsible for being nice.

Criticism is very closely associated with arrogance. What we think about other people in terms of how much we respect them affects the degree to which we will feel responsible for helping them or being nice to them. When we look down on others, we usually do not feel obligated to treat them well.

When we are arrogant (which we all are to some extent), we often think that other people do things wrong; they are bad or foolish, but we are smart and good. We tend to exaggerate other people's limitations and to minimize our own.

Once we see others as being bad or foolish, we have a tendency to see ourselves as being more important than they are. That allows us to feel justified to "put them down" and hurt their feelings. It also causes us to prioritize our own needs and interests more than other people's and to think we are not obligated to use our time, money, and energy to help others.

Acknowledging the Truth

The truth is that we all have limitations, and we all make mistakes. This fact gives us a context in which the other person's mistakes are more understandable and acceptable. The fact that it is understandable and justifiable does not mean that the person is not responsible for his behaviors, but the fact that the limitations are understandable has a significant effect on our respect for the person.

It is also important to recognize that even if someone's limitations are more significant than ours, that is not a reason to think that we are "above" them. It is certainly not a reason to think that we can treat them with less kindness and sensitivity.

It is not our job to punish others for their misbehavior. It is our job to help others; Hashem will determine whether, how, and when some-one should be held accountable for their actions. We do not have to get involved in that process ourselves, except in situations where the Torah specifically tells us that we need to do so.

Judging Others Appropriately

Some of the biggest deterrents to accepting our responsibility to try our best in our relationships relate to the way we interpret the behavior of the other person in the relationship.

When our spouse, child, or parent acts in a way that we do not ap-preciate, we often get upset, frustrated, or hurt. That will often lead us to think, "If they are not nice to me, why should I be nice to them?" or "If they are not a good person, why should I care about them?"

We have a tendency to vilify others. When we see unhelpful or inap-propriate behavior from another person, we will conclude that the other person is a "bad guy": He must be mean, selfish, lazy, or foolish to have behaved that way. When we view the other person with this perspective, it is natural to think we are not responsible for treating him well and that we are even entitled to hurt him with our words or behaviors.

These attitudes begin with a certain judgment of the other person's behavior. We see something they have done, and we infer their character or feelings about us based on their behavior. The way we judge their be-havior is based on the way in which we understand their behavior. When we witness their behavior and we conclude that the only interpretation of this behavior is that it is coming from someone who is a bad person or who does not care about us, then that is going to be our conclusion: They are bad, and they do not care.

For example, if someone raises their voice at us or strongly criticizes us, we may interpret their behavior as an indication that they are bad peo-ple who do not like us. If this happens repeatedly, then we will conclude that in general, they do not like us, and they are bad people. Similarly, if we ask someone to do something for us, and they do not, then we may think that it must be that they are being a bad person and do not care about us.

If they repeatedly do not listen, then we may conclude that this must really be a bad person and certainly do not care about us.

The reality is that our spouses, parents, children, and siblings are good people who do care about us. However, we each have our own needs, our own personalities, our own priorities, and our own limitations, which lead us to do things that are not always proper and can certainly cause us to do things that are not always in line with what our parents, children, or spouses would like us to do.

The reason we raise our voices at others, criticize others, and do not always help others in the way they request from us is not that we are bad people or that we do not care about our relationships. Rather, we yell because things are hard for us, and we have a hard time dealing with them. Even if we care about others, we may not respond appropriately when our feelings were hurt, when our needs are not met, or when we are in a bad mood. These behaviors are also not an indication that we are inherently bad; rather, we all struggle with these challenges.

When we have this clarity, we are much more likely to recognize our responsibility to help each other. We will know that we are the parent, the child, the spouse, and we are obligated to help each other. Even though we see that the other person is not always doing their part, we understand that they are good people who care about us and happen to have their own needs, interests, personalities, and limitations. The fact that they have these challenges does not mean that we are not obligated to try to do our part.

Negative Misinterpretations

When we hear information about others or when we see someone do something, we often do not know all the relevant information about the situation. Therefore, it is really difficult to accurately assess what is going on.

We have three options concerning how to deal with the fact that we do not have all of the information. We can recognize that are missing information and deal with the situation based on what we do know. Alternatively, we can fill in the information that we do not know in a positive way — or we can fill in the unknowns in a negative way.

The logical thing to do is to separate what we know from what we do not know, to recognize that we only know part of the story and leave the rest in doubt.

However, most of us have a strong tendency to "fill in the blanks" with a negative interpretation of the other person's thoughts, feelings, and behaviors. As we mentioned above, we have a tendency to jump to conclusions that vilify the other person. We conclude that the other person is a "bad guy" — that he is mean, selfish, lazy, foolish, etc. We are less likely to think that the other person is different than we are or that they are struggling.

It is important to understand why this tendency exists. Why is it that we often jump to negative conclusions? There are really two parts to this question: Why do we assume that we know the answer to things that we do not know the answer to, and if we do jump to a conclusion, why is it that we fill in information with a negative twist?

Understanding Human Behavior

As we mentioned previously, the Torah teaches us (*Vayikra* 19:15) to judge others favorably, and we are taught in *Pirkei Avos* (2:4), "Do not judge others until you have reached their place," which teaches us that the way to judge others favorably is to recognize the likelihood that we do not know the whole story and the possibility that if we knew more about the rest of the story, we would have a different opinion about the person.

This advice from *Pirkei Avos* is very true and very helpful. However, our understanding of human behavior also affects our ability to judge others favorably to a significant extent. It affects our ability to implement the Mishnah's advice in a productive way.

Some people think that the reason why people experience feelings of anger, fear, arrogance, intolerance, or jealousy is that they are bad people: They could have and should have avoided these bad feelings, which are inappropriate and unproductive. They certainly think that when someone *acts* in an unproductive and inappropriate way, it is because they are bad people who should have known better and behaved better.

When this is the way we understand human behavior, then when we see someone express these feelings or act in these ways, our natural conclusion is that they must be bad people. If we want to judge someone favorably, we need to be creative. We look at the situation in front of us, and we think to ourselves that the likely interpretation is that the person is a bad person. However, because we want to judge him favorably, we try to open our minds to include even the unlikely scenarios as part of our thought process.

There are many problems with this system. One of the challenges is that if we think that it is likely that the person is a bad person, and especially if we vilify them, then it is hard to be open to other possibilities of understanding what may have happened.

When we see someone who is upset, if we interpret it to indicate they are being mean, a bad person who does not care about us, then it will be hard for us to be convinced that they are different. We may tell ourselves that we need to be open minded, but if we think that most people who are angry are bad, then it is hard for us to be convinced that this situation is different.

Another problem is that when we try to be creative and assume that some unusual thing must have happened, it is usually not true. Rather, the usual thing usually happens. If we want to know how to deal with a situation productively, we need to know the truth. We cannot fix a situation properly and productively without a true understanding of what the real problems and challenges are.

In order to be able to judge every situation in a positive and productive way, it is helpful to understand these two key points:

1. Even great people are still human, and they have limitations and challenges.
2. Even people who love us have their own needs and their own personalities, and they will sometimes do things that are hurtful to us even though they love us.

According to this way of understanding human behavior, when we see someone doing something that is wrong or something that is hurtful to us, we will not have to work to reinterpret anything in order to not vilify them. There will be no reason to vilify them to begin with, because we always knew that even good people have limitations and challenges.

This does not mean it will not be difficult for us to maintain a good relationship with someone who does things that are hurtful to us. There will always be significant challenges in our relationships, especially our close relationships. When we combine the fact that each person in the relationship is emotionally needy (we need love from each other, and we need the other person to focus on our needs) and the fact that each person is naturally more focused on their own needs than the other person's needs, it is likely that we will be hurt sometimes.

However, even if our needs are often not going to be met, and we will often be hurt and upset, we will still be able to deal with our situation in a much better way. We will be able to recognize that our challenges are part of being in a relationship, and the existence of the challenges is not an indication that the other person is a terrible person or a person who does not care about us. Therefore, we will recognize that as a parent, child, spouse, or friend, we are still obligated to do our best to deal with our challenges properly and to be as pleasant, kind, and respectful to the other person as we can be.

Blaming Others

When there are challenges in our relationships, we often focus on questions like, "Who is the bad guy?" "Whose fault is it that we are arguing?" "Who needs to change?" With this thought process, we are either determining who is causing the problem or who is responsible for working on themselves in order to improve the relationship.

Very often, each person thinks that for the most part, the other person is the "bad guy." It is their fault that there is friction in the relationship — *they* need to change. They need to work on themselves, and it is their responsibility to improve the relationship. Each person may recognize that they are not perfect and hold some responsibility for the friction, but for the most part, we tend to think that the main responsibility to change lies with the other person.

Therefore, we are often not motivated to work hard to make changes within ourselves that could be helpful to our relationships. We often do not even feel compelled to change at all. If the other person, who holds most of the responsibility to change, is not working on themselves to change, then we feel that we are certainly not obligated to change.

Once we think that it is the other person's fault, and it is their responsibility to change and not ours, then we will not work on ourselves to try to change.

It is important to get out of the "Who is the bad guy?" and "Whose fault is it?" mentality in order to feel a sense of our own responsibility and not throw it all on the other person. In order to do so, it is helpful to try to understand where the other person is coming from. Why is it that they are acting in a manner that is upsetting to me? The more we understand where they are coming from, the easier it will be to be less critical of their behavior.

When we realize that when there is friction in our relationships and we are upset about what the other person is doing to us but we also realize that the other person is not a bad person and they do not hate us, then we will feel more obligated to work on changing ourselves. When we realize that the reason that they are not doing what we want has to do with their own needs and personality, we will not feel that it is the other person's fault or responsibility.

CHAPTER 4

PROPER ATTITUDES AND PERSPECTIVES ABOUT OUR RESPONSIBILITIES

Responsibilities, Obligations, Expectations, Accountability, and Consequences

When we want to determine the proper attitudes and perspectives regarding our responsibilities in our relationships, we have to begin by analyzing what the concept of responsibility refers to and what our responsibilities include.

The term *responsibility* can be used interchangeably with the term *obligation*. To say that we are responsible means that we are obligated.

Responsibility often comes together with *expectations*. Usually, when someone is responsible for completing or obligated to complete a task, there is someone else involved who expects him to get it done. Often, there is even someone who will hold the person *accountable* for completing the task. They may even create a set of *consequences* to enforce the fulfillment of the expectations.

All our relationships include many aspects of being responsible or obligated, having expectations, and being accountable. We are responsible for treating and obligated to treat every human being with compassion and respect, and we certainly have many responsibilities and obligations toward the people we have meaningful relationships with.

We are all familiar with these terms, but we may not understand and relate to them in a way that encourages us to embrace them productively. We may only fulfill our responsibilities out of an attitude of doing what we are forced to do rather than fulfilling them with desire and passion.

When discussing our attitudes about our responsibilities and obligations in our relationships, there are three different factors to consider:

1. our attitudes regarding giving, kindness, and helping others in general;
2. our attitudes about the specific applications of giving, kindness, and helping others that are relevant in each specific situation; and
3. our attitudes about the fact that we are responsible for helping and obligated to help others.
4. The way we relate to all of these aspects within our relationships will play a big role in the extent to which we fulfill our responsibilities and in how we do so.

A Good Thing

It is helpful to consider whether having responsibilities, obligations, expectations, and accountability is good for us or not. It is also important to have the self-awareness to recognize what our personal attitude is about these matters. Do we think about them as a good thing or not?

When we discuss what is good for us, we are discussing what we value and what we enjoy. Therefore, if we want to know whether we consider our responsibilities in our relationships to be good for us or not, we are asking ourselves whether we value and enjoy them. Do we value and enjoy helping others or giving to others?

The answer will depend on what we value and what we like in general.

The Idealistic View

When we think about our relationships objectively, we are often very idealistic — who does not want to be a great mom or dad, a great son or daughter, or a great husband or wife? We would all like to be selfless, and we want (and feel responsible) to be nice and kind to everyone, especially to our family and friends.

This is especially true in the beginning of a relationship. For example, when we bring our children into the world, we make a commitment to them to take care of them to the best of our abilities. When we get married, we make a commitment to our spouse to take care of them to the best of our abilities. The commitments that we make and the responsibilities that we accept are very real and far reaching, especially because our children and our spouse develop strong expectations of us to fulfill our responsibilities such that it is hurtful and painful when we do not fulfill them.

We often relate to the concept of responsibility in a very positive manner. We use the terminology of being a "responsible person" to describe a person who acts in an honorable and respectful manner, someone who does the right thing even when it is difficult and even when it is not popular. It means that a person has respectable goals and is committed to fulfilling them in all scenarios. It often includes a person who has a good moral and ethical character and whose commitment to their ideals and values motivates them to act in a manner that is appropriate and productive.

Everyone wants to live a life of morality, honor, respect, and dignity. We also recognize that in order to do so, we need to take responsibility and make good decisions even when it is difficult to do so.

Aside from our desire to act with morality and integrity and to live an ethical and appropriate life, we also we want our relationships to work out. We treasure few things more than our close relationships, and strong relationships require that we live up to our responsibilities and expectations.

However, in order to accomplish these goals, we need to focus on the following:

1. giving and not just receiving;
2. doing our best to help others even when they are not treating us so nicely; and
3. dedicating our efforts to our relationships rather than to pleasure and comfort.

When we do our best to prioritize these matters, we are properly fulfilling our responsibilities, and it is likely that we will have successful relationships.

Responsibility vs. Desire

What we want idealistically and what we want practically are not always the same. In the practical day-to-day interactions within our relationships, we are often less idealistic. We are faced with consistent challenges stemming from conflicts between our responsibilities and our desires. Even though we want to be the best husband, wife, father, mother, etc., there are many things that interfere with our dedication and desire to be the best person that we can be in our relationships.

The common denominator behind the factors that interfere with fulfilling our responsibilities in our relationships is the fact that our responsibilities often conflict with what we want to do. As a result, we are faced with a decision whether to do what we want to do or what we are obligated to do.

When faced with these decisions, we would like to believe that we will usually do what we are obligated to do; however, our temptations and desires can be very strong, and we often succumb to our desires despite the fact that it means neglecting our responsibilities. It is often difficult to do what we are supposed to do instead of what we want to do!

The conflicts between what we want to do and what we are responsible for doing not only make it difficult to fulfill our responsibilities but also cause us to resent our responsibilities and make it difficult to embrace them fully.

When we think about the concept of responsibility within our relationships, we often think in the following terms:

- our needs, interests, and desires vs. other people's needs, desires, and interests;
- our needs, interests, and desires vs. our responsibility to help others;
- our needs, interests, and desires vs. our ideals, morals, and values;
- our freedom to do what we want vs. our obligations to do things that we do not want to do; and
- what is easy and convenient vs. what is challenging and difficult.

These are all different ways of saying the same thing: We often think about our responsibilities as interfering with our own desires, which causes us to not be interested in pursuing them.

Wanting to Receive, Being Obligated to Give

One of the main things that interferes with our dedication to being the best person that we can be in our relationships is the conflict between our desire to "receive" versus our desire and responsibility to "give" in our relationships.

When we have a relationship, we hope and expect that the other person will help us fulfill our needs, interests, and desires. We especially expect that the people we have a close relationship with will be there for us to help us achieve our goals. A child certainly expects his parents to help him in any way that they can. A spouse will also generally have similar expectations.

It is very understandable for us to focus on what we are receiving in our relationships, whether it is from our parents, spouse, child, or anyone else. However, the focus on receiving often distracts us from being focused on giving.

The challenge is even greater when we are upset at someone but are still obligated to help them. Whenever our needs are not being met within a relationship, we will be upset, and we often will not be motivated to do our part to be helpful to the other person. If we are not receiving, it is even harder to give.

The Mesillas Yesharim (ch. 11) explains that when we are not treated with compassion and respect, it is emotionally very difficult for us to treat the other person with compassion and respect. It is common for us to feel hurt by the fact that others are not treating us properly, and that makes it difficult for us to treat them properly. This makes it difficult for us to do our job and to be nice to others much of the time.

Wanting Pleasure and Comfort

Some of the most significant challenges to fulfilling our responsibilities arise when our responsibilities conflict with our desires and temptations. We were created with many physical, emotional, psychological, financial, and spiritual needs, interests, and desires, and we are naturally very selfish. We want money, power, honor, and security. We desire many physical pleasures, including good food, nice houses, and other forms of comfort or pleasure. We have a desire for friendships and positive social experiences, and we want to have fun and enjoyment.

In general, we like to do what we want, and we like our lives to be comfortable and pleasurable. We prefer to spend our time, money, and energy on our own needs, interests, and desires rather than using them for the purpose of helping others. Our responsibilities often interfere with our ability to pursue what we desire, and they are often attached to the threat of undesired consequences (which are not comfortable or enjoyable) when they are not fulfilled appropriately. They also often bring pressure and stress.

We have frequent conflicts between our own needs, interests, and desires and our responsibilities to help others. Therefore, it is not surprising that we often do not think of our responsibilities as being good for us. Instead, we think of them as annoying obligations, we try to avoid responsibility, and we resent the responsibilities that we have.

The reality is that it is important for us to take care of ourselves. In order to function productively in life, our needs, interests, and desires must be taken care of. However, we are also obligated to do our part to take care of our children, spouse, or parents. It requires a lot of self-development to become the kind of person who can devote significant amounts of time, money, and energy to giving to others.

A New Outlook: Investing vs. Sacrificing

Fulfilling our responsibilities in our relationships will always be difficult. There will always be a conflict between fulfilling our needs and interests and helping others, and it requires hard work and sacrifice to prioritize other people's comfort and pleasure above our own. However, when we see the positive benefits that we receive from this process, then we will have a totally different outlook.

Dovid Hamelech teaches us, "Those who plant [invest] with tears, will harvest with joy" (*Tehillim* 126:5). He is teaching us that we have to "invest" in order to "profit." An investment requires giving something up in the short term for the purpose of benefiting from that investment over time. In his metaphor, the goal is clear: The farmer wants a successful harvest, and his challenge is to avoid getting distracted by the short-term benefits of pleasure and comfort, which can take his focus away from spending time working hard on planting his field.

Even though it is often difficult to do the right thing, it is important to realize that success and happiness are often the results of hard work. Very often, in the short term, we are not interested in working hard and would prefer the more comfortable route; however, looking at the big picture, we will not achieve happiness and success unless we put in the necessary effort to succeed.

When we appreciate the need to work hard and to give up certain pleasures and comforts in order to attain the long-term benefits that are good for us, we will look at our hard work as something that is good for us. When we work hard for something good and see it as an investment that pays great dividends, we will usually be happy about it. We will be more likely to work hard and give up on the pleasures and comforts, and we will generally do it with a smile and without resentment.

This same message is certainty true in our relationships. When we prioritize our desire for comfort and pleasure over our desire to be helpful, and when we choose to be critical and selfish in our interactions with others, it impacts our relationships in a very negative way and can have a significant impact on who we become as people throughout our lives.

When we recognize the positive impact of our focus on being the best that we can be in our relationships and realize that fulfilling our responsibilities will lead us to true success in our relationships and in life in general, we will appreciate that we need to work hard to fulfill our responsibilities in order to be successful. We will therefore not be distracted by our desire for pleasure and comfort.

A farmer generally understands the benefits of having a good harvest, so he appreciates the need to work hard and to sacrifice in the short term in order to achieve long-term benefits down the road.

However, it is often more difficult for us to value and appreciate the importance and the benefits of being a good person in our relationships, so it is harder to work hard and to sacrifice our pleasures and comforts in the short term in order to accomplish the goal of being a "giving person."

While the concept of responsibility is often understood as a battle between what we want to do and what we have to do, and we usually reserve the concept of responsibility for things we do not want to do but feel obligated to do anyway, there is much more to understand about the nature of responsibility.

When we only see the problems that are associated with accepting responsibility, then we avoid accepting our responsibilities, and we spend our lives resisting them and running from them. On the other hand, when we see the positive aspects of having responsibility — like the farmer — we will accept it and value it as an investment rather than a sacrifice.

Finding Value in Our Responsibilities

In order to find value in our job in our relationships, we need to learn about and to appreciate the positive aspects of our responsibilities. We need to figure out what the benefits are of being responsible and of fulfilling our responsibilities.

However, what we value in our relationships will depend on our general values; therefore, in order to find value in our responsibilities in our relationships, we sometimes have to adjust what our general values are in life.

Jobs, Missions, Goals, and Purposes

The way that we relate to responsibility is very much dependent on what our goals in life are. We all want to have purpose in our lives; it is pretty disheartening to wake up in the morning and not find purpose and value in our lives. Therefore, we are happy to have responsibilities, because they give us a mission, goal, and a purpose in life. The fact that we have responsibilities and we cannot just do whatever we want is an indication that we must have a purpose in life.

However, we do not value every job in the same way; therefore, we do not value all responsibilities in the same way. When we value the job, mission, goal, and purpose, then having the responsibility is a good thing.

The responsibilities that line up with our general values in life will be the responsibilities that we will embrace.

Different Types of Success

We often look up to those people who have power, fame, or financial success, such as a CEO of a large company. The job of a CEO comes with a lot of responsibilities. These responsibilities may cause a lot of stress, concern, and anxiety because of their magnitude, but the CEO is often proud of that responsibility and is happy to have it.

In such situations, we have a positive attitude about our responsibility for two reasons. First, we are happy to accept the negative aspects of having responsibility because the benefits of power, fame, and financial success make it all worthwhile. Second, the responsibilities often represent the fame and power, so having them makes us feel important. We feel good about ourselves when we feel the pressure and stress.

Many people also value tangible religious or moral successes. We can appreciate religious or moral accomplishments, many of which also come with a lot of responsibilities. To the extent that we value our religious observance and our dedication to our moral values, we can also see our responsibilities in a positive manner. The fact that we are obligated to live up to our religious and our moral expectations is something that can give us a sense of significance and purpose. We recognize that the way that we act matters because our lives matter.

The Day-to-Day: Part of True Success

The key to embracing the responsibilities we have in our relationships is to find value and significance in them. We need to find value in being kind to the people around us, especially the people we have a close relationship with.

We generally value being honest, loving, kind, compassionate, and dedicated in our relationships, but that often does not translate into finding value in the day-to-day responsibilities in our relationships.

We all value certain aspects of our jobs, but there are other parts that we do not find value in. Parents may feel accomplished when they take care of the family's finances, but they may not find the same value in cleaning up toys around the house. Parents may enjoy going to their child's graduation, but helping them with their homework is often less than the highlight of the week.

In many societies, there is not much honor associated with spending time with the family. There is certainly not much honor in spending much time working through the complications in our relationships.

The only way to really embrace our responsibilities, to dedicate ourselves to fulfilling them, and to fulfill them with happiness and passion is to value them and to enjoy them. Therefore, we need to appreciate the value in whatever the responsibilities are in our own personal lives, even when on the surface, our particular responsibilities seem to be relatively unimportant.

We can only find value in our daily responsibilities if we understand what true success in life really looks like. We need to recognize that a big part of our true success in life is related to how we treat others throughout our days and throughout our lives.

It is hard to find value in working on ourselves and addressing difficulties in our relationships productively. When we are hurt, it is especially hard to find value in helping others or being nice to them. However, if we are thinking, "Why should I help this person?" then we are not thinking about our mission and success in life properly.

We often think about the difficulties in our relationships as being annoyances that interfere with the needs, interests, desires, and goals in our lives. If we want to have a relatively easy and stress-free day, then any person we interact with who causes us hardship or stress is interfering with our needs, and we will resent that. If we want our spouse or child to be a certain way, we will be distressed if we see them acting differently than we want them to.

However, if we recognize that our mission and purpose in This World is to become better people and develop our good *middos,* then we will see that our greatest accomplishments are related to the kindness that we are able to do for others. When we have this perspective, we can approach the question of "Why should I help you?" differently. We will want to help. It is in our own best interests to help, since it is the vehicle for us to achieve our goals of being a good person and fulfilling our purpose in This World — not a nuisance that gets in the way of our ability to accomplish our goals.

The responsibilities we have in our relationships give us purpose, meaning, and significance. When we dedicate our lives to being a good parent, child, or spouse, then we will have that accomplishment with us throughout our lives. If we neglect our relationships or if we mistreat the other person, then that will be what we have. We will have created a bad relationship with someone we could have loved. We will always live with the results of our efforts. Whatever we make of our relationships is what we will get out of them. We can use that as a motivation to do our best to invest in the relationship from the beginning.

The Gemara (*Shabbos* 89b) demonstrates the value of our daily tasks and the challenges that we experience. The Gemara tells us that Yaakov Avinu had more dedication to the Jewish nation than Avraham Avinu did, because he experienced more difficulties in raising children. *Michtav Me'Eliyahu* explains that his difficulties in raising children caused him to be more dedicated to his children because he experienced more "giving" to his children, and giving develops love and dedication. Rashi and *Tosafos* in *Sanhedrin* (19b) argue about what type of difficulties Yaakov Avinu experienced that Avraham Avinu did not. Rashi says that the Gemara is referring to the fact that Yaakov Avinu had many more children than Avraham did; therefore, he spent more time taking care of his children's daily needs. *Tosafos*, however, says that it refers to the times of crisis that Yaakov Avinu's children faced. According to both understandings, Yaakov Avinu developed love and dedication to his children through the challenges that he faced when taking care of them.

The Source of Our Responsibilities

The value we see in our responsibilities depends a lot on what the source of our responsibilities is. We are often taught that we have responsibilities, but we do not usually spend much time reflecting on what that actually means.

What does the concept of responsibility refer to? What does the concept of responsibility within a relationship refer to? How can we identify the source and the nature of our responsibilities in general and of the responsibilities within our relationships in particular?

When we consider the nature of the concepts of responsibility, obligation, and expectations, we are trying to understand what the underlying concept is that tells us that we have to (or are supposed to) do a task or a set of tasks. What if we do not want to do a certain task? What is it that tells us we need to?

Relationships include many different areas of expectations, responsibilities, or obligations, including legal, moral, civil, social, financial, and spiritual obligations, and it is important to understand the nature of our expectations, responsibilities, and obligations in all these different areas. There are different ways to understand these concepts in a relationship, and how we understand them affects how they are implemented.

The foundation of our expectations, responsibilities, and obligations could be either the necessity to do something in order to achieve a desired result (i.e., positive or negative reinforcement) or a moral or ethical motivation.

Achieving a Specific Result: Positive or Negative Reinforcement

Our responsibilities are often related to positive or negative reinforcement. The nature of the reinforcement will determine how we deal with our responsibilities.

There is often a correlation between whether we perform a given task and the result that will come from performing the task. We will be motivated to perform the task by the desire to achieve a desired result or a desire to avoid negative results.

In this context, the concept of responsibility, obligation, or expectation is based on the reality that there is a relationship between cause and effect, regardless of why the effect will result from the cause. The fact that we want a particular outcome and that doing this particular task is a means of achieving that outcome motivates us to do the task in order to ensure that we get the outcome we are interested in.

We can find many examples of these types of expectations, responsibilities, and obligations within our relationships.

Most relationships contain agreements that are mutually beneficial for both parties. Each party makes a commitment to help the other, and when each person fulfills their commitment, the other party is likely to fulfill their commitment as well. These commitments can be described as responsibilities, obligations, or expectations, and they can be related to the responsibility to help each other in many different ways.

When we are thinking in terms of achieving the results that we desire, then our commitments will be based on the fact that if we want the other person to give us what we want, we need to give them what they want.

Bartering Responsibilities in a Relationship

Many relationships, such as a marriage or business partnership, can be transactional. Each party has a goal and an interest in the other person helping them, and they do what they must in exchange for that help. In order for a wife to receive what she wants from her husband, she commits to help him with what he wants from her. The employer agrees to pay the employee in order to benefit from the work that the employee will do for him. In these situations, they are "bartering" responsibilities.

In this context, each person can think of their obligations, responsibilities, and expectations as tasks that they would rather avoid but are necessary in order to achieve the result they want — receiving the desired benefits from the other person. Since the goal of the commitment is not coming from attributing a value to the task itself but is just a means of receiving the benefits that the other person will provide, it is unlikely that the task will be enjoyed or appreciated.

This mindset reinforces the perspective that responsibilities are a matter of doing what is necessary even if is not what we want to do.

As a result, many employees have negative feelings about their jobs. They work because they feel like they are forced to do it, but not because they want to do it. People can have the same feelings about any of their responsibilities in their relationships. The same perspective can apply to a spouse, parent, child, or any other person in a relationship.

Responsibilities Imposed by Authority

When we are obligated or expected to do something, there is often someone or something making us obligated or expected to do it. Therefore, how we relate to the person or being who is creating our responsibilities or the one who is holding us accountable affects how we relate to our responsibilities as well.

In many relationships, responsibilities are "imposed" on the other person. There is often someone who is in a position of authority, who creates a system of responsibility, obligations, expectations, and accountability. Therefore, the way that the authority figures in our life have taught us about our obligations, expectations, and accountability will have a strong influence on how we relate to them.

These concepts are often understood in terms of someone who is *superior* and someone who is *inferior*. Responsibilities can be understood as menial tasks that we would rather avoid, and they are only done because they are imposed by others. Having such responsibilities can create a sense of being inferior and less than others. This perspective certainly strengthens the concept of responsibility as a battle between what we want to do versus what we have to do.

In many cases, one person can hold a lot of power over the other person in a relationship. One person might need the other person to help them pay their bills, to feed them, and to take care of many of their needs. People need each other's love and emotional support. A parent, a spouse, or an employer can certainly hold a lot of power over their child, spouse, or employee.

The fact that one person has so much power over the other can create an unhealthy concept of responsibility, expectations, and accountability. Power can be misused if it comes together with bad *middos*. If the person with the power is selfish, arrogant, angry, manipulative, or narcissistic — or has low self-esteem — it can lead to a misuse of power in many forms.

When a person misuses their power, they can become demeaning or abusive to the other person in the relationship. The abuse can take place verbally, emotionally, financially, psychologically, or physically.

In addition to the bad *middos* that can certainly lead to abuse of power, there is also often a misunderstanding about what the "true rights" of authority entail. People often believe their authority as a parent, teacher, employer, or spouse gives them justification to treat others in a manner that is objectively abusive and unjustified but that in their minds is normal and appropriate.

The authority figure may think of themselves as being entitled and deserving of the right to control, manipulate, or criticize for various reasons. Sometimes, they may see themselves as being superior. In other situations, the authority figure thinks they are entitled to criticize or control because they need to act in that manner in order to do their job of teaching the child or student or of managing the employee's duties. At times, a parent or a spouse will feel entitled to control or mistreat the other person if they feel like the child or the other spouse has been bad or hurtful to them; therefore, it is okay to not have to treat them nicely.

Abuse is intertwined with responsibility, obligation, accountability, and expectations. An authority figure will communicate to a child, student, or employee that they have responsibilities, obligations, and expectations and that they will be held accountable for fulfilling them. If this communication is handled in a way that indicates they are inferior or less entitled than the authority figure, it will create an impression that responsibilities and obligations are a means by which a powerful and entitled person exerts control over a weaker and inferior person to get them to do things for them.

A More Productive Perspective

Obligations and expectations can be used in a positive manner. First, they can be used as a tool to help us to develop into the best and most productive person that we can be. When a child takes responsibility to learn how to spell or to read, this helps them develop skills that they need for life. An employee who takes the responsibilities of their job seriously and realizes that they are obligated to do their job well will be more likely to perform their duties well, and as a result, they are more likely to keep their job and be successful in their career. Even though it is possible to develop the skills or to do our job productively even without taking responsibility, such as because we enjoy it, we generally will not do it as well. We will often lose our motivation and interest over time.

Second, we can think about the correlation between a person's value and the degree of responsibilities, obligations, and expectations that are placed upon them. When someone is in an important position in their family, company, or society, they obviously will have a high degree of responsibility, and the expectations upon them will be significant. They will be held accountable for the job that they do, and there will be ramifications for them if they do not do a good job.

All people are important, and our job in This World is important. Therefore, we have great responsibilities. We are expected to work hard to fulfill those responsibilities, and we will be held accountable if we do not put in that effort. If there is an authority figure in our lives who has the proper appreciation of our value, and they hold us accountable for working hard in order to develop the perspectives and the skills that we need in order to be successful, they are doing us a favor.

The same is true within our relationships. We all have important jobs to do in our relationships. We are obligated and obligated to do our jobs properly, there are consequences when we do not do our jobs properly, and we will be held accountable if we neglect our jobs.

When an authority figure creates a set of expectations with the child's, the student's, or the employee's best interests in mind, their goal will be to help to create the success that is in the best interests of the other person.

When they hold the other person accountable, it is as a tool to encourage hard work, and the goal of hard work is the other person's success.

We are sometimes in a position to create responsibilities (including expectations and accountability) either for others or ourselves. Sometimes, we need to explain to someone else how to relate to their responsibilities, and other times, we need to deal with our own responsibilities. In all of these situations, it is important to look at responsibilities and accountability as means of and motivations for succeeding rather than as an annoyance and a system of control.

When a system has been created by someone else, we cannot control their attitudes or their implementation. In those situations, it is important to try our best to use the system as a means of succeeding. But we also need to be aware of the challenges that come along with authority that is critical, condescending, controlling, manipulative, or abusive, and we need to protect ourselves from this behavior. From a Torah perspective, we have a right and a responsibility to protect ourselves from being harmed by others. At the same time, we are not free from our responsibility to consider the other person's needs to the degree that is reasonable in each given situation. With the proper guidance, we often can navigate these difficult situations in a manner in which we will be protected from being hurt and can have a productive relationship as well.

One of the pitfalls in a situation in which we have responsibilities that are created by another person is that we may develop the mindset that we are only doing our job in order to achieve a positive result or avoid a negative result. This can hold us back from looking to find meaning and significance in the job itself.

Moral or Ethical Motivation

When moral or ethical factors are fueling our desire to fulfill our responsibilities, then we can have a good feeling about our involvement in the responsibility itself. We can do our job because we value the job.

Chovos Halevavos (introduction to *Sha'ar Avodas HaElokim*) explains that we have many moral or ethical responsibilities and obligations, and we are expected to fulfill them regardless of whether any reward or punishment is attached to our fulfillment.

Furthermore, according to *Chovos Halevavos*, the concept of responsibility is closely related to the concept of *seichel* (intellect). The recognition of our responsibilities in life is a sign of wisdom and good judgment.

Rav Chaim Shmuelevitz (*Sichos Mussar*, ch. 20) adds that recognition of responsibility is a sign of true wisdom, and the lack of acceptance of responsibility is a sign that we are missing that wisdom.

This perspective includes the first approach to responsibility: When there are desired results that are attached to a specific behavior, it is a sign of wisdom to behave in a manner that will achieve those results. However, Rav Shmuelevitz seems to be referring to our moral obligation to fulfill our responsibilities. It requires wisdom to recognize with clarity that we have moral and ethical responsibilities.

Determining How We Relate to Our Responsibilities

Everyone understands that people are obligated to lead moral and ethical lives. We all feel it intuitively, and we attempt to live our lives according to a moral and ethical code.

However, it is important to understand what it means that we are morally or ethically responsible for doing something. Why do we have to do what is moral or ethical? What is the logic behind our responsibility to act in a moral and ethical manner?

The Chovos Halevavos and Rav Chaim Shmuelevitz said that our responsibilities are a reflection of our *seichel*, but what does that mean? If we do not want to act with morality, why should we?

There are many perspectives about why we should feel obligated to act with morality, and each source will affect the degree of our commitment to act with morality. Therefore, it is important to understand the Torah's perspective about why we are obligated to lead moral and ethical lives and about what the benefits are of living a moral and ethical life.

The Positive Benefits of Responsibility in Our Relationships

From a Torah perspective, leading a moral and ethical life is both a responsibility and an opportunity.

Our responsibilities and our obligations are based on a true understanding of God, a true understanding of ourselves, and a true understanding of our purpose in This World.

The way in which we understand Hashem, or at least the way in which we relate to Hashem, is that He is the paradigm of all the proper moral and ethical *middos*. That is how we relate to Hashem and to His greatness. As humans, we each have a *neshamah* that has the same nature as Hashem. Therefore, we relate to our *neshamah* as an embodiment of all the proper moral and ethical *middos*.

These character traits of Hashem (and of our *neshamah*) are proper and appropriate due to an objective, fundamental truth.

Hashem created us for a reason, and He has given us great opportunities. Together with the opportunities that Hashem has given us, He has also given us significant responsibilities.

Chovos Halevavos (introduction to *Sha'ar Avodas HaElokim*) explains that our responsibility to fulfill what Hashem says is based on an innate truth that dictates that we are obligated to be grateful to Hashem for what He has given to us. Part of our responsibility of gratitude is to listen to Hashem when He tells us that we must fulfill certain responsibilities.

Our purpose and job in This World require us to act with the *middos* of Hashem. When we appreciate how much we were given and how much opportunity Hashem has given to us, then we can realize that our opportunity also comes with a significant responsibility and obligation as well. The fact that Hashem made the entire world in order to give us the opportunity to do our job and to receive the ultimate reward creates a tremendous obligation and responsibility for us to act in the proper way and to do our job.

From a Torah perspective, *chesed* is one of our greatest responsibilities and one of the greatest human achievements. When we appreciate that, we will be motivated to treat others with kindness and compassion.

Combining Love and Responsibility

In order to be able to treat others properly on a consistent basis, we need to love and care about others, and we need to feel the responsibility to help others.

We often avoid accepting responsibility in our relationships because it comes together with many difficulties and challenges. Responsibility often carries with it pressures, stresses, guilt, and shame. It also often comes along with a commitment to give of our time, energy, and money.

When we love someone and care about them, then we are much more eager to accept the responsibilities in the relationship because we feel good about working hard to care for the person we love. Therefore, even though the responsibilities may come along with the same challenges and pressures, we are usually more ready and open to embracing those challenges. On the other hand, in a situation where we do not have positive feelings for the other person, and certainly when we have negative feelings toward the other person, then we are more likely to resist accepting the responsibilities. If we are forced to accept them, we will often resent the hard work and the pressures that come along with them.

The Importance of Responsibility and Commitment in Our Relationships

Rav Shlomo Wolbe (*Kuntres Chassanim*) explains that commitment and responsibility are necessary both for the overall health of our relationships and for the day-to-day experiences of our relationships.

In order to maintain our relationship in general, we need to make a long-term commitment, and we need to feel obligated to keep it. If we think that we are only responsible for staying in our relationship as long as we feel motivated or as long as we are "in love," then our relationship or marriage will not last very long.

So too, in the day-to-day matters in our relationships, we need to recognize that we are responsible for being nice to each other even when we are not happy with each other. Otherwise, we will often feel justified to not be pleasant to each other.

Not by Love Alone

When a child is born, we feel endless love. We think and feel, "I love him so much! I will always love him, and I will always do anything for him." It may seem that our love will motivate us to always do our best to give our child whatever we can throughout our lives.

Similarly, when we get married, we often think and feel that we will do whatever we can for our spouse throughout our lives.

When these relationships begin, we often feel a lot of love for each other, and it would seem to be reasonable to rely on our love as motivation to take care of each other properly.

However, Rav Wolbe (*Kuntres Chassanim*) teaches that we need to be aware of the reality that at some point in the relationship, we are not going to feel so much love and we will lose a lot of our motivation to be helpful to each other.

The Mishnah tells us that "love that is dependent on a specific matter" will not last (*Pirkei Avos* 5:16). Therefore, Rav Wolbe warns us to not rely on love alone to be the main motivating force to care about others properly in our relationships.

He explains that even though love is an important component of our relationships, the feeling of love is not always going to be there, even in relatively good relationships. No couple feels love on a constant basis. Feelings of love come and go. They are sometimes stronger and sometimes weaker, and sometimes, we will be angry or upset with each other. Therefore, love is not reliable enough to use as the basis of our motivation to do our jobs in our relationships. When our commitment to each other is based on our feelings of love alone, then our dedication and commitment will come and go all the time.

Instead, Rav Wolbe encourages us to focus on our responsibilities in our relationships because when we commit ourselves to live up to our responsibilities, we are more likely to remain consistent in our relationships. If our commitment is based on a sense of responsibility, that may keep us committed to the relationship even when the feelings of love are not present.

Reliable Responsibility

We are obligated to do our job in our relationships even when we do not want to. There are times when we are not motivated to do our job, and there are times when we do not even feel responsible for doing our job, but we still need to do our best.

Rav Wolbe (*Kuntres Chassanim*) tells us that we need to prepare for the highs and lows of marriage, and we need to make a commitment that we will stick to the marriage even during the times when we are not feeling great about the relationship.

There are times when it is appropriate to consider ending a marriage because people need to be happy in their marriage, and marriage needs to be a productive aspect of a person's life. However, when we are committed to working on our marriage, it is often possible to create a positive, productive, and healthy relationship with our spouse despite the challenges that exist in the relationship.

We need responsibility and commitment to do our job in order to handle the daily experiences in our relationship properly and productively.

To whatever extent we think we should be responsible for being kind and helpful to our spouse, we can commit ourselves to try our best to live up to those responsibilities to the same extent, and vice versa.

Therefore, responsibility is only reliable to the level at which we feel the responsibility and commit to living up to it.

Bearing the Yoke

We are taught, "It is good for a man to bear the yoke in his youth" (*Eichah* 3:27). Rav Wolbe (*Kuntres Chassanim*) quotes a *midrash* that explains that this *pasuk* is referring to the yoke of marriage. Marriage comes together with responsibility, and it is necessary for our wellbeing for us to carry that responsibility. Rav Wolbe explains that the responsibilities of marriage include doing our best to fulfill each other's needs as much as we can.

Knowing that we are responsible for being kind and helpful does not automatically mean that we will commit ourselves to being kind and helpful. Similarly, even if we are committed to being kind and helpful, this does not mean that we will live up to our expectations. However, we have to do our best to recognize our responsibilities, commit to those responsibilities, and execute our responsibilities.

• CHAPTER 5 •

ACCEPTING RESPONSIBILITY FOR
OUR MISTAKES

Blame vs. Responsibility

When we have fights or friction in our relationships, such as between parents and children or between spouses, and feelings get hurt, the parties involved want to know how the problem happened. They often ask, "Whose *fault* was it that feelings were hurt?" or "Who is to *blame* for the problems that exist or have existed in the relationship?"

A similar way to ask these questions is, "Who was *responsible* for having created the problems?" and "Who is *responsible* for fixing the problem in the future?"

There are three parts to taking responsibility in our relationships:

1. taking responsibility for having created the problems that have existed in our relationships in the past,
2. taking responsibility for having created the problems that currently exist in the relationship, and
3. taking responsibility for dealing with future problems in the relationship.

It is important to analyze what we mean when we say that we are accepting *blame* or responsibility for what we have done, or "The problems that have occurred are my *fault*," or "I am *apologizing* for what has happened."

These terms all relate to how we understand the mistakes, limitations, and bad decisions that we make in our lives. They also relate to how we understand why we hurt people we have a relationship with, whether through doing things that they do not want us to do or through not doing things that they want us to do.

They also relate to how we understand what the ramifications of those mistakes should be. Should we be punished for our wrongdoings? If so, who should carry out the punishment? Do we lose our right to be treated with sensitivity and kindness?

A Typical Perspective on Mistakes and Apologies

We may think that our mistakes, limitations, and bad decisions indicate that we are "bad people" and that we do not care about our spouse, child, or parent.

The reason why we may think in those terms stems from how we understand what causes us to do things that are not proper or helpful to others.

Sometimes, we think the only reason why someone would act improperly is that they are a bad person and do not care about doing the right thing, or we think the only reason why someone would hurt a person they have a relationship with is that they do not care about the other person. We may also think there is never a good reason why someone would not care about doing the right thing or about helping others.

According to that way of thinking, when we act improperly, there is no good reason for it, and apparently, we do not care about doing the right thing. When we are not nice to those who are close to us, it is not for a good reason; rather, we must not care about our spouse, child, or parent.

Therefore, we often think that when someone makes bad decisions and does things that are wrong or hurtful to others, they do not deserve to be treated in a caring and respectful manner. They should lose the right to be treated well. They deserve to be punished and to be treated in a negative manner.

This line of thinking often goes together with the understanding that when we make bad decisions, it is for no good reason, and we only make these decisions because we are bad people. Therefore, it may feel justified to punish the other person for his bad behavior.

The above perspectives shape how we understand responsibility, blame, and fault — and their consequences — in our relationships. When we have a problem in a relationship, we will approach the issues of determining whether we were at fault and whether we should take the blame in the context of these perspectives.

We will think of an admission of fault or responsibility as an admission of being a bad person and that there was no understandable reason for our actions other than the fact that we are bad. We are also saying that we do not care about our child, parent, or spouse, and hurt them for no understandable or justifiable reason.

We also think that we deserve to be punished and treated without love and respect. In this context, we also think about apologies in the same way: By apologizing, we are admitting that we were bad for no reason, and we are opening ourselves up for punishment that we deserve. It also often seems to mean that we are accepting the responsibility to fix the problems in the relationship on our own.

An Improved Understanding of Mistakes and Their Ramifications

Even "good people" who care about their spouse, child, or parent make mistakes. They have limitations and make bad decisions.

We each have our own personalities and our own limitations, and we are far from perfect. We have character flaws that we need to work on, and we have needs, interests, and desires that interfere with our ability to make proper decisions. We often do things that are hurtful to the people we love because of our own needs, interests, and desires.

It is not easy to develop ourselves to the extent that we will not have negative *middos,* and it is difficult to develop the self-control that is necessary to overcome them all.

When we make bad decisions and do things that are wrong or hurtful to others, we do not lose the right to be treated in a positive manner, and we do not deserve to be punished or treated in a negative manner. There are two reasons for this. First, we are all human, every person is special, and we all deserve to be treated with respect and kindness. Second, everyone makes mistakes. It is really difficult to do everything right, and the fact that we make mistakes does not mean we are not trying to do what is right. Therefore, there is no reason why our mistakes should lead someone to not treat us properly. There is an understandable reason for our mistakes, and punishment is not justified.

Once we realize that everyone makes mistakes and it is normal for us to also make them, then admitting to a mistake just means we are admitting that we are human. Taking the blame and the responsibility means we recognize that we did have the ability to make a better decision, but it does not mean that we accept full responsibility to fix the problem or that we accept being treated without respect, because we did not do anything to give up the right to be treated properly.

Why We Avoid Taking Responsibility for Our Mistakes

We often prefer to avoid taking responsibility in our relationships. We do not like to take responsibility for having created the problems that we have had in the past or the problems that currently exist in our relationships. We also do not like to take responsibility for dealing with the future challenges that will exist in the relationship.

We would prefer to blame the other person for the challenges that have been created, and we would prefer for them to take the responsibility for problems that we will face in the future.

The Pain of Accepting Responsibility

The reason why we try to avoid accepting responsibility for having created the problems in our relationships is that it is often painful and uncomfortable to do so.

How we relate to our mistakes plays a big role in how uncomfortable and painful it is to accept the responsibility. If we relate to our responsibility properly, it is easier to accept the responsibility, and acceptance is more likely to happen.

The typical form of accepting responsibility can be very uncomfortable and very painful; therefore, we do our best to avoid accepting responsibility for our actions.

When we have friction in our relationships and face questions about how the problem happened, whose fault it was that feelings were hurt, whose job it is to fix the problems, and "Who is the one who has the problems that need to be fixed?" we are often also asking whether we are "good people" or not and whether we are worthy of respect, care, and concern or not.

When we put all these thoughts and feelings together, it is clear why we so often run away from accepting responsibility or blame or from admitting that the problems were our fault to a significant extent. The fact that it is overwhelming and painful to accept the blame makes it more likely that we will deny our responsibility.

A Healthier Understanding of Our Mistakes

If we have a more appropriate understanding of our human limitations and mistakes, then we will relate to responsibility in a more productive manner.

Mistakes are part of being human. Every person's individual nature, personality, and experiences come with their own set of challenges. It is our job to do our best to deal with our challenges in as productive a manner as possible, but realistically, we are all far from perfect.

With this perspective, we will be able to recognize that having limitations and making mistakes does not make us bad people. We can also recognize that our limitations can cause us to hurt the people who are close to us even if we really care about them.

Once we recognize that we are not compromising ourselves by admitting that we have done something wrong, then it is not so hard to admit our mistakes. We will be able to tell our spouse, our children, or our parents the following:

1. I recognize that what I have done has caused you pain;
2. I recognize that I could have worked harder to try to be more sensitive to your needs so that I would not have caused you that pain;
3. I feel really bad that I caused you that pain; and
4. I will do my best to make sure that I will not do it again.

We will be comfortable because we are merely admitting that we made a mistake, which is something that we all do. It does not mean we are fundamentally bad or uncaring.

The Complications That Accompany Acceptance of Responsibility

The questions about responsibility that relate to admitting to our mistakes would be hard enough to deal with on their own. However, these questions about responsibility often come together with other aspects of emotional pressure as well.

When we have friction in our intimate relationships, we often start to wonder, "Do you love me?" and "Do you respect me?" These thoughts can be very painful. It is painful for us to think that our spouse does not give us the kind of care, love, or respect that we want, need, and expect.

There are also often many fears that come to our minds, such as "Is our marriage going to last?" "What if we shouldn't have gotten married to begin with?" "What am I going to do if this relationship does not work out? How will I take care of everything that my spouse used to take care of?"

These thoughts are very much related to taking responsibility for the problems in our relationships. When we think that our spouse, parent, or child does not respect us or does not care about us, one of the ways in which we cope with our pain is to blame it on the other person. It would certainly be painful to blame our own pain on ourselves and to think that we brought about our own pain.

Our fears can lead to a similar reaction. When we are concerned about what is going to happen to us, such as when we are concerned about the future of our relationship, we often try to blame others. We do not want to think that we were the ones who messed ourselves up. We would prefer to think that it was someone else's fault.

There is also the element of guilt that we may try to avoid. When we struggle with our important relationships and there are others who are getting hurt through our behavior, we often feel a lot of guilt. We do not like to think that we caused our marriage to fall apart or our family to break apart. We do not want to think that we are to blame for our children's pain or our parent's or spouse's pain.

Therefore, we are motivated to push off the responsibility to someone else and to think that it was predominantly their fault, and not our own.

Self-Deception

We do not like to take the blame for the problems that exist within our relationships, and we do not like to take responsibility for fixing the situation, either.

Rav Chaim Shmuelevitz (*Sichos Mussar*, ch. 20) says that it is part of human nature to try to avoid taking responsibility for our wrongdoings. He says that we are all motivated to push off our responsibilities, and we generally work very hard to push away responsibilities and their ramifications.

He explains that one of the ways in which we "push away" our responsibilities is through justifying our actions. We justify them to others, to make them think that our actions were appropriate. We also justify our actions to ourselves, and we convince ourselves that our actions were appropriate. In order to justify our behaviors to ourselves and others, we often have to deceive others, and we often also have a lot of self-deception.

Rav Chaim Shmuelevitz highlights how much self-deception exists in This World. He quotes a *midrash* that says that even Kayin believed he was justified in having killed Hevel. When Hashem asked him why he killed his brother, he said, "It is not my fault!" To be able to justify cold-blooded murder is incredible. The fact that he found a justification shows us that when we are motivated, we can deceive ourselves and justify anything!

Closing Blessing

The extent of the shalom in our relationships is determined by Hashem. Let us merit that Hashem will send us continuous blessings in all of our relationships. Let us also do our best to fulfill our responsibilities in our relationships and to make our relationships productive. And let us be blessed to see the effects of our efforts.

– PART 3 –

FINDING CLOSENESS IN OUR RELATIONSHIPS

INTRODUCTION

IN AN IDEAL WORLD, WE would always feel the need, the desire, and the responsibility to do our best to make all of our relationships as good as possible, and we would have the ability to do so. We would love and respect everyone. We would have the best and most positive thoughts and feelings about others, and we would always treat others with kindness, compassion, and respect. Certainly, our most meaningful relationships would involve nothing other than positive experiences. Our relationships with our spouses, parents, children, and siblings would be among our most important priorities in life. They would be a source of happiness, comfort, safety, encouragement, and peace of mind for us throughout our lives.

However, in the real world, our relationships are very different. Even though they are often a source of great benefit to us, at the same time, we have many challenges and problems even in our closest relationships. Our closest relationships are often the greatest sources of stress, anger, pain, sadness, and unrest. Unfortunately, in many families, there are parents and children, siblings, and spouses that are angry with or are distant from each other for long periods of time.

We might assume that we would be extremely motivated to do our best to deal with conflicts in our close relationships productively and to attempt to improve our relationships. However, surprisingly, we often do not even feel like we want or need to work on improving these relationships. As a result, friction and distance can remain in the family without anyone expressing strong interest or feeling a strong sense of responsibility to improve the situation.

When challenges present themselves, we often lose the desire and the confidence to improve a relationship. When we feel angry at the other person or distant from them, we do not feel the desire to be close to them, and we do not feel confident that we can develop positive feelings for them again. The fact that we often lose the sense of responsibility to improve the relationship certainly makes it unlikely that we will be able to deal with the conflict productively.

As humans, we are emotional beings, and it is part of our nature to be hurt by what other people think about us, say about us, or do to us. It is also part of our nature to develop negative feelings toward the people who hurt us. We often get angry at them, we hate them, and we bear a grudge against them. We might even look to take revenge against them and to hurt them.

When we feel hurt and angry, we will often ask ourselves a number of questions: "Do I want to improve my relationship?" "Do I need to improve my relationship?" "Am I obligated to try?" and "Can I succeed?" We are often unsure what the answers are. We may have conflicting feelings about the issues, and we may switch from one feeling to another.

These are essential questions we must ask ourselves. It is important to look into them because how we think about these matters will determine the path we will take to deal with the challenges and conflicts within our relationships.

We will only be motivated to work on our relationships if we feel like we need our relationships to improve, we want them to improve, we are obligated to improve them, and we are capable of improving them.

Our relationships will obviously be much healthier if we work on them, so we need to develop the proper motivation to make that happen. Therefore, it is important to learn how to develop a desire for them to improve, to learn how to recognize that we need them to improve, and to realize that we are obligated to make them work and that we are capable of making them work. We also need to learn how to make them work.

The Torah educates us about all of these matters. The objective of this section of the book is to study the Torah's lessons that clarify our goal in our relationships — namely, developing the commitment, compassion, and devotion that can lead us to feel unconditional love in our relationships — and that offer guidance for dealing with the challenges that present themselves within our relationships.

• CHAPTER 1 •

UNCONDITIONAL LOVE AND COMPASSION

THE TORAH TEACHES US THAT we need to have unconditional compassion for others and to feel a connection with others. However, there are many times when our relationships are complicated and difficult. How can we be responsible for feeling compassion and connected in all situations, despite the challenges in our relationships?

The Importance of Unconditional Love and Compassion

We can learn many lessons from the laws of the Torah. We can learn what our responsibilities are, what our capabilities are, and what the proper and productive approach should be to fulfill our responsibilities. These lessons also affect how we should think about ourselves when we do have negative feelings toward others.

However, our ability to learn the proper lessons from the mitzvos of the Torah depends on our ability to interpret what the mitzvos are and to extrapolate the proper messages from our understanding of the Torah and the mitzvos. Therefore, we need to study the Torah carefully and to learn the appropriate laws and lessons.

The Torah teaches us that we are not allowed to hurt others in any manner ("Do not cause pain to another," *Sefer Hachinuch*, §338). It also teaches us that we are not allowed to feel hatred ("Do not hate your friend," §238), bear a grudge (§242), or take revenge (§241) against anyone. The Torah goes so far as to say that we have to love every Jew as we love ourselves ("Love your fellow like yourself," §243).

The *Mesillas Yesharim* (ch. 11) clarifies that the Torah is telling us that these same halachos apply even with regard to people who have hurt us. We even have a responsibility to do our best to love them!

Torah law seems to hold us accountable for loving everyone unconditionally!

The fact that the Torah teaches us that we are obligated to have unconditional love for others means that we are capable of doing so. Apparently, it is possible to love someone even when they have hurt us in a significant manner.

Generally, we know that we are both responsible for and capable of being nice to others. However, we see in *Chafetz Chaim* that there are many situations in which we do not feel obligated to be nice. The Chafetz Chaim gives the example of *lashon hara* and says we often think that we are allowed to speak about other people's deficiencies as long as what we are saying is true; as a result, we will often hurt others with our words. Furthermore, Rav Yisrael Salanter says that our ability to accomplish our goals is dependent upon our confidence that we can accomplish our goals. Therefore, when we do not have the confidence that we will be able to do a mitzvah or to avoid doing an *aveirah*, we will not end up doing the mitzvah, and we will do the *aveirah*. Even when we know something is objectively wrong, if we feel like it is too hard for us to overcome the challenge, then we will not even try.

Therefore, it is necessary and important for us to recognize that we are both capable of and responsible for having compassion for others even when they have hurt us because otherwise, we will be likely to cause them harm.

Just Do It!

The fact that the Torah teaches us that it is forbidden to have negative thoughts and feelings toward others seems to indicate that we can stop our negative thoughts and feelings from coming in the first place and that we can get rid of them even after they have come. We might conclude the following:

1. We can have a significant amount of control over our thoughts, emotions, and behaviors.
2. We are capable of having only positive thoughts and feelings toward other people and of always acting in a kind manner toward them.
3. We should feel guilty for any negative thoughts or feelings that we have toward others.
4. When we do have negative thoughts and feelings toward others, we should dismiss them, and they will go away.

The Gemara in *Yoma* (9b) seems to support this perspective. The Gemara says that the second Beis Hamikdash was destroyed because the Jews at that time had *sinas chinam*, which is translated as "hatred for no reason."

The concept of hatred that comes for "no reason" seems to support the perspective that negative thoughts and feelings are inappropriate, foolish, and harmful and that they should be able to be avoided or removed easily. If this negativity has "no reason," it seems to follow that any negative thoughts and feelings are totally unjustified and we should therefore feel really bad and guilty if we experience them.

As we mentioned, the Torah also holds us accountable for always treating others in a helpful, caring, and compassionate manner. We are obligated to always treat others in the same manner that we would want to be treated.

It would seem that the Torah is telling us that each of us is responsible for being the "ideal person" and capable of making it happen. In order to follow the laws of the Torah, we are expected to be kind, gentle, and respectful to all people, regardless of how they have treated us.

Challenging Relationships

The Mesillas Yesharim (ch. 11) discusses the negative thoughts and feelings that we have toward the people who have hurt us.

He says that due to the nature of our human psyche and emotions, it is very difficult to avoid feeling hatred, and it is difficult to not take revenge. We are very sensitive to being treated without compassion and respect;

the psychological and emotional pain that we experience is significant and can cause us to be in a constant state of psychological and emotional distress. When we have been treated with a lack of respect and compassion, it is extremely difficult to avoid feeling hatred and wanting to take revenge — and once we have those feelings, it is very difficult to remove them from our hearts even if we are extremely motivated to do so.

What the Mesillas Yesharim tells us about human nature seems to contradict everything we may have assumed based on the simple understanding of the mitzvos! From what he says, it seems clear that:

1. We do not have a significant amount of control over our thoughts, emotions, or behaviors.
2. We are not really able to only have positive thoughts and feelings toward other people and to only act in a kind manner toward them.
3. We should not feel guilty for having negative thoughts and feelings toward others.
4. When we have negative thoughts and feelings toward others, we cannot just dismiss them and make them go away.

However, according to this perspective, it is hard to understand what the Torah's expectations are. The Torah tells us that it is forbidden to hate others, we are not allowed to bear a grudge, and we are not allowed to take revenge. According to the *Mesillas Yesharim*, when we are hurt, we are not really able to not hate others, not bear a grudge, or not want to take revenge. Therefore, we need to understand what Hashem expects from us in these mitzvos.

The perspectives that the *Mesillas Yesharim* teaches are founded on many of the teachings that we see throughout the Torah and *Chazal*.

From the beginning of time, feelings of hatred and jealousy have been pervasive even among some of the greatest of people, and we see that they were not able to get rid of those feelings so easily.

We know that Kayin struggled with jealousy and was so upset that he even killed his brother because of it. Yosef's brothers had a similar experience: They were jealous of Yosef, and that feeling led them to decide to kill him. Even though they knew that jealousy is an inappropriate and a destructive *middah* and it is therefore good to get rid of it, apparently, they were not able to just make themselves not be jealous. We see a similar situation throughout the story of Shaul Hamelech: His jealousy of Dovid led him to want to kill him.

If these *middos* are so much a part of humanity, how do we understand what the mitzvos are telling us to do?

The Torah seems to be holding us responsible on two levels. In the short term, we have to try to avoid as many of the problematic *middos*, feelings, and behaviors as we can. In the long term, we need to try our best to develop ourselves and to improve our *middos*, feelings, and behaviors as much as possible.

Common Challenges to Compassion and Closeness

It is often difficult to have compassion for others and to feel close to them due to the challenges that we face in our relationships and in dealing with other people in general.

Most of the challenges within our relationships can be broken down into a few specific categories:

1. *Middos* challenges: *Middos* such as arrogance, self-centeredness, anger, jealousy, aggressiveness, and overconfidence interfere with our ability to have productive relationships.
2. A lack of respect: We often do not think highly of others or feel respect for them. This lack of respect is itself a problem, and it also often causes a lack of compassion for others.
3. A lack of love: There are some people we never had love for. There are others we do love, but our personal and selfish interests get in the way of our love. There are yet others we did love, but we have grown distant from them, or we have been hurt by them and our negative feelings overshadow our love.
4. Different perspectives, different personalities, or different priorities: These create distance and lead to us criticizing each other.

These challenges often stand in the way of our ability to have good relationships. It is difficult to make significant changes in any of these areas; therefore, it is difficult to make significant improvements in our relationships.

When we have so many challenges in our relationships, we may not even feel that we want to work on the relationship or that real improvements are even possible. We are often critical of the other person to the extent that we feel like it is impossible to have a productive relationship with them. Even when we want to make improvements, it is difficult to know how.

Fixing the Problems in Our Relationships

The problems within our relationships often seem to be significant, and it seems to be difficult to figure out what the solutions are. It is hard to make significant improvements in any of the above factors that can affect our relationships, and the task of making meaningful changes in a relationship sometimes seems to be insurmountable.

We learn from the *Orchos Tzaddikim* (Introduction) an important message about *middos* development: It is very difficult for anyone to change their *middos*. The Orchos Tzaddikim compares changing a *middah* to scraping rust off of a metal object that has rusted over a long period of time. The *middos* challenges that cause hardships in our relationships are not going away anytime soon.

It is also difficult to overcome a lack of respect within a relationship. How do we respect someone we simply do not respect? Motivation alone cannot create respect. If the reason for our lack of respect still exists, how are we going to change that? For example, if we think that someone is a bad person and we therefore do not respect them, how do we change our mind about that and respect a bad person?

In a similar vein, even if we are motivated to love someone or feel close to them, how can we do so if that is not how we feel? If we never felt close to them before, how can we begin now? It is certainly hard to bring ourselves to love someone who has hurt us or someone who has shown us that they do not care about us or about our relationship! If we feel distant, attacked, hurt, defensive, or disinterested, how can we over-come those feelings and feel compassion and love for the other person?

The challenges that come from our differences are usually also hard to fix. It is difficult to change our perspectives, personalities, or priorities, and it can be difficult to feel close to those who are different from us and to avoid criticizing them because of those differences.

When the problems come from a lack of focus or from a lack of motivation to be nice and to be compassionate, it is easier to overcome the challenges because those problems are not so deep or so difficult to fix. However, when the problems relate to who we are and to our deepest feelings, they are more difficult to change.

It seems unrealistic to expect ourselves to improve and change our outlooks, behaviors, and *middos* enough to significantly improve our relationships and to have more compassion for the other person. It also seems to require too much strength and commitment to follow through on making our relationships significantly better.

The Chafetz Chaim tells us (introduction to *Chafetz Chaim*) that we are unlikely to even work on improving ourselves when we do not think that we are doing anything wrong. That creates a big challenge because we are often very critical of others in such a manner that our negative thoughts and feelings seem to be justified. As a result, we are not motivated to change our thoughts and feelings. We often even justify negative behaviors toward others when we consider them to be bad people. It is especially easy to feel justified in our negative feelings toward others when we think of them as bad people or as people who have hurt us and do not deserve our compassion.

Sometimes, we are so critical of others that we may think, "It is impossible to have a productive relationship with this person." This assessment may sometimes be true, but often, it is not fully accurate — and it is really hard to work on doing our part to treat the other person properly when we have such thoughts.

We do not usually feel motivated to change when we do not think that we will be successful anyway. Therefore, since we often think that having a relationship with the other person will not be too productive (because they are "beyond hope"), we often will not even be motivated to try.

Even when we are motivated to make things better, it is often difficult to know how to do it. The problems are often very real and very complicated, and it is difficult to know how to change them. This is especially true because whatever caused the problems is still around, and it will likely cause the same problems again.

It is important to try to understand how we are capable of and responsible for working on our compassion and our relationships even when they have real challenges within them. Only then will we be motivated in and capable of making it happen.

• CHAPTER 2 •

THE TORAH APPROACH TO
DEALING WITH CHALLENGES IN
RELATIONSHIPS

THE TORAH GIVES US THE best guidance for improving our relationships.

In order to be able to improve our relationships, we need to be motivated to improve them, and we also need the knowledge of how to improve them. We need to have both the "Why?" (the motivation) and the "How?" (the knowledge) for improving our relationships.

The words of *Chazal* give us many insights that can help us to improve our relationships. They can motivate us to be kind and compassionate people and to do our best to improve our relationships. They can also help us understand how to build and maintain productive relationships and how to deal with many of the challenges that present themselves within those relationships.

As part of this process of improving our relationships, we need to

1. develop the proper ideals and values, goals, and perspectives about life in general and about our relationships in particular;

2. develop an appreciation of the importance of our responsibilities in our relationships, clarify what our responsibilities are within our relationships, and be motivated to fulfill them;

3. develop the proper perspectives and attitudes about working on our relationships;

4. work on ourselves (our own self-improvement) to make sure that we have the proper values in life, develop our *middos*, our *emunah* and *bitachon*, and develop our attitudes and perspectives (our success in our relationships is dependent on who we are as a person);

185

5. understand life, ourselves, the other person, and our relationship; and

6. develop the proper relationship strategies and skills to help us improve our relationships.

Part 2 of this book ("Responsibility in Relationships") mostly discussed the "Why?" — the reasons and motivation for working on our relationships. That section included discussions about what the proper ideals and values are in life and in our relationships; about appreciating the importance of our responsibilities in our relationships; and about what our responsibilities are within our relationships.

This section mostly focuses on the "How?" question.

Proper Perspectives and Attitudes in Working on Our Relationships

Our relationships are very much affected by our attitudes and perspectives that relate to working on our relationships. Therefore, it is important for us have the proper perspectives and attitudes about what our job is in our relationships, the problems that exist in our relationships, and what we are trying to accomplish by working on our relationships.

We need to realize that we cannot fix our problems ourselves, and we do not need to. Our job is not to fix our problems. Our job is to do our best to try to work on fixing them, and then, Hashem helps us.

Fixing the problems in our relationships is a very long and difficult process. However, it is important to recognize that success and peace in our relationships is determined by Hashem and is not dependent on our actions alone.

The help that Hashem gives us in our relationships is affected by our mitzvah observance, specifically our *davening*. A big part of what we can do to improve our relationships is to strengthen ourselves in this area.

We are taught in *Mishlei* (16:7) that when Hashem is pleased by the ways of man, all of his relationships (even the more challenging ones) will be peaceful. *Yalkut Shimoni* on that *pasuk* says that it refers to the important but challenging relationships that we have in our lives. Shlomo Hamelech is teaching us that even though we need to put our efforts into developing the wisdom and the tools to make our relationships as productive as possible, the real determination of the success in our relationships depends on our *zechusim* (merits) and on help from Hashem. This certainly highlights the importance of our doing our best to serve Hashem properly and to *daven* for His help in our relationships.

In Kaddish, in *Shemoneh Esrei*, and throughout our *davening*, we ask Hashem to bless us with peace. Hashem is in charge of everything, and that includes the success of our relationships. The same way we *daven* to Hashem for all of our other needs and for peace in general, so too, we ask Hashem to bring peace and success to our relationships.

It is important to recognize that Hashem is in charge of the success of our relationships, and it is our responsibility to *daven* to Hashem for His help. Even though we have to do our *hishtadlus* (effort) as well, our success is up to Hashem. Hashem helps us with the pain in our hearts — "He heals broken hearts" (*Tehillim* 147:3) — and brings peace between people.

Combining *Bitachon* and *Hishtadlus*

Rashi (on *Bereishis* 32:10) quotes a *midrash* that says the story of Yaakov Avinu's preparation to meet Esav teaches us about the importance of combining *tefillah* and *hishtadlus*. Yaakov Avinu wanted to have peace with Esav. He wanted to repair his relationship with Esav. Therefore, he did what he could to express his love and respect for him. However, he also *davened* to Hashem for peace.

Even though success in our relationships ultimately depends on Hashem, we are taught that when we deal with potential difficulties within our relationships, we cannot sit back and wait for Hashem to bring about whatever results He has in mind; rather, we have to do our part (our *hishtadlus*).

We are taught to prepare in three ways. When Yaakov Avinu was approaching Esav, he knew there was a strong reason to be concerned about the potential for a significant conflict, and he needed to prepare for it. He knew he might need to protect himself, so he prepared for battle. However, ideally, he was hoping to have peace. Therefore, he *davened* to Hashem for help, and at the same time, he did whatever he could to reach out to Esav in a manner that would make peace more likely.

In our relationships, it is important to know that ultimately, whether we have peace or not is determined by Hashem. However, it is important for us to do our *hishtadlus* as well. That includes doing *teshuvah*, *davening* to Hashem, and learning the lessons about improving our relationships.

Unconditional Love — to the Best of Our Ability

The Mesillas Yesharim (ch. 11) clarifies what the Torah's expectations for unconditional love are in a practical sense. To what extent does the Torah expect us to love others and to not hate them even when they have hurt us?

He says the Torah is telling us that we are expected to do our best to work on ourselves to remove negative feelings and to develop positive feelings even for people who have hurt us.

He also says that when we have been hurt, even if we do our best to remove our negative feelings, this will still take a long time. Even though we are responsible, in a way, for not having any negative thoughts, feelings, or behaviors toward others, we are not expected to do better than our best. Therefore, the mitzvah is not to remove the negative thoughts and feelings right away; rather, the mitzvah is to do our best to work on ourselves and slowly remove our negative thoughts and feelings, little by little, over time.

An Achievement to Celebrate

A number of stories about difficult relationships that are discussed throughout Tanach can shed light on this discussion; for example, the stories of Yaakov Avinu's business dealings with Lavan and Moshe Rabbeinu's dealings with Korach, Dasan, and Aviram.

We learn from the story of Yaakov Avinu and Lavan that our responsibility to act properly within a relationship is not dependent on whether the other person is also acting properly. Yaakov Avinu behaved with the greatest degree of integrity even though Lavan was constantly trying to swindle him. Yaakov Avinu recognized that his own personal integrity is his responsibility and does not depend on how he is treated.

Similarly, we see that Moshe Rabbeinu tried to reach out with an offering of peace to Korach and his followers, even though they were leading a major slander campaign and a revolution against Moshe Rabbeinu's leadership! Apparently, Moshe Rabbeinu's dedication to peace was not dependent on the other parties' behavior.

It is also clear that even if we do our best, we may not be able to create a productive relationship: Even though Yaakov Avinu had great dedication to integrity, Lavan continued to mistreat him, and even though Moshe Rabbeinu reached out, Korach, Dasan, and Aviram continued to push their rebellion. However, it is not our responsibility to make the relationship work. All we can do is our best.

This perspective helps us to avoid giving up due to what we would consider to be impossible and unrealistic expectations. The reality is that we are only expected to do our best, and that is something that we are capable of doing. There is no need to give up. There are times that we need to move on from a relationship, but as long as the relationship is intact, our job is merely to do our best.

Doing our best despite difficult challenges is very hard. We are taught to celebrate the great accomplishment of doing the right thing even when it is hard. *Chazal* say, "The reward [the accomplishment] is measured based on the difficulty" (*Pirkei Avos* 5:23). When we recognize the greatness of the accomplishment of treating others properly even when it is hard to do so, then we will be more motivated to do our best.

Helpful Challenges

We learn from the *Mesillas Yesharim* (ch. 1) that the challenges that Hashem gives us in life are for our benefit — our job in life is to follow the laws and the teachings of the Torah. However, when we need to overcome challenges in order to follow the Torah, our accomplishments are much greater. Therefore, Hashem puts us into challenging situations in order to give us the opportunity for greater accomplishments.

There are many mitzvos that relate to being kind, compassionate, and helpful within our relationships. It is by design that Hashem made it very difficult to fulfill these mitzvos. Hashem is giving us the opportunity to do the right thing despite the challenges. This gives us the greatest opportunity for growth and accomplishment.

When we see the challenges and difficulties that we face as opportunities to grow, to improve, and to accomplish in life, we are more likely to embrace the challenges and to serve Hashem in the ideal manner.

The Desire, Responsibility, and Confidence to Improve Our Relationships

Having the proper perspectives and attitudes about working on our relationships requires us to feel a desire and a responsibility to work on them. It also requires the confidence that we can be successful when we do work on them.

Motivation

We need to be motivated to improve our relationships in order to put in the necessary effort to work on improving them. If we do not think that our relationship with our parent, child, spouse, sibling, or neighbor is important and helpful for us, then we will not be motivated to work on improving it.

There are many lessons from the Torah about the importance and value of our relationships, especially with our families, that help motivate us to improve our relationships.

The Torah teaches us both the importance of the relationships themselves and the importance of treating others with kindness and compassion.

The Torah teaches that being part of a family and a community (social network) is generally an important goal within our Torah lifestyle, as is maintaining peace within the family. These relationships also help us to be able to follow the Torah productively.

The Torah teaches us many lessons about the importance of kindness and compassion. When we appreciate how important they are, we are more likely to work hard to treat others properly even when it is difficult for us to do so.

Responsibility

As we discussed above, Rav Shlomo Wolbe (*Kuntres Chassanim*) says that we cannot always rely on the love, care, and compassion that we have for the other person in a relationship or on our general desire to be kind and compassionate as motivation to work on our relationships. All of those motivations can come and go from time to time. Rather, we need to feel obligated to help others as well. When we feel responsible for helping others in an unconditional manner, then we will be able to be motivated to help them in all situations.

It is sometimes difficult to feel an unconditional responsibility to help. We feel justified in not helping others for various reasons, such as the fact that they hurt us, they are bad people, or merely because we are not close to them. However, the Torah teaches us that in reality, we have a relatively unconditional responsibility to help others. There are many practical considerations that we have to keep in mind to know how to deal with every situation. We cannot always be helpful to others; we have our own needs, and we are limited in our ability to help. However, our responsibility to help others is significant.

These reasons to improve them are relevant even when the relationships present difficult challenges.

Care, Concern, Respect

Among the many different possible motivations to work on a relationship, when our motivation comes from care, concern, and respect for the other person, it is most likely that we will make significant improvements in the relationship.

Shlomo Hamelech teaches us (*Mishlei* 27:19) "*K'mayim hapanim lapanim, kein leiv ha'adam la'adam* — Like water [reflects] the face to the face, so the heart of a person to another." Whatever we feel in our hearts will be communicated to the people around us. When we have friendship and love in our hearts, our friends and family will recognize that we feel that way about them, and they will respond in kind. When we are trying to improve our relationships, and we are not motivated by care, concern, and love but are only moved by a sense of responsibility or other goals, the other person will feel that, and our efforts will not be so successful.

Confidence

We also need to recognize that we are capable of improving our relationships so we will be motivated to work on them. In many cases, we do not have the confidence that we can improve our relationships because we think the other person has to change. "How can I improve the relationship if the other person has such problems and I do not have the ability to change them?" Based on that way of thinking, we give up on working on the relationship.

However, even though every person does have limitations, and realistically, we will not be able to change the other person, we can still make a lot of improvement within our relationships. The lessons from the Torah can teach us how to make these improvements. We will discuss some of them below.

When we put these factors together so that we recognize the value of having productive relationships; recognize the value of unconditional kindness; are dedicated to unconditional responsibility; are motivated by love and respect for the other person; and recognize that we are capable of improving our relationships, then we will be in good shape to successfully improve our relationships.

Productive and Appropriate Motivation

The proper attitudes about working on our relationships include having productive and appropriate goals and motivations for working on them.

Our motivation to improve our relationships can come from a variety of different sources. It can come from love, respect, or responsibility or from the desire for honor or some other result.

What we are motivated by will determine what we will create within our relationships. When we consider what we are looking for in our relationships, we will see the degree to which the basis of our motivations determines the nature and success of our relationships.

Sometimes, each person in a relationship is predominantly motivated by selfish desires. Each person is looking for the other person to help them fulfill their personal needs, comforts, and desires. When that type of relationship plays out, it will usually end up leading to a lot of challenges as people's individual needs and interests come into conflict.

Many things are necessary for a relationship to be successful, such as teamwork, open-mindedness, empathy, the willingness to make sacrifices, and the ability to compromise. If a person is mostly looking out for their own needs, then they are unlikely to do what they need to do in order to make the relationship succeed.

Conversely, when each person is motivated by the desire to care about the other person and their needs, then we can overcome many of the challenges we face in our relationships. When our motivations are related to a desire to work together for the betterment of both people and for the purpose of being a good person, then the relationship will reflect that.

When we combine all the factors discussed in this chapter, we will be in good shape to do our best to improve our relationships. We need to have the proper mindset about life, our relationships, the problems in our relationships, and what we are trying to accomplish by working on our relationships. We need to have productive and appropriate goals and motivations in life and in our relationships, and we need to feel, "I want to, I need to, and I can improve my relationships."

CHAPTER 3

SELF-IMPROVEMENT AS THE BASIS FOR IMPROVING OUR RELATIONSHIPS

EVERY PERSON BRINGS THEIR WHOLE self into each relationship, and every aspect of who they are as a person affects their relationships in a significant manner.

Most people begin their meaningful relationships with similar goals and similar commitments. Our goal is to create a relationship that brings happiness and success to both parties, and our commitment is to be dedicated to love the other person as we love ourselves. However, some people are able to achieve those goals and live up to their commitments better than others.

Our thoughts, feelings, perspectives, goals, ideals, needs, interests, *middos*, and personality are all part of who we are, and they all influence the way that we act. They all play a role in helping us to create great relationships, or they can cause us to have problems in our relationships.

Therefore, we need to develop each of these aspects of who we are so that we will be more capable of being kind, compassionate, loving, understanding, and trustworthy within our relationships.

It is certainly important for us to work through our own issues in order for us to be able to improve our relationships. If we are not happy, we do not feel good about ourselves, we have unfulfilled needs, interests, and desires, or we are struggling with any of our *middos*, we will not be able to act appropriately. Any of our problems that we are not addressing properly will hold us back from doing our job properly within our relationships.

The inner character (*middos* and values) of each of the people in the relationship is one of the main factors that determines whether we will find mutual happiness and success. We all want to be loving and kind, but our ability to do so is determined to a large extent by our *middos* and values.

The manner and the degree of our love and respect for ourselves will also play a big role. When we are struggling with our own happiness, self-esteem, stress, or sadness, it is difficult to be helpful to others. When our thoughts and feelings are generally more optimistic and positive, it is much easier to bring happiness and positivity to others as well.

Our perspectives and attitudes about ourselves, others, and life in general are a big part of who we are, and they play a major role in our relationships as well.

To a large extent, the most important thing we can do in order to improve our relationships is to focus on ourselves first. If we are able to become more positive people, develop more self-esteem, improve our *middos*, and develop more productive and appropriate perspectives, then our relationships will improve quickly.

What Determines the Success of Our Relationships

We do not have control over the success of our relationships — we can only control our own thoughts, feelings, and behaviors. The good news is that we are not in charge of the outcome, we are only responsible for our thoughts, feelings, and behaviors.

Our *middos*, values, *emunah*, and *bitachon* play a very big role in our ability to have the proper compassion and love for others and to treat others properly in our relationships, which definitely help our relationships in a significant manner.

We have the ability to develop our *middos*, our values, our *emunah*, and our *bitachon*, which generally will lead to increased happiness and success in our relationships. In fact, the greatest factor that determines the success of our relationships is the development of our character.

It takes time to make these changes, and during the process of working on ourselves, it will take time before we see significant improvements

in our relationships, but if we work on these changes, we can be very suc-
cessful in the long run.

There are a number of statements in the *mussar sefarim* that discuss
these matters. For example, the *Ohr Hatzafun* (vol. 1, p. 173) explains
that our ability to have productive relationships depends on our *middos*:
In order to treat others with love and compassion, we need to have love
and compassion, and in order to have love and compassion, we need to
have developed an internal *middah* of kindness.

The message of the *Ohr Hatzafun* seems to be very far-reaching. It
seems to mean that in order for us to have the types of thoughts, feelings,
and behaviors that are necessary for our relationships, we need to develop
the inner character that is the foundation for those thoughts, feelings, and
behaviors. When our inner character is rooted in kindness, that will lead
us to have and behave with compassion and love for others. If our inner
character is rooted in arrogance or a focus only on ourselves, then we are
not going to have much compassion and respect for others.

The general message of the *Ohr Hatzafun* is that even though it is cer-
tainly important for us to have the motivation to be kind and compassion-
ate, and it is important to learn about the perspectives and the skills that
are necessary for us to have a productive relationship, the foundation of
our relationships will always be our inner character. Therefore, we need
to focus on developing our inner character properly in order to fulfill our
responsibilities in our relationships and in order to build productive and
successful relationships.

The Chafetz Chaim, in his introduction to *Ahavas Chesed*, refers to
the fact that Michah Hanavi (*Michah* 6:8) teaches us that it is not just im-
portant to perform acts of kindness. It is also important for us to develop
a love of *chesed*. The love of kindness is an achievement on its own — it
is proper to care about others and to want the best for them, not mere-
ly to perform "acts of kindness," and it is also necessary to really want to
help them in order to realistically be able to help them in a consistent and
meaningful manner.

Throughout the *Orchos Tzaddikim*, we see explanations about how all of our *middos* challenges, such as lack of self-esteem, desire for honor, jealousy, anger, and selfishness, create all kinds of problems within our relationships.

The Orchos Tzaddikim says that *ga'avah* is the root (the source and cause) of most of our bad *middos*, bad decisions, and behaviors. It includes both the problems we have in our general mitzvah observance and the problems we have with regard to our responsibilities to other people.

He considers *ga'avah* to include arrogance; the need and desire for respect; selfishness; lack of self-esteem; and insecurities. All of these *middos* are interrelated, and they all cause many problems, including problems in our relationships.

Arrogance

The Orchos Tzaddikim quotes the Gemara in *Bava Basra* (98a) that says that arrogance creates problems in all of our relationships and makes it difficult to even get along with the people within our own house. He is teaching us that even though it is certainly in our best interests to get along with our families and friends, and we are motivated to do so, our ego will often get in the way. When we need and desire honor and respect, and we are insecure until we receive that honor and respect, we will end up thinking, feeling, and acting in a manner that is destructive to our relationships.

It is so common to see how families, communities, and countries suffer greatly from their disagreements and their fighting. Infighting within families, social groups, businesses, religious groups, and countries causes so much pain and suffering to everyone involved. The Orchos Tzaddikim explains that at the root of much of that suffering are the egos of those who are involved.

One example that highlights this concept is the rebellion of Korach and his followers. Shortly after the Jews received the Torah, while they were celebrating their special relationship with Hashem, there was a major "civil war" within the Jewish people. There was an attempt to undermine the leadership of Moshe Rabbeinu and to challenge the truth of *Torah miSinai*. *Chazal* describe the root cause of the insurrection as arrogance and jealousy. Arrogance led Korach and his followers to want to have power and fame. That led them to arguments, fighting, jealousy, and hatred!

Our arrogance often causes us to not be happy with our situation in life, and it causes us to get angry and nasty when things do not go our way. It leads us to have a hard time respecting others in our minds and to have a hard time treating them with respect as well.

The *Chovos Halevavos* also talks about how our arrogance causes us to have perspectives, attitudes, and feelings that are hurtful to our relationships.

He says (*Sha'ar Habitachon, ch. 5*) that when a person is arrogant, they are likely to attribute all of their success to themselves, and they will often blame their lack of success on others.

We also learn from *Chovos Halevavos* (*Sha'ar Hakeniah, ch. 9*) that an arrogant person will constantly be looking to be better than others and will often be in a race with others to surpass them. They will be happy when something happens that makes them feel like they are better than someone else, and they will be upset when they see other people's success. They feel threatened by others because they do not want others to be better than they are. They will often think critically of others and will often put them down. They certainly will not try to help others succeed. They will often feel like they have done more than their part in terms of their responsibility to help others.

Selfishness

In a similar manner, many of the challenges in our relationships relate to our being selfish, which causes us to lack consideration for others and to only be concerned with our own needs and interests.

Our selfish desires often create conflicts within our relationships because we often have to choose between prioritizing our own needs, interests, and desires versus other people's needs, interests, and desires. We will often prioritize our own more than we should.

We often do want to help others, especially the people we love, care for, and are responsible for. However, it is often more of a priority for us to pursue our own needs, interests, and desires as opposed to helping others. We do care about others, but not that much.

When we are selfish and narcissistic, even though we care about others and their needs, we are so focused on ourselves that we do not think about the other person's needs. We have a hard time recognizing or understanding the other person's needs. At times, we are not even aware of what their needs are to begin with.

The Ramban (*Bereishis* 35:22) teaches us an important message about how much our personal needs interfere with our desire to treat others well. He says that our egos often cause us to even make very self-destructive decisions.

He discusses the story of when Reuven disrespected his father Yaakov Avinu (by moving his bed inappropriately), and Yaakov Avinu had to decide whether to remove him from the tribes of Israel. Yaakov Avinu decided to keep him in the tribes despite his infraction. However, the Ramban explains that if it were not for Yaakov Avinu's humility, he would have thrown Reuven out. This is significant because we might have expected Yaakov Avinu to be more motivated by his ego when deciding to keep Reuven in the tribes. Reuven is Yaakov Avinu's son — Yaakov Avinu loves him and cares about him, and he probably does not want to throw him out. However, the fact that an aspect of his ego would have wanted to "get Reuven back" for having disrespected him could have led him to throw Reuven out. It would seem that our ego influences our judgment to the extent that we will often make bad decisions due to our egos.

Low Self-Esteem

When we have low self-esteem, we often look for reassurance from others that we are good, worthy, and competent. This can lead us to be insecure, anxious, and jealous. The Mishnah in *Pirkei Avos* (4:21) tells us that the desire for honor and the jealousy of others can "take us out of This World" — it causes us all kinds of problems, including problems in our relationships.

The *Mesillas Yesharim* (ch. 23) tells us that at the root of (a lot of) arrogance is a lack of self-esteem. Therefore, all of the problems that exist from arrogance really result from a lack of feeling good about ourselves.

The *Mesillas Yesharim* refers to the Gemara's metaphor that a coin in an empty jar makes a lot of noise (*Bava Metzia* 85b) and to a *midrash* that says a tree with no fruit has to make more noise than a tree that has fruit (*Bereishis Rabbah* 16:3).

Our self-esteem affects our relationships in many ways. It affects how we treat others, and it affects how we relate to others' treatment of us.

All of the skills that we use within our relationships are helpful, but our self-esteem plays a huge role in our ability to have productive relationships, and it even plays a big role in our ability to have good relationship skills. When we are consistently looking for love, honor, and respect from others, we will often find ourselves in conflict with others who are not giving us what we need. We are also less likely to cooperate with others and to focus on their needs. We often will not develop healthy boundaries and be assertive in a productive manner. We will sometimes be abusive, controlling, and critical of others as a means of trying to demand what we want in the relationship.

As the Orchos Tzaddikim says (*Sha'ar Haga'avah*), arrogance is the root of many of our bad *middos*; as a result, there are many ways in which our self-esteem affects our ability to be nice, kind, and compassionate to others.

Happiness

Pirkei Avos (4:1) says, "Who is wealthy? He who is happy with his lot." Being happy with what we have is the key to happiness in life in general, but it is also the key to being happy in our relationships. When we appreciate what we have and we see the positive aspects of every situation, this helps our relationships in many ways. It helps us be able to be happy with all the people we have a relationship with. We see the positive aspects of our parents, our spouses, and our children. Our happiness also helps our relationships because we are more likely to be nice to others when we are happy ourselves. When we are not in a good mood, we are usually not the best person to hang around with. If we are not happy, we often look to others to make us happy, and we will be upset when they are not able to do so.

General *Middos* Challenges

All of our *middos* challenges affect our ability to have compassion and consideration for others. Bad *middos* often destroy relationships. They influence our judgment and cause us to make inappropriate or unproductive decisions, and at times, they even cause us to make very self-destructive decisions.

Our bad *middos* cause us to act in a manner that is selfish, mean, aggressive, disrespectful, angry, antagonistic, or dishonest. As we discussed earlier, the stories about Kayin, the brothers of Yosef, and the rebellion of Korach certainly illustrate how our bad *middos* can lead to all of these destructive behaviors. There are many other examples of the damage that arrogance, anger, lust, jealousy, and other *middos* challenges have caused throughout the history of the world.

When we do not have good *middos*, there will always be problems within our relationships even when we are extremely motivated to make our relationships as positive as possible. The Midrash in *Bereishis Rabbah* (65:16) illustrates this point through the story of Esav and his wives. The Midrash tells us that Esav had a special coat that he valued dearly. He wanted to make sure that it was secure and safe, and he had to leave it in the hands of someone he trusted. He had a loving relationship with his wives but decided to leave it with his mother because he trusted her more. The Midrash explains that the reason he trusted his mother more is that she had better *middos*. Her integrity was greater than the integrity of his wives. His wives loved him dearly, but love without integrity is not reliable. Our good *middos* are generally going to lead us to make good decisions in our relationships, and our bad *middos* will lead us to make bad decisions in our relationships.

Our *middos* affect our thoughts, feelings, attitudes, behaviors, and priorities. Our good *middos* will lead to us having the types of thoughts, feelings, attitudes, behaviors, and priorities that are conducive to healthy relationships. We will have compassion, respect, humility, gratitude, and many other attributes that help our relationships in meaningful ways. At the other end of the spectrum, the negative effects of our bad *middos* impact many aspects of our lives. Therefore, it is so important to work on ourselves to improve our *middos*, and as a result, we will improve every aspect of our lives — especially our relationships.

The Importance of Proper Perspectives

For us to be compassionate within our relationships, in addition to having good *middos*, we also need to have the proper perspectives in many areas of life — about life in general, about ourselves, about others, and about our relationships.

Our perspectives are bound up with our *middos* as well. Working on our *middos* and values alongside working our perspectives will certainly improve our relationships.

Chazal provide us with many perspectives and insights that teach us about how to deal with many of the challenges that exist within our relationships.

The Torah teaches us what our goals and responsibilities should be within our relationships, such as loving others unconditionally, not bearing a grudge, not having hatred, and not taking revenge against others. The Torah also gives us insights that are helpful for dealing with pain, anger, hatred, grudges, and revenge. The Torah and *Chazal* also teach us many tools and strategies that can help us to achieve these results.

Our goals and responsibilities, how we deal with negative feelings about others, and the tools and strategies that can improve our relationships — all these things are rooted in our perspectives. Our perspectives about life in general, about ourselves, about each of our specific relationships, and about the other person in each relationship are all important elements.

When we develop our perspectives on our own or through sources other than the Torah, then we are likely to have misguided perspectives about our goals and responsibilities that will not effectively address our negative feelings or improve our relationships. The fact that people do often develop perspectives from sources that do not teach them the proper way to understand these matters leads to a lot of the problems in life in general and in relationships specifically.

However, if we learn the lessons the Torah and *Chazal* teach us and we incorporate them into our lives, then we can be well prepared to make the most of our relationships.

The coming pages will elaborate on the following important perspectives in life:

- Having *emunah* and *bitachon*: We are taught, "Everything Hashem does is for the good" (*Berachos* 60b). *Chovos Halevavos* (introduction to *Sha'ar Habitachon*) explains that we will have peace of mind when we know and trust that we are in Hashem's hands, He controls everything, and He does everything in our best interests. *Sefer Hachinuch* (§214) says that when we recognize that everything that happens to us (including everything that others do to harm us) is from Hashem and is actually in our best interests, we will not have the desire to take revenge against any person who caused us harm.

- Understanding what is truly important: We will see below how the *Kli Yakar* (*Vayikra* 19:18) shows us how we can deal with our anger and hatred toward others productively. We will recognize that very often, the things that happen to us are not really that important. We will also realize (the *Chizkuni*) how great it is that we have a relationship with Hashem — all of our problems will pale in comparison to that, and they will not interfere with our happiness and success. In general, the *Mesillas Yesharim* tells us that everything we do in life should be done based on decisions that we make with clarity and a focus on what is truly important for us.

- Having the proper appreciation for kindness, compassion, and forgiveness, and appreciating the necessity and importance of unconditional love and respect. The Mishnah (*Pirkei Avos* 5:16) teaches us that when our love is conditional, our relationships will suffer. We need to love and respect others based on the idea of the inherent value of every human being. Everyone is created in the image of Hashem, and that alone is enough of a reason to care for and respect them. Aside from that, in each of our meaningful relationships, with the right perspectives, we can always find reasons to have a baseline of love and respect that does not go away based on the day-to-day challenges and frustrations that we may face.

• There is a very big difference between the feeling of "I love and respect you, but I am upset, hurt, or disappointed by your behavior" and the feeling of "I don't love or respect you when you act in that manner." When our husband, wife, child, or friend knows that our love and respect for them is not dependent on their behavior, the relationship will be much stronger. They will feel much more loved and respected, and they will be more confident about the relationship.

The Helpfulness of *Emunah* and *Bitachon* in Relationships

The *Chovos Halevavos* (*Sha'ar Hakeniah*, ch. 10) says if we recognize that everything we have is from Hashem and all of our accomplishments only came about with His help, we will develop perspectives, attitudes, and behaviors that will be very helpful for our relationships.

We will feel gratitude and appreciation to Hashem. We will be humbled by the good things we have received and by everything we have been able to accomplish with Hashem's help.

We will also be happy for others to benefit from Hashem's help and to be successful as well.

Chovos Halevavos (*Sha'ar Habitachon*, ch. 4) adds that when we have *bitachon* and we recognize the fact that Hashem is in control of every outcome in our lives, this has a number of positive effects on our relationships.

We will realize that Hashem controls everything in This World, and Hashem will not cause us to benefit from doing anything that will hurt others. Therefore, we will treat others properly, and we will do our best not to hurt anyone. We will also be less likely to be upset at anyone for having hurt us, because we will realize that nobody could hurt us unless Hashem determined that it would happen.

In discussing our responsibility to not take revenge, *Sefer Hachinuch* (§241) explains that a big factor that causes us to be angry and upset at people who have hurt us is the fact that we think we would have been better off if the other person had not hurt us. On the surface, this seems to be true: The other person may have caused us to lose money, friends, reputation, or anything else through their words or actions. It is understandable for us to be upset with them since they hurt us and caused us to lose something important.

However, *Sefer Hachinuch* explains that the reality is that Hashem is the One who determines whether we will lose our money, our friends, or our reputation, and He has many different ways of making something happen. Whatever we are going to lose, we will lose regardless of what the other person decides to do.

When we have this perspective through our *emunah* and *bitachon*, we will recognize that we are not hurt by the other person. Our life would not be any better off even if the other person had not done what he did. That certainly helps us to put things into perspective and to be less upset at the other person.

There is also another factor to consider. When we are angry or upset at someone for something they did to us, it is not only because we think they were the ones who caused us to be hurt but also because we think we would have been better off if it had not happened. However, the Gemara (*Berachos* 60b) tells us we should always recognize that everything that Hashem does is for the best.

We are often upset because we think that what is happening in our lives is hurtful to us. However, the reality is that whatever happens to us is brought about by Hashem as a means of helping us in some manner. Hashem takes many things into account when determining what is good for us, and we often do not know all the factors or understand why a specific experience is good for us. However, Hashem is helping us and everything in our lives is given to us for our own benefit. When we recognize this reality, we have no reason to be angry about what has happened to us.

When we have the perspectives that Hashem runs the world, everything we have is from Hashem, and everything that Hashem does is for the best, then we can develop a "character" that enables us to approach our relationships in a very positive manner. We will be compassionate, grateful, respectful, accepting, and patient. It will be a pleasure to have a relationship with us. These are certainly important goals, and they will help us have productive relationships.

Priorities

The *Kli Yakar* (*Vayikra* 18:19) explains that the degree to which we get upset when things do not go the way we would have liked is dependent upon how much significance we attribute to the result we were looking for.

We learn from the *Kli Yakar* that when the Torah tells us not to be angry at others, hate others, or take revenge against others who have hurt us, it is telling us that we need to work on adjusting our priorities. We need to recognize that what is important in life is to do our best to serve Hashem in the situation that we are in. Everything else is not important in the same manner. Obviously, as part of the human race, we have many needs, interests, and desires, and when they do not work out the way that we would want them to, we will be upset. However, the more we appreciate the fact that these things are not really important in the context of our eternal life, the better our attitude will be when they do not work out as we wanted.

In a similar manner, Rav Henoch Lebowitz, my *rebbi, zt"l* (*Chiddushei Halev*), quotes the *Chizkuni*'s explanation of the *pasuk* in *Vayikra* (19:18), where the Torah seems to indicate that when we feel like we want to take revenge against someone, we should remember Hashem. The *Chizkuni* explains that the Torah is telling us that when we think about our relationship with Hashem, it will cause us to be extremely happy, and then, we will not be so upset with the other person anymore.

He seems to be saying that when someone hurts us, we get angry because we feel like we were hurt in a meaningful and an important manner. Either the insult was hurtful, or what we lost was hurtful — financially or otherwise. However, when we realize that we have a meaningful relationship with Hashem, everything else becomes much less important. It will no longer seem to matter that we were hurt in a relatively inconsequential manner. Rav Henoch Lebowitz explains this idea with a metaphor: If someone found out that he won the lottery, and at the same time, he found out that his business suffered a minor setback, he will likely be a lot less upset about the business setback because his overall financial situation has just improved dramatically. When we are able to really appreciate the great benefits of our relationship with Hashem, the relatively minor setbacks of life are not going to bother us so much.

Appreciating the Value of Kindness and Compassion

There are many statements of *Chazal* that teach us how important it is to act with kindness and compassion within our relationships. Many mitzvos of the Torah hold us responsible for being kind and compassionate to others in all situations.

When we do not appreciate the value of kindness, then we will face many situations in which it will be difficult to act with kindness. It is generally much more natural for us to focus on our own direct needs, interests, and comforts than to give of ourselves for others. We will also often feel justified in treating others negatively if we have had difficult experiences together. As a result, our relationships will suffer. We will not be as helpful, kind, forgiving, or compassionate as we could be to our friends, family, and neighbors, and we will not be as friendly and happy together as we could be.

The *Orchos Tzaddikim* (*Sha'ar Harachamim*) says we all know that compassion is an important *middah*. We know that the right way to think about others, to feel toward others, and to treat others is with compassion. However, it is difficult to truly appreciate how important compassion is, and we often grossly underestimate its true value. As a result, we do not prioritize it as much as we should, we do not feel so accomplished when we do act with compassion, and we are not motivated to be compassionate when it is difficult to do so.

The fact that *rachmanus* (compassion) is one of the *middos* of Hashem means that it is an aspect of true greatness and one of the greatest accomplishments that we can have in life. It is one of the defining characteristics of a true *tzaddik*, of true Torah observance, and of true spiritual success.

When we appreciate the true value of compassion and we recognize that behaving with compassion is one of the greatest accomplishments, we will overcome all the things that could potentially get in the way of our compassion and motivation to be as nice as possible in our relationships, and we will be able to significantly improve our relationships.

Furthermore, when we recognize how much we all desire to be treated with compassion and how beneficial it is for all of us, we will realize how important it is for us to treat others accordingly. However, if we underestimate how much we need and crave compassion, we are less likely to make sure that we treat others with as much compassion as they need.

It is also important to recognize how much of a responsibility we have to care about others. It is hard to know how much time, energy, and resources we are obligated to dedicate toward others, and we sometimes do not realize that our responsibility to have compassion includes a broad range of people — even animals.

Within our relationships, we often feel like our responsibility to be helpful to the other person should be limited to certain things at certain times. We draw lines in our minds to mark how much we should be obligated to do for others or which matters we should be responsible for helping with. Even though it is certainly true that we need to take care of ourselves as well and we need to have healthy boundaries as far as how much time and energy we dedicate to others, the starting point should be that we want to help, and we feel obligated to help as much as we possibly (and realistically) can.

The *Orchos Tzaddikim* says that all of these matters are often misunderstood, which leads us to not be as committed as we should be to helping others and to being properly compassionate to them. Developing our perspectives on these matters will improve our relationships greatly.

Appreciating the Value of Forgiveness

Forgiveness is a necessary component of a productive relationship. We all do or say things that are hurtful to others in our relationships, and they do the same. When we see the value in forgiving the other person properly, we will be motivated to do so, which will enable our relationships to function more productively.

We all know that it is appropriate to forgive others when they have hurt us and caused us pain. However, *Chazal* teach us important perspectives about forgiveness that we may not fully appreciate.

We often do not appreciate just how important it is to forgive others. The Gemara (*Yoma* 83b) teaches us that forgiveness is one of the *middos* of Hashem — it is an expression of the kindness of Hashem. The Gemara explains that when we appreciate the value of the kindness of Hashem and we emulate it through forgiving others, that is a great demonstration of our true love for Hashem.

We also often do not appreciate that we are obligated to forgive others. It is not just a nice thing to do — it is a responsibility. Forgiveness is an expression of Hashem's kindness, and we are responsible for emulating all of Hashem's *middos*.

We certainly often underestimate how far this responsibility goes. *Chazal* teach us that our responsibility to forgive others applies even to those who have hurt us in a significant manner.

When we put together these perspectives, we will recognize that Hashem holds us responsible for doing our best to forgive all those who have hurt us, and when we do forgive them, it is one of the greatest possible accomplishments!

• CHAPTER 4 •

UNDERSTANDING THE RELATIONSHIP AND THE PEOPLE IN IT

Understanding the Relationship, Ourselves, and the Other Person

In order to be able to improve our relationships, we need to understand ourselves and the other person. We also need to have a clear understanding of the problems within the relationship. Without this understanding, we will not know what is really causing the problems, and we will not know how to deal with the problems productively and appropriately. When we misinterpret what the problems are, even when we work hard to fix what we think is the problem, we will not be addressing the real issues.

We need to know what our needs, interests, and desires are, and we need to know how to fulfill them in a productive manner. We also need to know the same thing about the other person. We need to know what the consequences will be if our needs are not fulfilled and how to deal with them. We also need to identify our areas of vulnerability and weakness, and we need to know how to address them. It is also extremely helpful to know what our strengths are and how to use them to help us do our best in our relationships. It is also important to identify all these elements in the other person.

In addition to understanding each individual in the relationship, each relationship also has its own chemistry to it. There are many factors that are external to the direct relationship that influence the relationship; for instance, social, financial, spiritual, or environmental factors could affect

210

the situation in a significant manner. There are certainly also many factors within each direct relationship that affect the relationship. We are each affected by different people in different ways, and everything about one person's personality and their overall mode of behavior will affect the other person in a significant manner.

The more that we understand each of these dynamics, the better prepared we will be to use our knowledge to make improvements.

There is an additional benefit to understanding the problems correctly. The *Mesillas Yesharim* (ch. 11) tells us that when we are upset at someone and feel hatred toward them, the root of our feelings is often the fact that we feel hurt by them. The *Chizkuni* (*Vayikra* 19:18) tells us that even when we feel like we totally hate someone, we often really do care about them on many levels that we are not currently consciously feeling. It is important to look at what is really going on and not just focus on the actions or feelings we experience on the surface.

The way Moshe Rabbeinu dealt with the Jewish people throughout their travels in the desert highlights the benefits of seeing the true picture of what the problems are. He repeatedly saw that the Jews were angry and complaining about Hashem and about Moshe Rabbeinu and that they were not interested in following Moshe Rabbeinu. Yet Moshe Rabbeinu often responded to their fear (of the Mitzrim, of not having water, of being killed by their enemies, etc.) that was really behind the complaints. He recognized that they wanted to serve Hashem, to do the mitzvos, and to follow Moshe Rabbeinu's leadership, but they were often scared. As a result, they reacted with anger and criticism, but those were not their real feelings. When Moshe Rabbeinu helped them to address their fears, the other feelings melted away.

When we do not have the true understanding of a situation, we will often assume that the problems in the relationship are because either we or the other person is a really bad person or is hopelessly messed up. We will also often assume that the problems within the relationship are not fixable. When we do not really understand why we are getting upset, we will often conclude that it is because the relationship is beyond repair. If we think this way, it will be difficult to be motivated to work on the problems, and it will be difficult to connect with the other person in a loving manner.

However, when we have an accurate understanding of what the true problems are, we will often recognize that neither we nor the other person is so bad. Neither one is hopeless, and the problems in the relationship are not as difficult to manage as we once thought.

Every person has many levels of complexity. We have many needs, desires, and interests. We have many thoughts, feelings, and emotions. All of these also exist on both the conscious and subconscious levels. It is difficult to attain a true sense of self-awareness, and it is certainly difficult to have a good sense about what is going on within someone else's mind and heart. However, to truly grow and develop ourselves and our relationships properly, it is helpful for us to try to know ourselves and each other as much as possible.

Self-Awareness: Identifying Our True Feelings and Motivations

When we want to work on improving our relationships, we need to know what is going on in our subconscious minds and hearts, which often play a stronger role than our conscious minds in determining how we think, feel, and act overall. Therefore, if we are upset or someone is upset at us, and we want to figure out how to improve the situation, the changes that will be most effective will be those that address the issues in our minds and hearts — even the issues we may not be consciously aware of.

One example of this idea can be seen from what the Mesillas Yesharim says about conflict. He explains (ch. 11) that often, when we are angry with someone, we do not want to be friendly toward them, and we sometimes even want to hurt them. Those feelings are certainly not a recipe for a happy relationship. If we consider our thoughts and feelings toward that person at that specific time, we will often conclude that we do not like them, we do not want to be their friend, and it will actually make us happy to push away their friendship or even cause them harm.

The Mesillas Yesharim teaches us that the most powerful feelings we have in that scenario are really the feelings of being hurt by the other person. We feel the emotional pain of having been hurt by what the other person did to us through their words or actions. At our core, however, we may really want the closeness in the relationship. We do not really want to hurt the other person — we would be much happier if our pain and hurt would go away and we would be friends again.

These thoughts and feelings are often not so obvious, even to ourselves, while we are upset and feeling angry toward the other person. It requires real self-awareness to recognize that we are hurt and are therefore angry as opposed to just knowing, "I am angry!" There is a significant difference between those two ways of understanding ourselves. If we only focus on our anger, hatred, and desire for revenge, we will certainly not improve our relationship. On the other hand, when we recognize that our negative feelings are really rooted in the pain of being hurt, then we can focus on dealing with our pain and trying to rebuild the friendship.

There are times when we have an agenda that we are passionate about, and we are ready to fight for our opinion about that issue. However, in reality, we are motivated by a completely different matter that may even be buried within our subconscious minds. Once we have misinterpreted our own true motivations, even when we try to resolve the conflict, it will not help because we are not addressing the true issues.

When we do have multiple levels of problems, it is important to see beyond our surface-level thoughts and feelings and to be in touch with what is going on underneath them as well. That will allow us to address the deeper issues, which are often the more powerful issues.

As we mentioned above, a number of the Torah's stories about the Jewish people and their relationship with Moshe Rabbeinu demonstrate many of these points. The Torah records many stories about the conflicts that some of the Jewish people had with Moshe Rabbeinu as they left Mitzrayim and traveled through the desert for forty years. The *midrashim*, *Rishonim*, and *Acharonim* all explain that in many of these stories, the Jewish people had multiple levels of motivations and feelings, but often, they were only in touch with those on the surface, and that led them to be extremely upset at Moshe Rabbeinu. Had they been more aware of their deeper motivations, they could have dealt with their situations in a more appropriate and productive way. In many cases, we see that Moshe Rabbeinu did have a deeper understanding of the people who were upset at him, and that enabled him to guide them productively.

Judging Others Properly: Understanding the Other Person's Perspective

We make many judgments about others. We judge them to be wise or foolish, good or bad, capable or incapable, etc.

There is a mitzvah in the Torah (*Vayikra* 19:15) that teaches us the responsibility to "Judge your fellow with righteousness." This responsibility is echoed by the Mishnah in *Pirkei Avos*, which says (1:6), "You shall judge every person favorably" and (2:4) "Do not judge your friend until you have reached his place." In order to judge other people properly, we need to be "in their place."

It is possible to infer a number of important points from the Mishnah's statements.

- When we are making a judgment, we are assessing the information that we have and coming to a conclusion based on that information.
- It is difficult to understand another person's perspective, where they are coming from, or why they think and act the way they do.
- We often have a very small part of the information necessary to assess the information and come to a proper conclusion about another person. In order to make a proper judgment of the person, we would need to know their thoughts, feelings, and behaviors. We would also have to understand their nature, their environment, and what their environment and experiences have been throughout their lives. We obviously only know a tiny little piece of that information about most people. It is almost laughable to think we can come to definitive conclusions about other people.
- We often do not have enough expertise to be able to judge properly whether someone is wise or foolish, good or bad, capable or

incapable, etc., even if we did have all the necessary information in front of us.

- We have a tendency to be overconfident about our capacity to make the proper assessments and judgments.
- We have a tendency to be critical of others, and we often come to conclusions about others that are more derogatory than what the reality is.
- When we are able to understand where the other person is coming from, it helps us to be less critical of and be more compassionate toward the other person.
- We have a responsibility to be careful to not inappropriately judge others in a negative way.

The Benefits of Understanding the Other Person's Perspective

Many of the problems we face in our relationships are created by judgments that we made about the other person's thoughts, feelings, or behaviors. Based on those judgments, we conclude that the other person did something against us inappropriately (for no good or understandable reason), and that causes us to be angry or upset at the other person.

When the Mishnah in *Pirkei Avos* (2:4) says, "Do not judge your friend until you have reached his place," it seems to be telling us that it is extremely hard to really know and understand what is going on in someone else's world. We are unlikely to actually "reach his place." It is also telling us that when we do understand what is going on in another person's world, we will often be less critical of them. As a result, it is likely that we will be able to have more compassion toward them and to have a better relationship with them. So, if we do have that understanding, *then* we can judge them, because it will be a compassionate and productive judgment.

Often, someone will do something that seems to indicate that they are a bad person, they do not like us, we have good reason to be angry with them, and the relationship does not seem to have any hope.

Therefore, it is important to realize that there is often more to the story than we are aware of and we should not judge the other person so quickly because there may be a good reason for their behavior. Even if we do not know what that reason is, it is likely that there is one. They may not be such a bad person, they may like us more than we thought, there may not be any real reason to be angry at them, and there may be a lot of hope for the relationship.

The fact that there is a lot about the other person that we do not know or understand can motivate us to learn about the other person so we can have a better understanding of what the other person's experiences, struggles, and accomplishments have been. We can also gain a better understanding of why they have not been successful in some of their experiences in life. When we have new information about the other person, we will often end up being more understanding of them; more compassionate and empathetic toward them; and more respectful of them.

Overall, our relationships will certainly be improved when we do not prematurely jump to negative conclusions and judgments of others, especially when we learn more about the other people in our relationships and understand them better.

We can see many of these messages clearly from some of the previously mentioned stories about the interactions between Moshe Rabbeinu and the Jewish people.

When the Jewish people left Mitzrayim and approached the Yam Suf, they found themselves trapped. The sea was in front of them, and the Mitzrim were behind them. When they realized they were in danger, they began to complain to Moshe Rabbeinu and to criticize him.

"And they said to Moshe, 'Was it for want of graves in Mitzrayim that you brought us to die in the wilderness? What have you done to us, taking us out of Mitzrayim?'" (*Shemos* 14:11)

They were criticizing him for taking them out of Mitzrayim and putting them into a state of danger. However, the reality was that Moshe Rabbeinu had not been the one to decide to lead them out of Mitzrayim — he was merely following directions from Hashem. Moshe Rabbeinu was also leading the Jews out of Mitzrayim due to his love, care, and concern for them, as he demonstrated over and over by risking his life to save them from the Mitzrim.

Moshe Rabbeinu could easily have responded to the complaints against him by arguing that he did not do anything wrong. He could have shown them that they were being rude and ungrateful.

Instead, Moshe Rabbeinu told them, "Have no fear! Stand by and witness the deliverance that Hashem will work for you today; for the Mitzrim, whom you see today, you will never see again" (*Shemos* 14:13).

At first glance, Moshe Rabbeinu's response seems strange. The Jews were complaining that Moshe Rabbeinu's motivation to take them out of Mitzrayim was due to his selfish interests, and Moshe Rabbeinu responded, "Do not be afraid." They did not say to him, "We are afraid," they said, "We are angry!" Why did he respond to the fear?

It seems that even though they were saying, "We are angry," Moshe Rabbeinu understood that at the core, the main issue was their fear. He knew that if he was able to alleviate some of their fear, then their anger would dissipate.

It is amazing to contrast the two possible responses that Moshe Rabbeinu could have given in this scenario and to recognize the benefits of the approach that he decided to take. Having seen the Jews complaining and criticizing him despite everything he had done for them, Moshe Rabbeinu could have berated them for being ungrateful, and he could have focused on defending his actions and his leadership decisions. This would not have helped them to be less scared, and it probably would have made them less likely to turn to Hashem with *tefillah* and *bitachon*. However, when Moshe Rabbeinu focused on helping them alleviate their fears and rely on Hashem and on giving them emotional support and the confidence that they would be safe, that led them to respond by *davening* to Hashem, having *emunah* in Hashem, and even risking their lives based on their *bitachon* in Hashem (as they walked straight into the sea, led by Nachshon ben Aminadav).

If we were in Moshe Rabbeinu's situation, and we interpreted the Jewish people's behavior as being ungrateful and antagonistic, we would have been tempted to respond to them with criticism or at least by focusing on defending ourselves from their attack. However, understanding that their main concern was really their fear would make it much easier to respond with compassion, reassurance, and encouragement, as Moshe Rabbeinu did.

This same type of situation can present itself in many different ways. Often, a situation itself can be interpreted in extremely different ways, and our determination of how to deal with it will depend on our interpretation. As we see from Moshe Rabbeinu and the Jewish people at the Yam Suf, being able to see a situation in a positive manner can be extremely beneficial.

Both aspects of a situation can be true: On the one hand, we may be motivated by noble and productive motives, and on the other hand, we may also be motivated by inappropriate and unhelpful motives. Or sometimes, our motives may be good, but the way we deal with them may not be productive.

One of the challenges we face in seeing the positive aspects of a situation is the fact that often, the more obvious way to see the situation is in the negative manner. For example, in the previous situation, the Jews were complaining that Moshe Rabbeinu had created a situation in which they were going to be killed. The only way Moshe Rabbeinu was able to see the situation more positively and understand what would improve it was by seeing past the obvious surface anger to the other aspects of the story.

The *Chizkuni* tells us that the Torah teaches us a similar idea about the benefits of understanding other people's perspectives in order to get along with them properly. When the Torah tells us we should not take revenge against someone who had hurt us, it says that we should love the person instead (*Vayikra* 19:18). The *Chizkuni* explains that the Torah is not only telling us what we are responsible for doing but is also teaching us how to do it: by focusing on our love for this person and using it to overcome our negative feelings toward him.

According to the *Chizkuni*, the Torah is describing a situation in which we were hurt by a spouse, child, friend, or neighbor, and we want to hurt them back. In that situation, we usually feel like the person who hurt us is a bad person, they do not like us, and they hurt us without any justifiable reason. Therefore, it would seem that we should have a legitimate reason to be angry at them, to dislike them, and to want to hurt them.

However, the Torah tells us that the reality is that when we look into the situation better and consider the context of the whole relationship, we will often realize that there is more love than we are noticing at the moment, there is less reason for negativity than we may be feeling at the moment, and we are likely underestimating the positivity that each of the people really feel toward each other. It is not really accurate to say, "He does not like me, and I do not like him."

When we do not misjudge the situation, we will often recognize that even though there is a problem and something happened that was hurtful to us, that should not lead us to jump to the conclusion that there are no positive feelings for each other. Very often, we do care about each other, we do find value in the relationship, and despite the fact that there are problems, the relationship can still be significantly improved.

The Mishnah in *Sotah* (1:4) teaches us that at times, when a woman is suspected of being unfaithful to her husband, she goes through a process of interrogation in order to determine whether she actually committed the sin. The Mishnah describes the process the Sanhedrin uses to motivate her to admit to her sin. They begin by warning her that if she is guilty but does not admit to it, she will die an embarrassing death. Then, if she still has not admitted her sin, the Sanhedrin switches tactics. They tell her that even if she did commit the offense, she should not overestimate her guilt. It is often more understandable for her to have done what she did than she may be giving herself credit for.

Chiddushei Halev points out that sometimes, we do not take responsibility for our actions because the guilt that is associated with taking responsibility is too great. Therefore, it is important to see the true context of our guilt — and it is often much less than we had originally imagined it to be.

When we look into the sins that we have committed or those that others have committed, and we understand the context and the circumstances that led to the sin, we often will be much more understanding of why the person sinned, and we will not look at the sinner in such a negative manner.

The same is true in our relationships. When we do not properly understand the context of the other person's thoughts, feelings, and behaviors, we will often overestimate the degree of evil intent. When someone has hurt us, if we can understand the context of the circumstances that led to their behavior, we will often be much more understanding of why the person hurt us, and we will not look at them in such a negative manner. It will also often help us to feel less hurt by their actions when we understand the context of their behavior better.

Understanding Conflict within a Close Relationship

The Mishnah in *Pirkei Avos* (1:12) teaches us to love peace and to pursue peace, just as Aharon Hakohen did. The Midrash *Tanna D'vei Eliyahu* (*Avos D'Rabbi Nassan* 12:1) explains that Aharon Hakohen was proactive in helping people rebuild relationships that had been in a state of conflict. It says that Aharon Hakohen would tell each of the parties that even though the other person hurt them, they recognize that they were wrong for doing so, they sincerely regret what they did, and they really want to reconnect. It says that Aharon Hakohen would sit with each of them until they were ready to reconnect. As a result, they would give each other a hug, and they would end their fight.

It is unclear what Aharon Hakohen's method really was. How did he help people who were angry at each other to be happy with each other? How did he get people who hated each other to have compassion and love for each other? What was the message that he shared with each of the parties? What did he speak with them about when he sat with them?

Seeing the Big Picture

Aharon Hakohen must have used a lot of wisdom in order to help people to mend their relationships. His messages probably included the messages taught to us by the previously mentioned *Chizkuni,* along with other messages that were related to us by *Chazal.*

Let's look deeper into the lessons from the *Chizkuni* that relate to Aharon Hakohen's discussions.

The *Chizkuni* says the reason why the Torah teaches us the responsibility "Love your fellow Jew" right next to where it teaches us "Do not take revenge" (*Vayikra* 19:18) is to teach us an important strategy about how we should deal with conflict within our relationships. The Torah is teaching us to allow the love we have for the friend to override the hatred we feel that would lead us to take revenge.

We can learn a number of important lessons from the *Chizkuni* about conflicts within our relationships. First, when we have been hurt by something that a friend did to us, we get upset, we think about all the problems we have with the other person, and it is difficult to imagine being friends again. Even though the big picture of a relationship often does include positive feelings for the other person, we often have tunnel vision, and we do not think about the big picture. It is common for us to only focus on one aspect of the picture, and we often focus mostly on the negative aspects of the situation and will feel angry and upset at the other person.

However, we can overcome the problems if we have productive perspectives and attitudes about the relationship.

We can break this message down further and learn the following from the *Chizkuni*.

- When we think about the big picture of the relationship, we will recognize that we have many layers of thoughts, feelings, and experiences beyond the ones we are focusing on.
- Relationships often include both good parts and bad parts (e.g., love and hate, compassion and animosity). Even after we have been hurt in a relationship, we are still capable of finding love and compassion.
- Finding the love and compassion (the good parts of our relationship) is the most beneficial way to deal with the pain and anger (the hard parts within our relationship).

On the Same Team

The *Talmud Yerushalmi* (*Nedarim* 9:4) tells us that when we get upset at someone for what they did to us, it is because we see the other person as our enemy or as our competitor. When our enemy or competitor has done something to hurt us, we get angry at them, and we often want to hurt them.

The *Yerushalmi* tells us that the reality is that all of the Jewish people are connected and are part of the same team — we are not enemies or competitors. The Gemara gives an analogy: If a person's right hand hurts his left hand, his left hand does not get angry with his right hand, and it certainly does not take revenge against it.

When we have this perspective, we are much less likely to be upset at our family, friends, and neighbors, because we can see them as being "on our side" and "part of our team," as opposed to seeing them as being against us.

One of the reasons why this perspective is helpful is that it prevents our ego from being hurt. When we feel like our ego is being threatened, we become very defensive, and we end up working really hard to protect it. When someone has done something to hurt us, it is easy to feel threatened and to feel that our competitor has hurt us or has the upper hand over us. However, the reason our ego is hurt so much is that we identify ourselves as being totally separate from the other person. When we are able to think about the person as our teammate, then our ego is not threatened as much anymore.

It is certainly very difficult to really see the other person as being so close to us to the extent that we are not hurt by their words, but trying to think of them as being on our team will minimize the pain to a certain degree.

Managing a Relationship Between
People Who Are Different

Every person and every relationship will involve unique dynamics. Happiness in a relationship depends on the people involved understanding each other, respecting each other, loving each other, accepting each other, and working together.

One of the reasons why it is difficult to be happy in long-term committed relationships is that there are always differences between the two people in the relationship. Different personalities, values, and life experiences make it difficult for them to understand each other, love each other, respect each other, accept each other, and work together on a long-term basis. Expecting either person to change themselves enough to solve the problem is usually not realistic, and it is not a good idea.

How We Understand the World

Our understanding of human behavior is generally seen through the prism of our nature and our personality. It is hard to think of something as being normal and appropriate if we do not see it that way in our own lives and experiences. We often project our own expectations of what would be "normal" for us onto others as well. As a result, we are often critical of their behaviors based on our own perspective of what is proper and appropriate.

These differences often lead to a lot of criticism because each person thinks there cannot possibly be a good reason for the other person's behavior.

They can also lead to disagreements about values, priorities, and decisions in life. The disagreements can come up especially about matters that are important and/or constant.

Sometimes, the different personalities or values will make it hard to find shared interests, ambitions, and goals, causing distance in the relationship. Without shared interests, ambitions, and goals, it is difficult for the two people to create a bond!

It is very challenging to create a positive and productive relationship and to avoid having consistent conflict in the relationship because people are so different and cannot change who they are. However, it is possible to create positive and productive relationships. There might always be a certain degree of conflict, and it is unlikely that people will change in a significant manner, but if the situation is approached with wisdom, it can be done.

Dealing with Differences Productively:
The Confidence and Strategies for Success

Our ability to deal with a relationship productively is dependent on our recognition that we have the ability to make it work. If we think there is nothing that we can do about the relationship and we are subject to continuous conflict, we will never try to improve it.

If we think that in order to succeed, we need to either change ourselves, change the other person, or totally fix the problem, then we will give up because none of those things are realistic. We need to have appropriate and realistic goals in order to have the confidence that we can succeed.

It helps to think about the situation in two parts: (1) the challenge or problem and (2) how we will deal with the challenge. We do not have control over the fact that there will be challenges within our relationships. However, our focus should be on the part that we can control, which is how we deal with the challenges that we have.

We can also remember that doing our best to deal with the challenges properly often reduces conflict significantly. When our focus is only to do our best, we can be confident that we will succeed in accomplishing that and making significant improvements in the relationship despite our differences.

To really address the problems in a relationship, it is important to realize that the problems are not really created by the differences between the two people in the relationship, and the solutions to the problems are not dependent on one person changing to become exactly like the other person.

Getting along with others is difficult, and we would have challenges even if one person in the relationship had the same personality as the other person. Our problems are actually created by our *middos* challenges. The differences between our personalities aggravate our challenges, but they are not the source of our challenges.

The Importance of Good *Middos*

Our happiness and success in a relationship depend more on having good *middos* than on having the right combination of personalities. When we have good *middos* (such as faith and trust in Hashem; humility; compassion; patience; respect; and understanding), then we are able to have great relationships with others even when our personalities are different. We can deal with all of our frustrations within our relationships productively, and we are able to find closeness and love despite our differences. However, when our *middos* are not so good (such as arrogance, selfishness, and anger), and we are quick to criticize and not so quick to be compassionate and understanding, then we will never be able to have good relationships. Even if we find someone who has similar values, goals, and interests, we will still experience friction in our relationship with them.

The first step in achieving happiness in our relationships is to work on our *middos*. It is not easy to make significant improvements in our *middos* either, but with effort, we can improve them enough to help us improve our relationships in a meaningful manner.

Uniqueness

Everyone has a different nature and a different personality. Therefore, it is expected and appropriate for each person to have different thoughts, feelings, needs, and actions.

The term "personality" can refer to the characteristics a person has that significantly affect the way he thinks, feels, and acts. Each person also has their own individual "nature," which also affects our thoughts, feelings, desires, and behaviors. It is common for our nature and our personality to be intertwined — they work together and team up to be a powerful influence on our thoughts, feelings, and behaviors.

Even though Hashem created us with *seichel*, which gives us the ability to make our decisions based on objective measures of right and wrong, to a large extent, our actions are influenced by the many internal and external forces in our lives.

When we realize that the other person's thoughts, feelings, perspectives, and behaviors are influenced by their nature, their experiences, and their personality, we will understand where they are coming from to a greater degree. We will be more likely to recognize that their behaviors are appropriate (or at least understandable) for who they are. This can help us to be less critical, more respectful, and more compassionate toward the other person.

Every personality has some aspects to it that are appealing and some that are less appealing. There are times when we focus on the less appealing aspects of the other person in the relationship, yet we see other people who have a type of personality that seems more appealing to us. This leads us to think that we would be much happier if we were in a relationship with someone who had a different type of personality.

However, when we look at each person's personality as a whole, we will see that the same personality that can sometimes be annoying can also have aspects to it that are very appealing, and the two parts often come together.

A classic example of different personalities would be an introvert and an extrovert. An introvert enjoys spending time alone, prefers quality time with smaller groups more than spending time in bigger groups, and spends a lot of time thinking and processing his thoughts. An extrovert has the opposite tendencies. He likes to spend time with others, enjoys big crowds, is outgoing, talkative, and likes to be the center of attention.

Often, someone who is an introvert appreciates the benefits of quality time, thinking about life, and processing decisions slowly and carefully. As a result, he may be critical of the extrovert's desire for attention and his lack of careful thought. The person who is an extrovert will appreciate having passion and energy and the ability to be courageous and confident about his decisions. As a result, he may be critical of the introvert's quiet, thoughtful, and careful approach toward life and decisions. (These are merely very general examples and there are many nuances within every situation.)

It is important for each person with each personality to recognize that there are advantages and challenges that come along with either personality.

That perspective often helps us see that in the big picture, the personality is not all bad; rather, it is part of the picture of the whole person, whom we can appreciate in some ways even if not in others.

It also helps to recognize, when we do think about finding someone else who may seem to have the perfect personality for us, that we would have to deal with the less pleasing aspects of that person as well. The way to find happiness is not to find the person who has a personality that is totally appealing, which is impossible. Rather, we need to try to have a positive attitude toward the other person despite the fact that we find them annoying at times and to work on our *middos* to deal with those situations appropriately.

Managing Differences, Not Changing

None of the challenges within a relationship that relate to different people and different personalities will be solved through either party changing who they are in any significant manner. We cannot change our personalities so easily! Therefore, many of the problems will remain, and they need to be managed rather than solved.

Compromise is a big part of managing differences productively, as are acceptance, respect, understanding, and compassion.

Communication is also certainly helpful and necessary to make the situation as good as possible. Through healthy communication, we can explain ourselves to each other, and we can understand each other better. That helps the other person service our needs better, and it helps us to share our true thoughts of respect and love without being misunderstood.

Understanding, Acceptance, Compassion, and Respect

We need to accept each other, respect each other, understand each other, and have compassion for each other despite personality differences. We also need to make some changes in our behaviors in order to make the relationship easier to handle for both people.

Accepting the other person includes both not trying to change the other person and not resenting the other person for not changing. Respecting the other person and having compassion for them is the next step, wherein each person can appreciate the other and value them for who they are.

Understanding the other person and their perspective is often necessary in order to have compassion, respect, and acceptance. It is hard to have these attitudes about someone who seems to be acting in an inappropriate or annoying manner. However, when we understand why they are acting the way that they are, it is easier to develop positive perspectives and feelings.

Recognizing the challenges in our own personality also helps us accept the other person's limitations. Our arrogance is often what stands in the way of our respect and compassion for others, and ultimately, it stands in the way of our happiness with our family and friends.

Working Together

The greatest success in our relationships comes when we work as individuals to improve ourselves and when we work as a team to improve the relationship.

If we care about each other and each other's best interests; we share the goal of having a happy and productive relationship; and we want both people to benefit from it, then we can join together and work as a team to create the best possible situation for everyone involved. That includes compromise, putting the other person's interests ahead of ours, and helping the other person however we can.

When we work well together with someone else, we will find many benefits to the fact that each person has their own nature and their own personality. In that situation, the two people can complement each other so that each person's unique abilities add to their overall shared success. When one person is organized and the other is creative, one of them is proactive in conversations and the other is a good listener, when one is generous with their money and the other one is careful, in all of these situations, when the two people work well together, they can each offer the perspectives, guidance, and abilities that the other person lacks.

◆ CHAPTER 5 ◆

DEVELOPING TOOLS AND STRATEGIES FOR IMPROVING OUR RELATIONSHIPS

PREVIOUS SECTIONS OF THIS BOOK have discussed many of the tools and strategies that *Chazal* have taught us that can help us to improve our relationships and deal with the challenges that present themselves within those relationships.

Many of them relate to *self-development:* developing ourselves so that we are more capable and more motivated to be the best spouse, parent, friend, etc. These include the following:

- We need to have proper and productive values and priorities in life, such as *emunah* and *bitachon* in Hashem; kindness; compassion; integrity; dignity; humility; gratitude; and dedication to family and community. We must not prioritize pleasure, comfort, honor, or power. It is especially important to properly value and prioritize kindness and compassion for others, especially for the people we have close relationships with. We need to have the proper value for kindness and compassion; recognize our responsibility to act with kindness even when the other person has hurt us or has done something wrong; and recognize that we are capable of acting with kindness even when we have been hurt or we have become distant from the other person, in order for our relationships to succeed.

- We need to develop the *middos* that fit with those values. It is important to have *emunah* and *bitachon* in Hashem as well as to be a compassionate, kind, humble, generous, and honest person who has integrity and gratitude. We must avoid the *middos* that collide with those values, such as arrogance, selfishness, and callousness toward others.

- We need to work to be happy, with a healthy and appropriate sense of self-esteem and self-confidence.
- We need to find the proper motivation to improve the relationship, in line with our *middos* and our values.
- We need to have the confidence that we can improve ourselves and our relationships.
- We need a clear understanding of ourselves, of the other person in the relationship, and of the relationship itself, including what the problems and challenges are.

These self-development tools can put us in a very good position to approach our relationship and to try to develop it productively. However, the following relationship development and management tools are important as well:

- Love and respect are very powerful forces within a relationship, and they are the forces we should use to improve our relationships.
- It is important to understand the dynamics of conflict, even in a close relationship. This understanding covers several important points:
  - It is important to try to feel like we are on the same team despite our challenges;
  - It is important to try to see the big picture of love and respect in the relationship, not just the negatives immediately before us; and
  - Relationships often consist of combinations of love and friction as well as respect and criticism.
- Productive communication is very helpful in expressing positive feelings and putting things into context as well as helping each other understand where we are coming from.
- We need to judge others favorably and try to understand the other person.
- Accepting our situation and making the best of it.
- We need to be assertive but not aggressive.

These are all important lessons that we learn from *Chazal* about how to improve our relationships, aside from the essential lessons about the need to *daven* to Hashem for peace and the need to work on improving our *middos* as a means of improving our relationships. Many of these lessons were discussed above, and some of them will be discussed now.

Developing the Relationship Productively

We want to create healthy relationships that are productive and appropriate and that help us achieve our goals in a manner that is good for us.

Relationships are created for a variety of reasons. Many people who are in productive relationships share common goals, interests, or hobbies. Therefore, they develop the relationship in a manner that will help them reach their goals, and they pursue their common interests and hobbies together. Many close relationships include a key goal of creating a meaningful emotional connection within the relationship. Each person makes the other person feel cared for, valued, appreciated, accepted, understood, respected, and emotionally fulfilled.

In order to develop a relationship, we need to work together to create common goals and work together to achieve them. In order to develop an emotional connection, one of the shared common goals has to be to have a meaningful relationship. We also need to work on caring for, valuing, appreciating, understanding, and respecting the other person.

In addition to shared goals, shared experiences also play a big role in developing a relationship. Sharing experiences and spending quality time together can strengthen the relationship and increase the bond between the two people. It is often especially helpful to bond over something meaningful, fun, or challenging.

There are many elements that affect how a sense of closeness and friendship is created between two people.

The Power of Love and Respect in Improving Our Relationships

Above, we discussed the explanation of the *Chizkuni* (*Vayikra* 19:18) that we often have conflicting emotions. We can be angry at someone and have hateful feelings toward them and at the same time have layers of love and respect for them. Love and compassion can exist even during difficult times — there are times that the positive feelings are overt, but they remain in our subconscious minds and hearts even at other times.

At the beginning of *Parshas Vayishlach*, the Torah discusses the relationship of Yaakov Avinu and Esav as well as the dramatic confrontation between them. Esav was so upset and hurt by what Yaakov Avinu had done to him that he wanted to kill him, and Yaakov Avinu needed to escape to a distant land. After many years, Yaakov Avinu was on his way back to Israel and knew that he was going to face Esav. As it turned out, Esav was still so upset at Yaakov Avinu that he hired an army to come with him, and his intention was to murder Yaakov Avinu and his entire family.

As Yaakov Avinu approached Esav, he needed a plan. He needed to figure out how to reconcile with Esav. This is perhaps the clearest case where the Torah discusses the concept of reconciliation within a relationship that has conflict. Therefore, this is one of the best sources we have for learning the Torah's lessons about conflict and reconciliation.

The Chizkuni and the Ralbag describe how Yaakov Avinu attempted to improve the relationship by reaching out to Esav with respect and love. In their descriptions of the story, Yaakov Avinu knew that at the foundation of Esav's pain was a feeling of not being respected and cared about. If Yaakov Avinu could make him feel respected and cared about, he could change the dynamics from the root of the relationship. Even if the problem was not specifically limited to Esav not feeling cared for and respected, Yaakov Avinu realized that love and respect could still help to improve the relationship. Therefore, Yaakov Avinu demonstrated, through his gifts, his overt displays of respect, such as bowing to Esav and his words that he sincerely respected and cared about him.

The way Rashi explains what happened in the story is that Esav did end up allowing the hatred to leave his heart, and he reconciled with Yaakov.

The story is astounding! Esav had such deep hatred for Yaakov Avinu. He was planning his murder for twenty-two years, and now, he finally had the opportunity to do it. He was marching with his army, and he was determined to finally fulfill his mission. Then, Rashi says, when Yaakov Avinu reached out with respect and love, Esav's heart melted.

Esav was a warrior. He was not afraid to kill, and he was very determined to carry out his plan. He also did not like Yaakov Avinu. He did not want this love and respect. He did not want the relationship at all! How could respect and love have changed Esav's mind so dramatically?

It seems that even though Esav's hatred for Yaakov Avinu was very real, at the same time, deep down, he really did have feelings of love, care, and concern for his brother. As we see from the *Ohr Hachaim* (*Bereishis* 32:5), Esav responded to the fact that Yaakov Avinu reached out to him as a brother. A part of Esav still felt brotherly love for Yaakov Avinu, and he responded in kind when Yaakov Avinu appealed to that brotherly feeling.

We see that when the inner feelings of love, closeness, and respect are brought out from within, they can be strong enough to remove some of the most powerful feelings of negativity and hatred.

Apparently, even when people are extremely angry at each other, there are often still inner feelings of love. Those feelings of love are accessible, and they are powerful.

The *Ohr Hachaim* and the Ralbag are teaching us to use our positive feelings and connect with the other person through our underlying love and compassion as well as to use our connection to overcome the challenges that exist within our relationship.

As *Avos D'Rabbi Nassan* (1:2) says, Aharon Hakohen seems to have used a similar approach as he tried to bring people back together again. He helped each person recognize that the other person really did care about and respect them. The painful experiences are real, and they do not go away easily. However, Aharon helped them get in touch with their positive feelings for each other and connect with each other. He helped them feel their deep-down closeness, care, and concern, which enabled them to face their challenges in a more productive manner.

Rabbeinu Bachaye (introduction to *Parshas Vayigash*) discusses a similar situation where there was a dramatic confrontation. He talks about the confrontation between Yehudah and Yosef in Mitzrayim. At the time, Yehudah was under the impression that he was facing an aggressive and vindictive viceroy of Mitzrayim, who had kidnapped one of his brothers and who had been treating him and his family unfairly and unjustly. He was also under the impression that the viceroy was going to hold Binyamin as a slave.

Yehudah needed a plan — he needed to figure out how to communicate with the viceroy. Rabbeinu Bachaye tells us that one of the main parts of Yehudah's strategy was to treat the viceroy with respect. As Shlomo Hamelech teaches us (*Mishlei* 15:1), "A soft response quiets anger, but speaking harshly causes more anger."

Shlomo Hamelech is teaching us how to handle a situation where we have been hurt by someone. We may be upset at them, we may want to get them to recognize that they have done something wrong to us, and we may even want to get them to fix the problem. Rabbeinu Bachaye says we are naturally driven to express our feelings in an angry and aggressive manner in order to show the person how wrong they were; how guilty and sorry they should feel; and how motivated they should be to apologize to us and to fix the problem.

However, the reality is that communicating angrily is not productive. *We need to speak with respect.* When we do not communicate with respect, the other person is less likely to take responsibility for his actions, to admit that he needs to change, or to make the constructive changes that will improve the relationship.

Getting in touch with our positive feelings for each other and connecting with each other helps us through the process in many ways. When we recognize that even though we have challenges and difficulties in our relationships, very often, we also have positive feelings for each other, and our whole perspective on the relationship will be different. Instead of thinking there is no hope for this relationship because we clearly do not really care about each other, we will see our positive feelings and be motivated to get past the problems and do what we can to improve the relationship.

We will also feel more support and encouragement from our positive feelings. Feeling connected provides *chizuk* and motivation for us to work on the relationship. Working on a relationship is often difficult and painful. The negative experiences that we have experienced within the relationship can be painful, and they can take away our motivation to work on making improvements. The process can sometimes be long and drawn out as well, and that can cause us to lose our inspiration to work to make improvements. However, the love, respect, and connection that we feel can continue to inspire us to keep putting in the necessary work to take each step toward our goal.

The care, concern, empathy, attention, compassion, and respect that we have for each other in a relationship constitute the essence of the relationship itself. The nature of a relationship between parents and children, husbands and wives, friends, or any other relationship with meaningful closeness is built on these factors. Therefore, as we try to build or rebuild a relationship, it is important to slowly develop these feelings, rather than trying to somehow develop the relationship and hoping for the closeness to follow.

The Great Need for Respect and Love

Rav Shlomo Wolbe (*Zeriah U'binyan B'chinuch*) compares a human being's need for love, care, concern, compassion, and empathy to a plant's need for water, soil, and sunlight. We need love in order to function productively. We can live and breathe without it, but we cannot function well without it. We crave it, we need it, and we search for it. When we do not receive it, we tend to try to compensate for it in other ways that are usually not helpful.

With this understanding, we can see how important it is to try to give that love to the other people within our relationships and how much we should try to be open to receiving love from them as well. Rav Wolbe's message also clarifies for us how helpful it is for the success of the relationship when we are able to connect in a meaningful, compassionate, and loving way.

Accepting Our Situation

When we find ourselves in a situation that we would prefer to not be in, it is really important to deal with the situation appropriately. Situations come up very often within our relationships where we might think, "I wish that I were not in this relationship at all" or "I wish that the other person in the relationship were different in certain ways." We may find ourselves saying, "Why did I get stuck in this relationship?" or "Why can they not just be different?" When we do so, we are complaining about the other person, and we are blaming them for our problems. Sometimes, we are also expecting the other person to change. It is true that with the proper communication and teamwork, things can change, but very often, things are not likely to change — especially when we criticize, blame, and complain about them.

Underlying the reason why we start to communicate in unproductive ways about our situation is the fact that we resist accepting the reality that we are stuck in a situation we do not want to be in, so we distract ourselves and focus on criticism, blame, and complaints, even though they usually do not help us get the results that we were looking for.

In order to begin to focus on more productive means of dealing with the challenges in our relationships, we need to accept the reality about our situation. Criticism, blame, and complaints are not going to help us deal with our situation in a productive manner. Expecting unrealistic changes is also not going to help us deal with the situation productively. Rather, we need to accept the reality of our current situation, and then, we can determine what we can realistically expect to change and what we probably are not going to change. Then, we can figure out a plan for how to make the proper changes, and we can figure out how to make the best of the current reality.

When we think about our relationships in an optimistic manner, it is more likely that we will be able to accept the reality of our situation. The reason we resist accepting the reality is that we think of our situation as being bad for us and do not want it to be that way. We are either unhappy with the relationship as a whole or with parts of the relationship.

Even though there are problems that exist in our relationships, there are generally many positives in each relationship as well. If we focus on the good parts as well, it helps us to be happier.

It is also helpful to recognize the reality that Hashem runs the world and that every situation that we have experienced in our lives was planned by Hashem specifically for our own benefit. When we have that recognition, we will realize that Hashem gave us the exact parents, children, spouse, and clients that are the best for us. They are not always the best for us in all ways, but they are the best for our spiritual growth.

Communication

The Torah teaches us about the benefits of communication. For example, "Do not hate your brother in your heart" (*Vayikra* 19:17) — we are not allowed to hate others, even when we are tempted to hate someone because of how they have treated us. The Ramban, Rashbam, and others explain that the reason why the Torah says, "You shall surely rebuke your friend" right afterward is to teach us that when we feel compelled to be upset at someone for having hurt us, we should talk to the person about the hurt they caused. When we communicate with them in an attempt to solve the problem, it will likely enable us to resolve some of our difficulties.

Sometimes, when we communicate with others when we are upset, we are actually making the problems much greater. But if we are able to communicate in a proper and productive manner, then we will be able to improve the situation and avoid negativity and hatred.

The *Rishonim* explain that there are two potential benefits we can attain from speaking to the person about the fact that they hurt us. Sometimes, the other person will recognize what they did and sincerely feel bad about the fact that they had hurt us. They will then be able to show us that they do care about us, they do respect us, and they will commit themselves to treating us more appropriately in the future. There are other times when, through the conversation, they will be able to clarify to us that they always really did care about and respect us, and whatever happened was really the result of a mistake or misunderstanding of some sort.

Either way, communication helps in allowing the two people to become much closer to each other.

There are many aspects of communication that can be helpful, and there are many ways it can be unhelpful.

For example, communication works together with some of the other concepts that the Torah teaches us about our relationships, such as judging others properly and understanding where other people are coming from. These tools work together very well.

Relationships are often strained when people hurt their friends, neighbors, or family members, and they do not understand the overall context of their behaviors. That leads people to attribute a context to the other person's behaviors that is much more negative and hurtful than the reality.

However, when we judge others appropriately and have an accurate understanding of their perspective, then we will be able to assess their behavior more positively. In order for this process to work properly, we need to communicate productively.

Be Assertive, Not Aggressive

Rabbeinu Bachaye (introduction to says that along with being respectful when he spoke to Yosef, Yehudah was also assertive about the fact that he thought that he was right, and the viceroy should allow Binyamin to go free. We see from here that it is true that there are times when we need to be assertive, but being assertive is different from being aggressive.

The Process of Growth

Developing a productive relationship takes time. Growth and change within a relationship will not happen overnight.

Certainly, once the challenges in a relationship surface, and there have been hurt feelings, improving the relationship will involve a difficult process. There is no quick-fix or easy ten-step strategy that can be used in order to make the situation better. There is also no great motivational speech that will make us have the ability to have a good relationship. Rather, there are many perspectives, *middos*, and skills that are necessary for improving our relationships. Each takes time to develop.

Working on ourselves is one of the most important parts to improving our relationships, but improvement in that area will certainly take a while.

Changing our priorities in life takes time. Improving our *emunah, bitachon,* compassion, and kindness takes time. Developing better *middos* is a long process. It is not easy to work on our arrogance, selfishness, or desire for power, respect, and honor. It is hard to become more understanding, more generous, or more honest. Developing a healthier sense of self-esteem requires a lot of work. It is hard to understand ourselves properly and to develop a good sense of self-awareness. It is also hard to get to know and understand the other person properly. It takes time to learn the skills for how to deal with relationships in general and to learn to apply them to each specific relationship.

The Mesillas Yesharim (ch. 11) discusses the process of growth in relation to negative feelings. He explains that feelings of anger, resentment, and hatred toward others who have hurt us do not go away easily. It is hard to make any meaningful improvements without time and hard work. In order to change our negative feelings, we often need to develop a high degree of *emunah* and *bitachon*; we need to work on developing a more meaningful connection within our relationships; we often need to learn how to deal with pain productively; we need to work on our perspectives in life; and we need to work on a variety of different *middos.* These are all important projects to work on, and they take time and effort in order to make significant progress.

All of the *Mesillas Yesharim* is about the process of self-development. The Ramchal explains throughout his *sefer* how a person's growth in *avodas Hashem* requires a process, and we cannot skip steps. In his introduction, he first clarifies for us what our goals should be in our service of Hashem: to love Hashem; be in awe of Hashem; follow in His ways; dedicate our entire minds, hearts, and actions to serving Hashem; and keep all of the *mitzvos.* After that introduction, he structures his entire book according to a step-by-step process of growth that is needed in order to achieve those goals. It seems clear that growth often requires a process, and we need to follow the process in order to achieve our goals.

The same is true within our relationships. Even if our goals are noble, pure, and productive, we still need a productive process in order to reach those goals.

It is important to maintain expectations that are in line with the reality and with the process. When our expectations for success are not in line with reality, a number of things can go wrong. On the one hand, we may give up because change seems to be impossible. We may look at the challenges that we currently face and think they are insurmountable, but that is often only true when we are thinking about what can happen within a short amount of time. There is often no way to heal pain or to remove anger and resentment within a day, a week, a month, or a year. However, if our goal is to try to heal our pain and remove our anger over the amount of time that is necessary for that particular emotion in that particular situation, then we may not give up so quickly.

Alternatively, we may have the opposite response. When our expectations are for quick changes, and we try to make the changes quickly, then we try to push things in unproductive ways. The process needs to be done in the manner that is appropriate, and when we try to fix things too quickly, this often leads to frustration, resentment, or other problems, and eventually, we will give up.

Aside from giving the process the right amount of time to unfold, we also need to follow the proper steps in the process of developing productive relationships. *Toras Avraham* (pp. 390–395) teaches us that we need a specific type of process for how to develop each *middah*, and the *Mesillas Yesharim* teaches that there is a specific order to our development in *avodas Hashem*; so too, it is important to use a productive process in improving our relationships. There is not one specific way to improve our *middos*, our *avodas Hashem*, or our relationships, but whatever process it is that we are using, it is important to do so productively.

For example, within our relationships, it is important to communicate about the challenges that we face. It is also important to work on being less critical of each other, and it is extremely helpful for our communication if we are working on being less critical at the same time. If we prioritize communication with the goal of working on our criticism later, then our communication will not lead to the results that we were hoping for. As a result, we may walk away with the conclusion that communication is useless and only makes things worse. That will lead us to abandon it in the future.

Another challenge we face when addressing problems in our relationships is the overconfidence that we develop when we see some progress. A little progress can often lead us to stop working hard at improving the relationship. Issues within our relationships are often deeply rooted, and short-term success can lure us into a mindset of complacency. We can be overconfident and stop working on the slow process of long-term growth.

For example, when Yaakov Avinu was on his way to greet Esav, he knew that there were many problems in their relationship. Therefore, Yaakov Avinu developed a plan to communicate love and respect for Esav in order to rebuild the relationship. According to Rashi (*Bereishis* 33:4), his plan worked to a certain extent, and Esav gave Yaakov Avinu a hug and a kiss as a genuine expression of care and closeness. However, as Rashi also says, this closeness did not last. Esav's hatred for Yaakov Avinu was too deep, and despite the short-term reconciliation, the feelings returned. Long-term success requires a long-term gradual process.

Similarly, Shmuel Hanavi (*Shmuel I* 17) tells us the story of Shaul Hamelech, who was convinced that Dovid should be killed and made various attempts to kill him. At one point, Shaul Hamelech's son Yonasan spoke to his father and convinced him of Dovid's innocence. As a result, Shaul Hamelech swore that he would not hurt Dovid, so Yonasan told Dovid that he was safe. It seems that Yonasan was convinced that his father had changed his mind and that Dovid was therefore safe. A short time later, however, Shaul Hamelech resumed his efforts to try to kill Dovid.

We see from these stories that when the problems are deeply rooted, it is possible to be inspired to change and to have a sincere short-term reconciliation based on "seeing the light," but long-term improvements in the relationship require a long-term process of growth and development.

This is true when the problems relate to *middos* challenges (such as

Esav's), emotional challenges (such as Shaul Hamelech's, according to some *mefarshim*), or any other deeply rooted challenges. There are no quick magical fixes for deeply rooted problems.

Improving our relationships is doable, but it takes time and requires a productive process.

Passion, Persistence, Patience, and Purpose

Some of the most important parts of the process require passion, persistence, patience, and a sense of purpose. Making significant improvements in our relationships is a difficult task that requires a lot of passion and motivation. However, passion and motivation do not necessarily last. When we are working on our relationships or any other long-term project, we need to maintain a combination of passion, patience, persistence, and effort over a long period of time.

Passion and patience are two traits that do not often come together. When we feel a strong motivation to reach a certain goal, we can have the passion to do what we need to do in order to reach that goal even if it is difficult. However, the fact that we are so passionate will often cause us to not have the patience necessary to reach our goal.

There are some projects that are short term but difficult. For those projects, we need to have passion, but we do not need so much patience. Other projects are long-term projects, but each task within the project is not so difficult. For those projects, we need patience and persistence but not as much passion. Our relationships are long-term projects; therefore, they require patience and persistence — but there are often many difficult short-term challenges involved along the way, and addressing those requires a lot of passion as well.

It is especially hard to have patience in our relationships because many of our unfulfilled needs and our uncomfortable experiences cause us a lot of emotional pain. It is difficult to stay positive and to keep our passion, our optimism, and our motivation when the progress of improvement in our relationships is often slow and hard to see; the pain is not removed so quickly; and there are continuous setbacks along the path toward the goal. All of these factors, especially the setbacks, can easily drain our optimism, our motivation, and our passion for improvement.

The only way to be able to continue to work hard over a long period of time, despite the challenges that we face along the way, is to identify a valuable purpose for why we want to pursue the relationship. We need to recognize the value of the relationship and the value of doing our part in it. When we see the benefits of the relationship and we take responsibility for doing our part, this gives us a sense of purpose, which will help us find the consistent passion to work hard to do our part in the relationship. When we have the purpose and the passion to improve the relationship, it is easier to find the strength to persevere and to work through all the challenges that stand in the way of improving our relationships.

Strength and Confidence

Improving our relationships in a significant manner requires a lot of strength and confidence.

Many of our challenges can cause us to lose confidence in our ability to make improvements. It is also hard to have the emotional and psychological strength to do what we need to do to improve them.

Many of the challenges in our meaningful relationships involve a lack of love or respect from those who are close to us. Sometimes, a child feels like he was neglected or mistreated by their parents, or a parent feels like they have not been respected properly by their child, or a spouse feels like they have not been treated properly by their spouse. Often, it is not one occurrence that causes the person to feel this way in the relationship; rather, there is a consistent pattern of behavior over years. This causes the person who is hurt to feel that the problems are too entrenched to reasonably expect that anything will change. In addition, since the negative experience has existed for a long time, there may have been so much accumulated pain that it is difficult to find the strength to work on the relationship.

When we combine the lack of strength to work on the relationship with the fact that we do not have the confidence that we will be able to improve the relationship, it is not likely that we will get very far.

In order to find the strength to persevere and put in the effort necessary to work on a relationship despite the pain, we need to have a purpose in continuing the relationship. If we value the relationship and the responsibility that we are taking when we work on our relationship, then we can find the passion and the determination to work through the challenges productively.

When we are feeling hurt by an apparent lack of love and respect, it is important to see the big picture as well. Even when there are many challenges in a relationship, love and respect are often present as well. When we realize this, despite the friction, we will be able to find the strength to work through the challenges in our relationships. We can focus on that love, and it can give us the courage and the desire to develop the love and the relationship and to try to make the necessary improvements. Focusing on the love and respect can also give us the confidence that we need in order to be successful.

By finding value and purpose within our relationships as well as connecting to our positive feelings in our relationships can help us find the strength and confidence to be able to work hard and do our best to make the relationship as successful as possible.

Using *Chazal's* Concepts and Strategies Productively

Even though all of the previous concepts and strategies can help us find peace and happiness within our relationships, each of the lessons needs to be understood and applied properly in order to be useful. When they are misunderstood or misapplied, they can be unhelpful and even hurtful to our peace and success in our relationships.

In order to apply a concept from *Chazal* properly, we need to understand the concept properly; understand both parties in the relationship properly; and understand the specific dynamics of the situation. Therefore, it is necessary to study and clarify each concept from *Chazal* properly, to work on our self-awareness, to try to understand the other person properly (through productive communication), and to consider the particulars of the situation as well.

When we feel hurt, and when we think that someone has done something wrong to us, the Torah (*Vayikra* 19:17) teaches us to communicate as a means of mending our relationships: "Do not hate your brother in your heart. You shall surely rebuke your friend." However, in the same sentence, the Torah also teaches us how damaging such criticism can be and how careful we have to be: "Do not bear sin regarding him." *Mishlei* (15:1) tells us that communicating with criticism usually makes the disagreement much worse than it was: "Speaking harshly causes more anger." Therefore, it is necessary to figure out how to communicate properly and productively. Thankfully, the beginning of that *pasuk* tells us how to navigate such a situation: "A soft response quiets anger." Shlomo Hamelech teaches us to communicate about the fact that we were hurt in a soft and respectful tone.

On the other hand, when we are taught to communicate in a soft and respectful tone, we will often focus so much on not hurting the other person that we will end up not protecting ourselves, and we will be hurt again by the person who hurt us in the past. However, we are taught, "If he came to kill you, kill him first" (*Sanhedrin* 72a). When we are threatened by someone, we are allowed to protect ourselves. How can we be soft and respectful and still protect ourselves? As we discussed previously, Rabbeinu Bachaye teaches us that Yehudah was able to accomplish this feat by being assertive but not aggressive. It is possible to be soft and respectful as well as to be assertive at the same time.

One of the most challenging aspects of many of the lessons of *Chazal* that we quoted above is that the Torah teaches us there are many feelings and *middos* that are objectively foolish, bad, and damaging. Therefore, we are taught that we should avoid developing these *middos* and feelings. We are taught to not bear a grudge, to not judge, and, in general, to not have negative thoughts and feelings about others. We are taught to not be angry, jealous, or arrogant. Similarly, the *Kli Yakar* tells us that one of the ways to avoid conflict is to recognize that whatever was done to us is objectively not such a big deal, and we should therefore not be too upset. *Chazal* teach us that when we have the right perspectives, we will realize that everything that happens to us is from Hashem, it is for the best, and there is therefore no reason for us to be upset.

Based on these concepts, it would seem that we should not pay too much attention to our thoughts, perspectives, and feelings, and we should get rid of our negative feelings. We may think, "Do not make a big deal about it," "Do not think about it," "It is not important," or "Just get over it."

However, the *Mesillas Yesharim* (ch. 11) teaches us that being human involves valuing many comforts, pleasures, interests, and desires even if they seem to be unimportant and petty from a Torah perspective. Being human also includes getting upset, angry, and jealous. We bear grudges, and we have many negative feelings toward others who have hurt us. We cannot realistically avoid having these thoughts and feelings, even if we want to.

So, even if we try to ignore our feelings, the pain will remain. We will have unresolved pain, frustration, discomfort, and unrest. At times, we may think that we do not have the feelings anymore, and we may not even acknowledge that we had them to begin with, but in reality, the feelings do exist, and we are dealing with them through denial or suppression.

These existing feelings often lead to stress, anxiety, or depression. Dealing with our emotions by ignoring them often leads to our being significantly affected by them without our even realizing it!

If we learn the messages from *Chazal* that tell us that feelings such as anger and hatred are bad and damaging and consequently try to ignore our feelings, we will end up feeling miserable and will likely lash out in ways that are very damaging.

The *Mesillas Yesharim* also teaches us that as long as we have these feelings, we will need to deal with them, and we will be looking to find peace with those feelings. We will try to find that peace in a variety of ways, some of which will include aggression and behavior that is hurtful to others.

In order to avoid living with unresolved pain and all of the ramifications that come along with that, we need to find a way to deal with our feelings productively. Even if we would prefer to not have had these feelings to begin with, and even if we would prefer to remove them, that is not a possibility, so we must find a better way to deal with them. Dealing with our feelings more productively requires a more nuanced understanding of what the Torah is teaching us when it says not to get angry or jealous. What is the Torah telling us to do when it says we should not hate anyone? It cannot mean we should just ignore our feelings, so what does it mean?

When someone loses a parent, Torah law teaches us the importance of going through a process of mourning. The process includes a seven-day period, a thirty-day period, and then a lighter mourning period for the rest of the year. The Torah recognizes the importance of dealing with our emotions in a manner in which they can be influenced — they cannot just be removed. The *Mesillas Yesharim* says the same thing about feelings of hatred and negativity toward others. These feelings, too, can be influenced, but they cannot just be removed. In order to deal with our feelings productively, we need to have a proper understanding of how our feelings work and how to deal with them productively. Each of the messages from *Chazal* is real, true, and helpful, but each one has to be properly understood in the context of the big puzzle of our inner selves.

CHAPTER 6

A TORAH-BASED STRATEGY FOR
REBUILDING OUR RELATIONSHIPS

WE CAN USE ALL OF the concepts from the previous chapters to help us develop a productive strategy to build (or rebuild) a productive relationship that can thrive despite the challenges that may arise.

The chapters taught us self-development tools for becoming more capable and motivated to be the best spouse, parent, or friend, putting us in a good position to develop our relationships productively. They also taught us many tools for developing and managing our relationships.

Chazal teach us to follow the guidance of Aharon Hakohen concerning how to navigate challenges within our relationships. Aharon Hakohen's role as the *kohen gadol* is well known, his role as a *rebbi* who taught Torah to the nation is well known, and his role as a relationship therapist is also well known. There is a lot we can learn from the wisdom and the strategy that he used to help others to improve their relationships. However, his methods still require clarification.

Aharon Hakohen's Method for Mending Relationships

The Mishnah says (*Avos D'Rabbi Nassan* 12:4) that Aharon Hakohen helped many people to repair their friendships and marriages that had gone bad. He was so successful at helping people to keep their marriages intact that thousands of parents named their children Aharon as a sign of gratitude and recognition of the fact that these children would not have been born if Aharon Hakohen had not helped them save their marriages.

The Mishnah also tells us (*Avos D'Rabbi Nassan* 12:3) what Aharon Hakohen's method was for helping people get along: When two people quarreled, Aharon would go and sit down with one of them and say to him, "My son, know that your friend has said, 'Woe is to me! How shall I raise my eyes and look at my friend? I am ashamed before him because I have sinned against him.'" Aharon Hakohen would sit with him until he had dispelled the ill feelings from his heart. Then, Aharon Hakohen would go and sit with the other one and say to him, "Know that your friend is saying, 'Woe is to me! How shall I raise my eyes and look at my friend? I am ashamed before him because I have sinned against him.'" Aharon Hakohen would sit with him until he had dispelled the ill feelings from his heart. When the two friends later met, they would embrace and kiss each other.

Often, when two people are fighting, they are angry and upset with each other. Each of them thinks that the other person is wrong, and each is upset that the other party hurt them. The Mishnah seems to be saying that once they hear that the other person regrets their words or actions, then they will be ready to forgive the other person. The fact that the Mishnah states that the two people embraced each other and kissed each other when they were "making up" seems to indicate that the hard feelings were gone and that they had warm feelings for each other again.

The way the Mishnah is describing the typical situation that Aharon Hakohen was involved in is hard to understand. First of all, what happened to their previous feelings of anger or pain — how did they just go away so easily? Also, how did they remain friends, when it should not take long for them to realize that their initial opinions are still the same? Whatever differences existed initially are still there!

A Simple Approach

The simple understanding of this *mishnah* implies that the hard feelings went away rather quickly once each person thought that their friend had apologized, so it would seem that fights and hard feelings can come and go very easily.

If fights and feelings can change so quickly, it seems the only conclusion is that most are based in foolishness; therefore, if you can help people wake up from their foolishness, then they will be able to have their relationship back.

The term "baseless hatred" (named as the cause for the destruction of the second Beis Hamikdash) is often used in this context to refer to people hating each other for no real reason. Many people say things like, "There is no reason for you to feel the way that you do," or "You are overreacting — there is no reason for your feelings to be so intense." These expressions represent this way of thinking: Feelings are "made up" and have no real cause. If hatred comes for no real reason, it should be able to leave easily as well.

However, the truth is that hatred is not based on "nothing." Every feeling that we have has a cause, and the cause of our feelings is often significant.

The Mesillas Yesharim (ch. 11) gives context for understanding where our feelings of hatred and anger come from as well as how difficult they are to remove.

He says that when we hate someone or are angry at someone, it is because we are very sensitive, and it is very painful when we are insulted or criticized. When we are insulted or criticized, it is hard not to allow the pain to turn into anger and hatred. Once we do have feelings of anger and hatred, it is difficult to remove those feelings. This is human nature.

Therefore, we see that the concept of baseless hatred cannot mean that there is no reason for the hatred. Hatred is usually a reaction to an insult, which is a very strong reason. The Mesillas Yesharim also clarifies that there is no easy way to overcome our feelings of hatred toward others.

The Beis Hamikdash was not destroyed because people hated each other for no reason. There is no such thing. Rather, even though people had very understandable reasons to hate each other, they should have been more motivated to try to overcome those feelings and to eventually like each other.

It is clear that the Mesillas Yesharim would say that Aharon Hakohen's message was not "Get over it — it's not such a big deal." As the Mesillas Yesharim explains, most fights are a big deal, and it is difficult to overcome disagreements and pain.

It also does not seem realistic to assume that the Mishnah is really saying that Aharon Hakohen helped everyone resolve their issues, revert back to the highest levels of love, and give each other a big hug and kiss. Most problems within our relationships are too deep to be solved through a single conversation. Therefore, it seems clear that Aharon Hakohen's initial conversation with the people who were in conflict was only the first step. That conversation helped them begin the process of resolving their conflict and rebuilding their relationship. Aharon Hakohen was able to help them with the first step, but they needed to do their part to take the additional steps afterward.

What were these steps? What did Aharon Hakohen do in his conversation with them? And what did the people need to do themselves afterward? We cannot know the exact answers to these questions, but we can make an educated guess based on what we have learned.

Step 1 — Getting Things Started

Aharon Hakohen clearly recognized that it is important for us to work on repairing our relationships. However, in order to do so, we need the motivation, confidence, and strength to work on them.

When conflicts present themselves within our relationships, we often lose both the interest and the confidence to work on improving them, and we do not even begin to work on improving them. Even after we begin to work on our relationships, a lot of emotional and psychological strength is required to do what we need to do to improve them. We often do not have the strength that is necessary to work hard enough to sufficiently improve our relationships, especially because the conflict drains our motivation. The fact that we do not have the motivation and the confidence to improve the relationship makes it even harder to have the strength to follow through when we are working on it. Therefore, even though we need to have the motivation, confidence, and strength to be able to improve our relationships, it is very difficult to do so.

The first thing that Aharon Hakohen needed to accomplish when he met with one of the people who was in a conflict was to encourage them and help them develop the motivation, strength, and confidence to work on their relationships. However, he needed a means by which he could teach them how to do so.

Aharon Hakohen had the benefit of having Torah values and Torah-based wisdom. Those values and that wisdom enable us to help ourselves and help others to find the motivation, confidence, and strength to work on improving their relationships.

Some of the wisdom and values from the Torah that help us or others to develop the motivation, confidence, and strength to work on our relationships properly have been discussed previously in this book.

These messages include several key points:

- It is beneficial for us to work on our relationships.
- We have a great responsibility to work on our relationships.
- Even within a difficult relationship, we can uncover love, respect, and connection, and when we do, we will be able to rebuild our relationship.
- We can find purpose in working on our relationships, and that can be very fulfilling. Having a sense of purpose can be a strong motivation for us to work on our relationships.

Overall, the message is that despite our challenges, we can feel like we want to, we need to, and we can improve our relationships!

Motivation

From a Torah perspective, it is important and valuable to improve our relationships (especially within our families), even when the relationships present difficult challenges.

The motivation to improve our relationships comes from recognizing both the benefits and the responsibilities of working on improving them.

We are often motivated by both of these factors. We know that there are many ways in which we benefit from having a productive relationship, and when we appreciate those benefits and focus on them, developing productive relationships becomes a priority. As a result, we are much more likely to celebrate the rewards that come from having a good relationship. Similarly, we often feel a sense of responsibility to work on our relationships, and that motivates us to fulfill our responsibilities.

However, we often do not focus on the benefits of working on our relationships and our responsibility to improve them. We also often do not have the confidence that we will be able to improve the relationship, or we do not have the skills or tools that we need to be able to improve it, so we are not so motivated to work on ourselves and improve the relationship. We are also often not so motivated to work on our relationships during the times when we are upset at each other. During those times, we often do not see the benefits so clearly — we do not think that we will be happy together anyway, we are not so motivated to be nice to each other, and we do not feel so obligated to be nice to each other either. During these times, we are angry, negative, and self-centered, so we have a hard time working on compassion, connection, and cooperation.

In order to get the strength to persevere and to put in the effort that we need in order to work on our relationship despite the pain, we need to really focus on the benefits and our responsibility to improve them. We also need to find purpose in working on the relationship. If we value the relationship and the responsibility that we are taking on when we work on our relationship, then we can find the passion and determination to work through the challenges productively.

It is important to develop productive and appropriate goals and motivations (in line with the proper values and *middos*). Unproductive or inappropriate motivations do not lead to healthy and stable relationships. This also often holds us back from feeling the motivation or confidence that we can succeed in achieving our goals in a relationship. If our goals are very selfish, it may not be realistic to achieve them. When our goals include a healthy balance between giving and receiving, then it is more likely that we will be able to achieve the results that we are looking for.

As we discussed above, Rav Shlomo Wolbe (*Kuntres Chassanim*) tells us that in order to be motivated, we cannot always rely on our love, care, and compassion for the other person or on our desire for kindness and compassion. All of those motivations can come and go from time to time. Rather, we need to feel obligated to help others as well. When we feel an unconditional responsibility to help others, then we will be motivated to help in all situations.

It is sometimes difficult to feel an unconditional responsibility to help. We feel justified in not helping others for various reasons, such as the fact that they hurt us, we think they are bad people, or merely because we are not close to them. However, the Torah teaches us that in reality, we have a relatively unconditional responsibility to help others. There are a number of considerations that limit our responsibilities, such as the fact that we have other responsibilities that conflict with our responsibility to help others and the fact that we have our own needs ourselves. However, our responsibilities to others are very significant.

One aspect of our responsibility to work on our relationships is the importance of acting with kindness. When we appreciate how important kindness and compassion are, we are more likely to work hard to treat others properly even when it is difficult for us to do so.

The goals of improving our relationships also include the fact that the relationships themselves are an important goal within our Torah lifestyle. Being part of a family and a community (social network) and having peace in our family can often help us to follow the Torah productively.

Even though there are many different things that can cause us to be motivated to work on our relationships, when our motivation comes from an appreciation of the value of our relationships, we are more likely to make significant improvements in our relationships. When our motivation is combined with care, concern, and respect for the other person, we are even more likely to succeed.

Shlomo Hamelech says (*Mishlei* 27:19), "*K'mayim hapanim lapanim, kein leiv ha'adam la'adam* — Like water [reflects] the face to the face, so the heart of a person to another." He is telling us that whatever feelings are in our hearts will be shared with the people around us. When we have friendship, love, care, and concern within our hearts, then our friends or family will recognize that we feel that way about them. When we are trying to improve our relationships because of other goals, the other person will feel that, and our efforts will not be so successful.

There are often many things within our own world that we need to work on in order to be motivated to work on improving our relationships.

We need to prioritize family and relationships more than our jobs, hobbies, or general interests. When we appreciate the importance of family, we will be much more motivated to improve our familial relationships.

It is likely that Aharon Hakohen shared all of these messages that can help a person be motivated to work on their relationships. They are even helpful to someone who is currently struggling in their relationships because working at improving relationships brings purpose, happiness, and connection.

Confidence

In order for us to be and to remain motivated to improve our relationships, we need to develop the confidence that we have the ability to improve ourselves and our relationships.

We also need to recognize that we are capable of improving our relationships in order to be motivated to work on improving them. Otherwise, we will certainly give up. The Torah not only tells us that we can improve our relationships (even the difficult ones), but it even gives us guidance on how to do it.

Often, we will not have the confidence that we can improve our relationships because we will think, "How can we improve our relationship when the other person is such a bad person or has such problems? In order for the relationship to improve, I need them to change, and I do not have the ability to change them!" Based on that way of thinking, we will often give up on working on the relationship.

However, the reality is that there is a lot of room for improvement within our relationships. Even though every person does have their limitations, and realistically, we will not be able to change the other person in a relationship, we can still make a lot of improvement within our relationships. The lessons from the Torah can teach us how to make these improvements.

Aharon Hakohen must have known that we have reason to be confident that we can improve our relationships when we work on them, and he must have shared that with them.

When we put these factors together, and we (a) recognize the value of having productive relationships; (b) recognize the value of unconditional kindness; (c) are dedicated to an unconditional responsibility to treat others well; (d) are motivated by love and respect for the other person; and (e) recognize that we are capable of improving our relationships, then we will be in good shape to embark on a successful project of making the proper improvements in our relationships.

Positive and Negative Feelings

"I am upset. My spouse/friend is so mean! Look at how I was treated! No respect, no care or concern! It is a consistent problem for me. Who needs this?!"

The reality is that even when two people care about and love each other, at the same time, they often feel like they do not care about or love each other. Even though it seems impossible to love someone and hate them at the same time, the reality is that it is actually a very common phenomenon in relationships.

Both people in a relationship have the desire and the need to love and care about the other person as well as the desire and need to be loved and cared for by the other person. On its own, this would seem to be a recipe for success. When both people give each other a lot of love and respect, that lays the foundation for a strong and productive relationship.

However, even in the best relationships, even though there is often much love and respect, there will be many times when they do not treat each other properly, and that will cause a lot of friction and distance. That can sometimes cause each person to feel that they are not loved, respected, or cared for.

There are several reasons why people who are in a good relationship might treat each other poorly. Humans are naturally very selfish. We have many personal needs and desires that are really important to us. That often causes us to focus on our personal needs and desires instead of focusing on the needs within the relationship. This creates many conflicts of interest in our relationships. Additionally, we all have a strong tendency to be critical and arrogant. Furthermore, even though we all have many great *middos* that are helpful for our relationships (integrity, kindness, responsibility, gratitude, etc.), we also all have many *middos* challenges that get in the way of our relationships (anger, jealousy, a desire for pleasure, etc.).

The fact that we care about and respect someone helps our relationship, but at the same time, our *middos* challenges, selfishness, and criticism hurt our relationship.

All of us crave acceptance and respect, but the way we were created leads to an explosive combination. We need acceptance and respect, yet it is hard for us to really respect each other properly!

However, if we can recognize that we really still love each other, that can allow us to feel the other person's love, care, and concern, and we can avoid the feeling that there is no love and respect in the relationship.

When we are feeling hurt by a seeming lack of love and respect, it is important to see the big picture. When we recognize the love and respect that exist in the relationship despite the fact that there are challenges, then we can find the strength to work on making improvements. We can focus on the love, and it can give us the courage and desire to develop the love and the relationship as well as to try to make the necessary improvements. When we see the big picture and recognize that our relationship has a lot of love even when there is also a lot of friction, it can also give us the confidence that we need to be successful.

We saw in the preceding chapter that the *Chizkuni* and the *Ohr Hachaim* (and others) teach us important lessons about the nature of our conflicts within our relationships, and they teach us an important strategy for working on our relationships.

They explain how Yaakov Avinu was able to ease Esav's anger and hatred even though he had harbored a deep-rooted hatred of Yaakov Avinu for decades, waiting for an opportunity to murder him: Yaakov Avinu reached out to Esav and told him that he loved him, cared about him, and respected him. He was trying to reconnect with him, and as the *Ohr Hachaim* says, reaching out in this manner can "melt a stone heart." According to Rashi, it actually helped: When Esav greeted Yaakov Avinu, it was with a genuine embrace of friendship and love. Yaakov Avinu had reconnected with Esav!

The *Chizkuni* tells us that the most effective way to overcome our desire to take revenge within our relationships is to use our love for the other person to overcome our hatred of them.

At first glance, it seems hard to understand these messages.

The *Ohr Hachaim* is talking about the feelings that Esav had for Yaakov Avinu. He hated Yaakov Avinu! How was Yaakov Avinu able to melt his heart by reaching out with love? What happened to the hatred and anger that he had in his heart for the previous two decades?

The *Chizkuni* is talking about a situation in which we have feelings of hate toward the person, not feelings of love. There may be levels of love, and there may be levels of hate, and there are times when we may partially love or partially hate someone, but how can we have both feelings within us at the same time?

We can learn a number of important lessons about relationships from these explanations:

Lesson 1: Love and hate can exist within the same relationship!

Lesson 2: At times, we focus on our negative thoughts and feelings, and we are not in touch with our positive thoughts and feelings, which causes us to hate the other person.

Lesson 3: Even when we are only feeling hatred for the other person, it *is* possible to also access our positive thoughts and feelings.

Lesson 4: The way to overcome our feelings of hatred is through accessing our positive thoughts and feelings that had been buried within our subconscious.

Lesson 5: When we access our positive feelings, it can create a meaningful connection and can also help us to remove our negative feelings.

Understanding the Context of the Problems
in a Relationship

A challenge that often presents itself is the fact that it is hard to understand why we are treated without the respect and care that we expect. This difficulty often leads us to consider the other person to be a bad person or at least someone who does not care about us.

The knowledge that it is normal for good people who like each other to have negative feelings for each other is helpful, but since it is so hard to really understand, we often go back to thinking that it is not true, and we question whether we really are loved and cared about.

The more we understand our specific challenges and those of our spouse or friend, the easier it is to believe this perspective.

For example, sometimes, a husband and wife find themselves constantly being upset at each other about their daily family life. They may think that they must not respect each other or care about each other too much. The reality may really be that they have different needs and interests concerning how they would like their houses to be. These needs and interests may be based on major parts of each person's nature, personality, and experiences. One person needs their house to be fun, laid back, and loose, yet their spouse needs their house to be structured and efficient. These differences will lead to conflicts and frustrations. We need to be able to recognize and understand that even though we care about each other, our needs are real, they are a part of us, and we cannot change them so easily. Therefore, the fact that we have a strong reaction when our needs are not met is not due to a lack of desire to be kind or respectful; rather, it is due to the difficulty of dealing with the fact that our needs are not being met, and most of us do not handle those situations with such grace.

This perspective can help in a situation in which we have already had a disagreement or fight. At the time of the fight, we were each thinking of ourselves and telling each other, "You do not care about me" and "You do not respect me." However, if we can look back and say to ourselves, "I know that I really care about my spouse, and they really do care about me. Based on understanding each of our needs and our personalities, it makes sense that in this situation, we both ended up both thinking, feeling, and acting the way that we did" then we can focus on the fact that we do love each other, and our relationship is very important to us. That can motivate us to reconnect emotionally and to make the challenges in our relationship into secondary issues.

Based on these lessons, we may have some insight into what Aharon Hakohen's method and strategy may have been and what Aharon Hakohen may have been saying to the people that he met.

Accessing Love, Connection, and Positive Feelings for Each Other

Aharon Hakohen would help a couple realize that they really do love each other and that one spouse's thoughts, feelings, and actions do not really show that they do not care about the other spouse; rather, the spouse's nature, together with the specific situation, caused them to react in this fashion. However, since then, each spouse has thought about what happened and has recognized how much they care about their spouse. Each spouse feels terrible about the pain the other spouse was caused and really wants to bring the close relationship back again.

Aharon Hakohen would help them understand the challenges within their relationship and see that each person's behavior does not mean there is no love between them. He would help them realize that even though there are complications in their relationship and they may have many negative feelings toward each other, they have many positive feelings in their relationship as well.

He helped them reestablish the foundation of the relationship, put the challenges into a more appropriate context, and dedicate themselves to work through their challenges over time.

Aharon Hakohen was able to help them feel their love for each other (as *Avos D'Rabbi Nassan* [1:12] says that they embraced and kissed) *despite* their existing disagreements and hard feelings. Feeling connected is itself helpful for the relationship and puts disagreements into a more productive context.

When Aharon Hakohen would tell each party that the other person truly feels bad about their role in the disagreement, the message was, "I understand that my words or actions were hurtful to you and caused you to feel like I did not love you, care about you, or respect you. I wish that you had not felt that pain, and I certainly wish that I had not been the one who caused you to have that experience. I do care about you, and I do respect you, and it is important to me that you know that and that you feel that. Additionally, I will commit to do my best to avoid making the same mistake in the future."

This message can really help the other person be reassured about the love and respect that they desire. As the *Mesillas Yesharim* explains, the emotional pain underneath the hatred comes from feelings of being criticized and not being cared about. Therefore, when someone is told that they really are respected and cared for, it provides the reassurance that they were looking for.

The combination of finding value and purpose within our relationships together with connecting to our positive feelings for each other can help us find the strength and confidence to be able to work hard and do our best to make the relationship as successful as possible.

Step 2 — Sitting with Them

Even though we can understand that feeling connected is extremely beneficial despite the existence of challenges within the relationship, it still seems like a difficult task for someone to change their thoughts and feelings, especially in such a short amount of time! If a married couple is experiencing challenges that threaten their marriage, how do they change the way they think about each other and the way they feel about each other? Prior to the conversation with Aharon Hakohen, couples were upset with each other and felt the other person did not love or respect them. To hug and kiss each other after one conversation is a quick switch. How does that work?

Additionally, when someone hurts his friend and feels justified for having hurt him, it is difficult to help him realize that he should feel bad about what he did. How did Aharon Hakohen's approach work? If they did not change their feelings, would they not each spouse that the other was not really remorseful when they eventually saw them after the meeting?

Outside Guidance

For someone who is upset to be able to see the big picture and understand the relationship in a better context, a healthy perspective from a proper mentor is required. Even with a proper mentor, it often takes time for the mentor to be able to help them see the picture differently. That may be what Aharon Hakohen was doing when he "sat with them."

They may have asked him some variation of these questions: "How can you say that he cares about me when he was so mean to me? How can you say that he is a good person — do you know what he did to me? How can I feel close to this person when we have so many problems? How do I access my positive feelings for the other person when I am so upset at them? How do I solve the problems that I have and that we have? They are too big and too challenging!"

Aharon Hakohen would sit with them, and he would help them come to the understanding that there really are many positive aspects to the relationship and there is hope that they can reach a good place together.

As Aharon Hakohen sat with them, he taught them, heard them out, and encouraged them to do what they needed to do to significantly improve their relationship.

Every person is different, every relationship is different, and the problems and challenges that every couple faces are different. Therefore, Aharon Hakohen could not merely have one specific speech lined up to give to all the different couples. He had to "sit with them" and listen to the specific details that each person was able to share with him, and based on their specific stories, he was able to guide them, inspire them, and answer their questions about how to have a healthy and optimistic approach toward working on their relationship.

Step 3 — Dealing with Our Feelings

When Aharon Hakohen was helping those who were struggling in their relationships, he certainly had to help them deal with their feelings of hurt, anger, and resentment. These are feelings that we all need to work on when we are trying to repair our relationships.

When we are angry and upset at someone, it is difficult to even begin to work on making our relationship better. It is difficult to let go of our feelings even when we want to, but what makes it even more difficult is that we often do not even want to let go of them. We do not want to forgive the person who hurt us and made us upset. Even when there are many positive aspects to the relationship, it is difficult to access them when we are upset, and it is difficult to become less upset when we do not want to. How do we even begin to start to feel or think about things differently when we really do not want to?

The good news is that the positive aspects in our relationships can be accessed even if we are not feeling them at the moment due to our anger. This phenomenon is part of our nature — feelings change over time. One of the clearest examples of our emotions changing over time is seen from the laws of Jewish mourning. When someone loses a relative, they generally experience pain and sadness. However, over time, those feelings fade. The same type of experience can be seen with feelings of anger and pain. However, anger and pain can be different. Those feelings can remain over decades and even generations if they are not dealt with productively.

Over time, we process our situations both consciously and subconsciously, and the thoughts, feelings, and *middos* within us often determine what will happen to our external feelings. When our inner feelings are conducive to compassion, love, and forgiveness, then gradually, as we process the situations both consciously and subconsciously, our anger will slowly dissipate, and we will be in a better position to want to forgive and to improve the relationship.

Talking It Out

Our pain and anger often become more manageable when we are able to verbalize our feelings to others. We are taught, "One who has emotional pain in his heart should verbalize it to others" (*Mishlei* 12:25, explained in *Yoma* 75a). The Vilna Gaon (on *Esther 1:12*) explains that there is an extreme qualitative difference between the anger we feel when we are able to speak out an issue and a situation where we cannot speak it out.

What is even more beneficial is when we can discuss problems with someone who will empathize with us. When someone expresses meaningful emotional support for us in our time of pain, it is extremely helpful to us.

When we are hurt and angry, it is really helpful to have someone to talk to who will enable us to verbalize our feelings, offer us support, and sometimes give us guidance and encouragement to help us move in a good direction.

On the other hand, Hillel teaches us in *Pirkei Avos* (1:14), "If I am not for myself, who will be for me?" No one can solve our problems for us. We each need to do this ourselves. Rabbeinu Yonah (*Pirkei Avos* 1:14) explains that true growth in life is dependent on us alone. We certainly benefit from other people's empathy and encouragement, but our ultimate growth comes from within ourselves.

Therefore, we need to process our feelings and situations; to decide to do whatever we can to deal with our feelings productively and appropriately; and to make meaningful improvements in our relationships to the best of our ability.

When we are hurt very badly and are extremely angry, it is very difficult to improve a damaged relationship in a significant manner. Even if we receive a lot of help and support, and even if we want to make things better, it is still difficult to improve the way we feel. The *Mesillas Yesharim* (ch. 11) tells us that the process of improvement is long and difficult. Even the process of getting to the point at which we are ready to be open to having a positive relationship often takes time. We cannot rush the process. We can only do our best. We need to allow the process to take the time that it needs. In the meantime, we need to try to strengthen ourselves and receive support, empathy, and encouragement from others.

The *Mesillas Yesharim* tells us that when we feel hurt, our initial feeling is hatred, and our desire is for revenge. That is the first thing we need to work on. Only after we go through the process of dealing with those feelings can we start to move toward having a healthy and productive relationship with the other person.

Step 4 — Tools and Strategies for Long-Term Success

To improve our relationships, we need to find both the "why" (the motivation) and the "how" (the tools).

We obviously need to be motivated to work hard to overcome all of the challenges that stand in our way. We often are not motivated enough to put in the work; therefore, we need to develop the motivation to be kind and compassionate to others and to improve our relationships. If we do not have enough motivation to improve our relationships, then the knowledge of how to improve them will not be helpful.

However, even if we are extremely motivated to improve our relationships, we also need to understand how to have productive relationships and how to deal with the challenges that present themselves within those relationships.

The Responsibility of Aharon Hakohen's Couples to Continue

This step is extremely important, because even if Aharon Hakohen was successful in helping people find the motivation to improve their relationships and in putting the relationship in a better context so they could reconnect and find love, care, and respect in their relationship despite their challenges, that positivity will not last long. The same factors that caused the problems in the first place will resurface over time unless the necessary changes are put into place to make things different in the future.

As long as we have not changed our goals, values, *middos*, and perspectives on life, we will fall back into the same traps into which we fell into before.

Therefore, it is important and necessary for both people to continue to work on their goals, values, *middos*, and perspectives on life in order to be able to make long-term meaningful improvements in their relationships.

It is also necessary to learn about the nature of relationships and to learn productive strategies to help develop our relationships productively.

Therefore, it would seem that Aharon Hakohen would encourage the people he was working with and teach them that in order to have long-term success in their relationships, aside from reconnecting with each other, they need to develop their *middos*, tools, and strategies. There is nothing that anyone (including Aaron Hakohen) can do for us or teach us that can replace the need for each of the people to work on themselves throughout their lives to improve themselves and, as a result, improve their relationships.

Combining All the Tools and Strategies for Long-Term Success

Each of the ideas mentioned above can help us be able to improve our relationships. However, when they are combined, they are much more effective. Therefore, we will conclude with a summary of these tools that can help improve our relationships so we can try to combine them and implement them productively.

Aside from developing the motivation, there are two parts to working on our relationships. Our success in our relationships is dependent on who each person is as an individual and on how each person relates to the other in the relationship. Therefore, we need to both work on ourselves and work on the relationship. There are systems, strategies, and specific tools that relate to working on ourselves (self-improvement tools), and there are also systems, strategies, and tools that relate to working on our relationships (relationship tools).

Self-improvement includes:

- fine-tuning our values, attitudes, perspectives, and priorities in life;
- developing our *middos* to fit with those values, including our *emunah* and *bitachon;*

- building and developing our emotional health and a productive way to deal with our emotions;
- working on our happiness, self-esteem, and confidence; and
- having a keen sense of self-awareness.
- Our work on the relationship includes:
- understanding ourselves, the other person, and the nature of the specific relationship;
- understanding the dynamics of conflict in relationships; and
- developing the proper strategies and skills to help us improve our relationships.

Fine-Tuning Our Values, Attitudes, Perspectives, and Priorities in Life

When we have proper and productive values, attitudes, perspectives, and priorities in life, we are much more likely to have good relationships. Most of the problems in our relationships revolve around the fact that our values, attitudes, perspectives, and priorities are generally not proper or productive. Even though many of our values are proper and productive, we also often have unproductive values as well. These values are not necessarily objectively bad; however, when we focus on them or pursue them at the wrong time, to the wrong extent, or in the wrong manner, they become problematic and can be damaging. We often value power, strength, attention, wealth, control, comfort, pleasure, and fun more than we should or in a manner that is not productive or appropriate.

Our attitudes and perspectives on life are often founded on selfishness or arrogance, without an appreciation of the value of kindness and giving or of the fact that Hashem created us and gave us everything we have. These attitudes and perspectives are often very detrimental to our relationships.

We often prioritize money, pleasure, comfort, honor, and power, and we spend our time, money, and energy on these pursuits. None of these priorities motivate us to be kind, compassionate, nice, and helpful to others in a relationship. Rather, they generally will cause us to deal with our situations in life in a manner that is not beneficial to our relationships.

When we want to make meaningful improvements in our lives, we need to realize that our values and priorities are not fully in the right place, and we need to find true clarity about what is really important and valuable in life. We can achieve that clarity temporarily, but it will go away unless we work on ourselves over time to improve our *emunah*, *bitachon*, and value system in a manner that will stick with us for good and will be more likely to improve our relationships.

It is appropriate to appreciate the value of kindness, compassion, integrity, dignity, humility, gratitude, and dedication to family and community.

Kindness and compassion are especially important, especially toward the people we have close relationships with. We need to understand the value of kindness and compassion and to recognize our responsibility to act with kindness even when the other person has done something wrong or hurtful.

Our attitudes and perspectives should be based on our recognition of the fact that Hashem created the world, Hashem has given us everything we have, and it is our job and responsibility to emulate the ways of Hashem, which are the ways of kindness and compassion. Acting this way is the source of our success and accomplishment in life, and it will lead us to our greatest benefits in This World and the Next World. (Of course, we have to take care of our own needs as well, and we cannot only focus on helping others, but recognizing our responsibility to help others will motivate us to do as much as we can.)

Our priorities in life should include doing our best to care about others and to help them out in whatever way we can. Our close relationships, especially our family relationships, should certainly be among our top priorities in life.

Besides having the proper values and priorities in life, we need to appreciate the extent of the importance of each of these values. There is nothing in the world that is more important than having good *middos* and being kind and helpful to others! When we appreciate the true extent of the value of kindness, then we will prioritize the improvement of our *middos* and kindness properly.

When these are our values, we will be able to consistently do our best to be nice and compassionate to everyone around us. Knowing our values will help us do what we can to deal with all the situations and challenges that we face in our relationships.

Developing Our *Middos* That Fit with Those Values

In order to improve our relationships, we need to improve the *middos* that fit with those attitudes and values. It is important to have trust and faith in Hashem as well as to have compassion, kindness, humility, generosity, honesty, integrity, gratitude, and patience. All of these *middos* are helpful for our happiness in our relationships, and the more we improve these *middos*, the better our relationships will be. When we are arrogant and selfish, and we are critical, condescending, antagonistic, and callous toward others, it is not possible to have good relationships. Similarly, if we have a tendency to get angry, jealous, or anxious, it will interfere significantly with our relationships. We need to improve these *middos* in order to improve our relationships.

Emotional Health

Our emotional health has a big effect on our relationships. We all have emotional needs — we need love, affection, attention, appreciation, and respect. We need a sense of purpose, value, and meaning. We need family, friends, and community. We need safety, security, and control of our wellbeing as well.

These emotional needs are actually the basis for our relationships. They help us feel close to others, care about others, and be devoted to others. However, when our emotional needs are connected to shame, anger, pain, and a lack of self-worth, our needs are not healthy and can be very destructive to our relationships. They can lead us to feel more anger, resentment, hatred, and aggression. We can also feel extremely sad, worthless, or depressed. We can feel anxious, scared, or timid. This can cause us to be mean and nasty or distant and detached.

Working on our emotional health is a very important part of improving our relationships.

We also need to have a healthy and productive approach to dealing with our emotions in order to deal with our relationships productively.

We all have many different experiences in life, and these experiences create many different emotions in us. The way we deal with these situations and with the emotions that come with them has a major impact on our relationships.

Working on Our Happiness, Self-Esteem, and Confidence

Our relationships are much better when we are generally happy and when we have a healthy and appropriate sense of self-esteem and self-confidence.

When we are not happy, we have a hard time with our spouses, children, and others. Our relationships suffer because we are not happy in general. General unhappiness is also often a sign of other problems, which are themselves a cause for our lack of happiness. The more we have the *middah* of being *samei'ach bechelko* (happy with our lot), the more likely we are to be happy with the other people in our relationships. Similarly, the less critical we are of others, the less arrogant and entitled we feel. And the less angry we are when things do not go our way, the happier we will be, and the better our relationships will be as well.

When we do not have a healthy sense of self-respect or self-confidence, it will cause us to be very sensitive to how we are treated in our relationships. We will feel very hurt and angry when we do not receive the respect that we desire, and this will result in a lot of emotional pain and suffering. When we are suffering, in pain, and desperate for love and affection, we will generally not act in a manner that is conducive to developing productive and healthy relationships. We will often be selfish, demanding, critical, and aggressive, or at least passive aggressive, in our quest for attention. None of these approaches are productive or appropriate, and they will not help us get the type of attention, respect, and connection that we really need. These approaches usually actually make matters worse for us and for our relationships.

Developing a Keen Understanding of Ourselves

Self-awareness refers to having a conscious knowledge of our character, ideals, values, thoughts, feelings, behaviors, motives, and desires.

It also involves an understanding of why we are the way we are. Why is our character the way that it is? Why do we have these ideals, perspectives, values, and thoughts? Why do we feel and behave the way that we do? Why are we motivated to do what we do, and why do we desire to do what we do?

In order to make improvements in any area of life, we need more than motivation alone. We also need to understand what it is that we want to improve. Just as a lot of wisdom is required for a doctor to know how to diagnose and treat our physical ailments, so too a lot of wisdom is required for us to know how to diagnose and to treat our *middos* ailments. The motivation to be physically healthy alone will not cause us to be healthy, and it may not even guide us to knowing how to be healthy; rather, we need to understand medicine in general and our body specifically in order to know how to be healthy.

Similarly, we cannot rely on motivation alone to be able to have good *middos* and good relationships. We need to have a good understanding of how people work and how *middos* work in general, together with a specific understanding of ourselves and our specific *middos*.

We all have our own *middos* challenges, and they affect us in significant ways. They certainly affect our happiness and relationships. Even when we recognize that our happiness and relationships are being hurt by our *middos* challenges, it is still difficult for us to diagnose what the problems are and to know what we should do in order to improve them.

There are many things that go into making the diagnosis and the plan to improve ourselves, but self-awareness is certainly a big part of the picture if we want to work on ourselves productively.

Understanding Ourselves, the Other Person, and the Relationship

Before working on the skills that relate to mending our relationships, we need to understand the fundamentals of human behavior in general. In a relationship, we need to understand ourselves and the other person in the relationship very well in order to be able to diagnose our specific needs and problems correctly. We also need to have a proper understanding of how relationships work in general, and we need to understand how to develop and deal with the specific dynamics of the relationship.

We need to understand ourselves well in order to become better people. If we do not understand ourselves well, we will not know what needs improvement and how to improve ourselves, so we will not be able to make the necessary improvements.

Every person is different; therefore, we need to understand the specific dynamics of each person. If we do not understand the other person's specific personalities, needs, and challenges, then we will not be able to work well together.

Aside from understanding each person independently, it is important to understand the specific dynamics of the relationship. Relationships are complex, and it is important to understand the specific complexities of each relationship that is being worked on.

Understanding The Dynamics of Conflict in Relationships

It is important to realize that there is almost always conflict, even within close relationships. Relationships often consist of a combination of love and friction and of respect and criticism. Even though we often only focus on what we see in front of us, which is sometimes quite negative, when we see the big picture of the relationship, we will see that there is also a lot of love and respect. We can and need to feel like we are on the same team as the other person despite our challenges.

Conflict comes in many shapes and forms. Every relationship has its own set of dynamics — every person and every situation is unique. The more we understand the dynamics of a specific conflict, the better we will be able to deal with it.

Working on Our Strategies and Skills

In order to improve our relationships, aside from working on ourselves to improve personally and to become better equipped to have good relationships, we need to work on the proper strategies and skills that relate specifically to relationships. We need to work on skills such as productive and appropriate communication, empathy, active listening, integrity, fairness, loyalty, and conflict resolution.

When we have these tools, we are in a very good position to approach a relationship and to try to develop it productively. However, everyone is different, each of our challenges is different, and we need to work on different things in different ways in order to improve ourselves and our relationships. We each need an individualized approach toward improvement alongside the above concepts and strategies, which are helpful for everyone.

The previous discussions were about general tools, perspectives, and strategies, but there are also many applications to each of these tools. The better we get at developing all of them, the better our relationships will be.

When we put everything together (our ideals, values, goals, purpose, mission, *middos*, skills, and strategies), then we will be equipped to put in our best efforts to developing great relationships.

Final Blessings

Our relationships play a major role in our lives. Our spouses, siblings, parents, and children are certainly important parts of our lives. Extended family, friends, community members, and general acquaintances are also important to us. The friendship, encouragement, and assistance that we receive and that we give to others is essential for our happiness and success in life.

However, relationships are difficult, and it is easy for us to run into conflict. When we deal with those conflicts productively, we will be able to maximize the benefits of our relationships despite our conflicts, but if we do not deal with our conflicts productively, it is easy for these conflicts to cause our relationships to fall apart.

It is up to us to work hard to do our best to learn how to do what we can to work on ourselves and be more equipped to do our part to have productive relationships. Then, we need to work hard to actually be the best that we can. Together with trying to do our best, we can also turn to Hashem and ask Him to help us to be happy and productive together.

We should all be blessed with peace, happiness, and success in all of our relationships and in life in general.

CPSIA information can be obtained
at www.ICGtesting.com
Printed in the USA
BVHW091122270922
648083BV00013B/1232